Tort Law in Romania

Tort Law in Romania

Laura Toma-Dăuceanu, Ioan Ilieş Neamţ

This book was originally published as a monograph in the International Encyclopaedia of Laws/Tort Law.

Founding Editor: Roger Blanpain
General Editor: Frank Hendrickx
Volume Editor: Britt Weyts

Wolters Kluwer

Published by:
Kluwer Law International B.V.
PO Box 316
2400 AH Alphen aan den Rijn
The Netherlands
E-mail: lrs-sales@wolterskluwer.com
Website: www.wolterskluwer.com/en/solutions/kluwerlawinternational

Sold and distributed by:
Wolters Kluwer Legal & Regulatory U.S.
7201 McKinney Circle
Frederick, MD 21704
United States of America
E-mail: customer.service@wolterskluwer.com

ISBN 978-94-035-4941-5

e-Book: ISBN 978-94-035-4702-2
web-PDF: ISBN 978-94-035-4463-2

This title is available on www.kluwerlawonline.com

The Authors

Laura Toma-Dăuceanu is currently a Judge at the Bucharest Court of Appeal and a Professor at the Faculty of Law of the University of Bucharest.

After graduating the Law Faculty at the University of Bucharest and the French—Romanian Law College of European, she continued with her master studies at the University Paris I Pantheon Sorbonne in general private law. In 2013, she obtained a double doctor's degree from the University of Bucharest and the University Paris I Pantheon Sorbonne after completion of her thesis titled "Unilateral Termination for Breach of Contract." The legal paper has been published in 2016 at IRJS Editions, Paris.

Since 2011 she had a constant academic activity working at the Faculty of Law—University of Bucharest where she held lectures and seminars in Civil Law—Property Rights and General Theory of Obligations.

She has published and participated in various conferences regarding civil law topics. In the matter of civil liability notable published works are: *The Moral Damage Suffered by Individuals* —an analysis of the doctrine and jurisprudence after ten years of the New Romanian Civil Code, Bucharest, RRDP No. 3-4/2021; National Rapporteur at the Grerca Seminaire in 2018 (*La reforme du droit de la responsabilite en France et en Belgique*, Regards croises et aspects de droit compare, Belgium) and 2019 (*Les dommages de masse, Roumanie*, coauthor); National Rapporteur at the Journees Internationales de l'Association Henri Capitant in 2019 on the theme "Solidarite et indemnisation," coauthor; *The Characteristics of the Medical Civil Liability*, Travaux de l'Association Henri Capitant, Istanbul, 2016; *The Damage Caused by the Loss of Chance*, Bucharest, Curierul Judiciar No. 10/2011.

The Authors

Ioan Ilieş Neamţ is a judge at the County Court of Maramureş (Tribunal) and editor-in-chief at Revista de Dreptul Familiei (Family Law Review). After graduating from the Law Faculty of Babeş Bolyai University in 2011, he pursued the master studies in National and European Business Law at the same university, in which he graduated in 2013. In 2017 he received, at the same University, his doctoral degree in law with *summa cum laude* for the thesis, *The Class Action as an Instrument for Repairing the Mass Torts. A Comparative Law Analysis*, which was published the same year at Universul Juridic, Bucharest.

As a judge, he is practicing mostly in family law, civil law and labor law. From 2017 to 2020 he was assistant professor at Babeş-Bolyai Faculty of Law, holding seminars in Obligations and International Private Law.

Also, he published more than 20 legal studies in certified law reviews, mainly in the field of civil obligations, civil procedure and family law. In the matter of civil liability, some of the most relevant papers published are: *Is the Fear of a Future Damage Likely to Be a Sufficient Basis for a Current Tort Liability. An Insight into Pandora's Box*, in RRDP 3/2020; and *Old Instruments for New Issues. Mass Damages Face to Face with Civil Liability. Convergence or Antinomy?* in RRDP 2/2020. He also coordinated RRDP 2/2020, a volume dedicated to civil liability.

For the published books and studies he was awarded with *Simion Bărnuţiu* of Romanian Academy, *Henri Capitant* of Revista Română de Drept Privat (Romanian Private Law Review) and twice with *Octavian Căptăţână* of Revista Română de Drept Privat (Romanian Private Law Review). Starting with 2019 he has been one of the scientific organizers of Conferinţa Naţională de Drept Civil. Familia (The National Conference on Civil Law. The Family).

Table of Contents

Table of Contents

List of Abbreviations

A.D.	Anno Domini
C.C.	Civil Code
EU	European Union
No.	Number
O.J.	Official Journal
O.U.G.	Government Emergency Ordinance
RCA	Răspundere civilă auto (Automobilistic Civil Liability)

List of Abbreviations

General Introduction

§1. GENERAL BACKGROUND OF THE COUNTRY

I. Geography

1. Romania is situated in southeastern Europe, to the north of the Balkan Peninsula. Its surface covers 238,391 km^2, and it is the twelfth largest country on the continent, being a member of the European Union (EU) since January 1, 2007.

2. Romania is bordered by Ukraine in the north, Moldova, Ukraine and the Black Sea in the east, Bulgaria in the south, Serbia in the southwest and Hungary to the west. The south border, for most of its length, follows the course of the river Danube.

3. The majority population is formed approximately 90% of Romanians. The minorities include Hungarians (the largest number approx. 6.6%), Germans, Romani, Turks, Tartars and Bulgarians. The national language is Romanian.

4. With a population of approximately 2,155,000 inhabitants out of 22,175,000 total inhabitants,[1] Bucharest is the capital and it is located in the southeast of the country.

5. The relief is varied and has a rather symmetrical and egalitarian distribution between its mountains, hills and plains organized around the Carpathians mountains that form the Transylvanian Basin situated in the center of the country.

6. The climate is moderately temperate with four distinct seasons. However, given its location and relief, in certain parts of the country the climate is altered by humid Atlantic climatic influences, continental East European Plain or sub-Mediterranean influences. Normally, in the summer, the maximum average temperature is between 22 and 24 degrees C, while during the winter the maximum average temperature is between –3 and –5 degrees C.

7. The territory of the country is organized since 1968 into forty-one counties to which is added the municipality of Bucharest that constitute administrative divisions of Romania.

1. According to the National Institute of Statistics, graphics, July 2020.

II. History

8. Romania has a millenary history that goes back thousands of years, as though scarce, first signs of human activity in this region being recorded around 40,000 years ago. Already during the Stone Age, the entire region was populated, and in Neolithic period, the population flourished and developed into complex cultural, political, religious and social systems, the best example being Cucuteni civilization or Hamangia which date during that period. Archeological evidence shows that as far as 2,000 B.C. geto-dacian, whom the Greek historian Herodotus referred to as being "the most courageous and fair of the Thracians," were organized in complex political alliances.

9. Under the rule of King Burebista, in first century B.C., the geto-dacian tribes had united for the first time into a large state, named Dacia, that covered the entire nowadays Romania and Moldavia, and major parts of Bulgaria, Serbia, Hungary and Ukraine. Dacia survived after the death of King Burebista, in 44 B.C., and was further ruled by several kings during which it continued to flourish. Having as neighbor the Roman Empire has led to both a series of cultural and political transformations and a number of military conflicts. After several battles, a part of Dacia was conquered on 106 A.D. by the Roman emperor Trajan and was transformed into a Roman province. The Roman occupation lasted until 273 A.D., when the Roman emperor Aurelius decided to retreat the Roman administration and army and set the borders of Roman Empire to Danube river.

10. Despite the fact that the Roman occupation was short and partial, it nevertheless had significant impact on the local population, fundamentally shaping its language and culture. A major argument in this regard is that although after Roman retreat multiple nomadic invasions and influences followed, the locals continued to speak a Latin-based language, Romanian being nowadays the only Latin language in the region.

11. After the Aurelian retreat from Dacia, the regions was invaded by multiple nomadic people such as Goths, Huns, Gepids, Avars or Slavs and the archaeological and historic sources are scarce until late early Middle Age, when some sources reveal the existence of several local small states.

12. During the late twelfth and thirteenth centuries, on the region once occupied by Dacia, three different states started to emerge: Transilvania, Moldova (the nowadays eastern part of Romania and the Republic of Moldavia and the southern part of Ukraine) and Ţara Românească. After the fall of Constantinople, in 1453, because of their geographic position, the three states were on a continuous threat by the Ottoman Empire. Several major battles were carried, and the rulers of Transilvania, Moldova and Ţara Românească managed, on several occasions, to prevent the advancement of Ottomans into Europe. Though after losing some battles the states were placed under Ottoman suzerainty, the three were never a pashalic.

13. For a very short period of time, in 1599, Transilvania, Moldova and Ţara

Românească were united under the rulership of Mihai Viteazu, but after his killing, in 1600, they became different entities with different rulership.

14. The same geographic position, at the edge of different empires, meant that the three small states were, along their history, either occupied by their neighbors or at least under some form of influence. Thus, for periods of time, Transilvania was either a part of Hungary or Hapsburg Empire, or was under their influence. Parts of Moldova and Ţara Românească were also under the occupation of the same Austrian Empire, while a large part of Moldavia (what is today the Republic of Moldavia) was occupied by the Russians.

15. The first real reconstruction under one state took place in 1859, when Alexandru Ioan Cuza is elected as ruler by both Moldova and Ţara Românească, and this election, and the union of the two states into one, named Romania, is later recognized by the large European powers of the time. Alexandru Ioan Cuza initiates a series of large reforms, among which are the adoption of first Civil and Criminal Code and the building of two Universities in Iaşi and Bucharest.

16. In 1866 the German prince Carol de Hohenzollern-Sigmaringen is proclaimed as ruler of Romania. A decade later, in 1877, Romania achieves independence from the Ottoman Empire and in 1881 it becomes a Kingdom. Under the rulership of Carol, Romania undergoes a broad series of judicial, political and economic reforms, becoming a major force in the region, despite being neighbored by three large empires (Ottoman, Russian and Austro-Hungarian).

17. As the First World War brought an end to the Russian and Austro-Hungarian Empires, it also set the proper conditions to reunite all the territories where Romanians were majoritarian under one state. Thus, during 1918 the regions formerly occupied by the two empires (Transylvania and Norden and Eastern Moldavia) united with Romania.

18. The period between the two World Wars was marked by both ups and downs. Besides some undisputable social, economic and judicial progresses, that strengthened the position of Romania in the region, the large economic crisis in 1929 and the political instability and tensions had also marked the period.

19. The Second World War majorly reconfigured Romania's border and history for the next half a century. In 1940s, in less than a year, Romania lost a major part of its territories to Russia, Hungary, Ukraine and Bulgaria. Willing to recover its territories occupied by Russia, in 1941 Romania enters into war as an ally of the Axis, but in 1944 the King Mihai decides to change sides and fight together with the Allies, and Romania manages to contribute decisively to the defeat of the Germans. As recognition of its merits, after the war Norden Transylvania is returned to Romania, but the Norden and Eastern Moldavia and Southern Dobrogea remain under Russian and Bulgarian occupation.

20. In 1946, after fraudulent elections, the communist party forms the first communist government, and the communism installs in Romania for more than half a century. In 1947 King Mihai is forced to abdicate by the communists and Romania becomes a communist republic. From the end of 1940s through the 1950s to the beginning of the 1960s the communist party completely reshaped Romanian society: all the previous cultural, intellectual and politic elites were prisoned and most of them died in prisons; private property ceased to exist and most of land and houses once belonging to former middles and high class was confiscated; the political pluralism ceased, as the only remaining party was the communist one, etc.

21. In 1967 Ceauseşescu became head of state. After a short relaxation, he soon transformed his regime into one of the harshest in the communist bloc, putting in a militia that was supervising and controlling everyone, closing the borders so that leaving the country was prohibited and setting an extreme level of austerity for the people.

22. December 1989 marks the end of the communist regime in Romania. After a bloody revolution, in which thousands have died, the communist regime is overturned, and democracy is installed. Although the evolution was not linear, once the communist regime ended, the adherence of Romanians to the western values and democracy is undoubtable. As an expression of this, in 2004 Romania became part of North Atlantic Treaty Organization and in 2007 part of EU.

III. Political System

23. Romania is a semipresidential representative, democratic and social republic. The Constitution of 1991, adopted after the fall of the communist party and revised in 2003, establishes a democratic republic form of government of the Romanian State that is organized on the principle of the separation and balance of the three powers: legislative, executive and judicial within the framework of constitutional democracy.

24. The Parliament is the supreme representative body of the Romanian people and it consists of the Chamber of Deputies (332 members) and the Senate (137 members). The mandate of its members takes four years.

25. It is also the sole legislative authority of the State. However, legislation delegation is admitted in certain conditions provided by the Constitution. Thus the Parliament may pass a special law enabling the Government to issue ordinances in fields outside the scope of organic laws. Also, the Government can adopt emergency ordinances in exceptional cases, the regulation of which cannot be postponed.

26. In accordance with its government program accepted by the Parliament, the Government ensures the implementation of the domestic and foreign policy of the country and exercises the general management of the public administration. Special central public administration can be exercised by ministries or other specialized agencies. The local representative of the Government is the prefect, appointed in each county and in the Bucharest Municipality. The prefect directs the decentralized public services of ministries and other bodies of the central public administration in the territorial administrative units.

27. The Prime Minister directs the Government actions and co-ordinates activities of its members, under observance of the powers and duties incumbent on them.

28. The President of Romania is elected for a five-year term, with the possibility to be reelected once, by universal, equal, direct, secret and free suffrage. The President has mainly a role of representation of the Romanian State and safeguard of the national independence, unity and territorial integrity of the country. It will also act as a mediator between the powers in the State as well as between the State and the society. The Constitution also grants him special powers in matters of foreign policy, defense and emergency measures.

29. Judicial authority comprises the courts of law, the Public Ministry and the Superior Council of Magistracy, whose role is to guard the independence of justice. Justice is administrated by the High Court of Cassation and Justice and 245 other courts set up by the law: courts of appeal, tribunals and district courts. Within the judicial activity, the Public Ministry represents the general interest of the society and defends legal order, as well as citizens' rights and freedoms.

IV. Economic and Social Values

30. After the fall of communism, in December 1989, Romania turned from a communist economy, dominated by the state, to a capitalist economy based on private initiative. The evolution was by no means a steady and linear one, by contrary. Many of the state companies which have been privatized in the 1990s soon went bankrupt, the agricultural infrastructure was destroyed, unemployment increased dramatically, the level of inflation were skyrocketing and social tension was building up.

31. Nevertheless, after a harsh beginning, things were slowly leveling up, as the economy started to recover, to the point where now the gross domestic product is several times higher than in 1989, with Romania having one of the fastest economic growths in the EU and one of the lowest public debts levels. It is still far to the point where one could say that things are working perfectly, but the evolution is certainly taking place. The main economic sectors are agriculture, services, production of assets (such as cars, household items, furniture or cloths) and information technology. The economic sector is dominated by private companies, even though some public companies still exist, but only in marginal areas, such as postal services or energy.

32. Because of its history, Romania is a multicultural society, with multiple nations and ethnic groups leaving together in pace. Except some minor and local cases, no major conflicts existed among the different groups, and the atmosphere is one of tolerance and acceptance. Furthermore, despite being quite a conservatory and highly religious country, the level of tolerance and acceptance also manifests in relation to other minorities, such as sexual ones. As an evidence in this regard, a national referendum, carried in 2018 and having as a goal prohibiting by Constitution the same sex marriages, met a very low popular support and ended up rejected, although it was strongly supported by all major parties and the orthodox church. Thus, values such as family, religion and tolerance form the core of social values.

33. Another landmark of Romanian society is its adherence to traditions. In many parts of Romania, century old traditions, as those referring to major religious celebrations, life events or social activities are carefully preserved and passed to further generations as an important cultural, social and religious heritage. Among others, one can still find regions in which the locals use for special occasions traditional clothes, play traditional songs or practice different traditional activities.

34. Finally, it must be mentioned that after the fall of the communism and the opening of borders, many Romanians, especially youngsters, left the country and settled abroad. This phenomenon manifested more intensely after Romania became part of EU, to the point where it is estimated that more than 4 million Romanians have now their residence abroad. Though most of them still regularly visit Romania and plan to return one day, the high level of migration impacted Romanian society on all levels: the labor force declined; many children, some only a few months old, were left behind with relatives, mainly grandparents; entire communities were depopulated; schools were closed because of the lack of children, etc. These situations led local authorities to emplace different measures in order to encourage the return of Romanians from abroad, but so far with little result.

§2. Legal Systems

I. Primacy of Legislation and Codification

35. Romania's legal system is part of the large family of juridical systems of Romanic tradition. Therefore, the law is eminently written; there is a hierarchy of the sources of the law and a division between the public and private law as well as a certain division on branches.

36. The (written) Constitution of 1991, revised in 2003, consecrates the principle of supremacy of Constitution and laws. However, there are two exceptions to this principle. First, where any inconsistencies exist between the covenants and treaties on the fundamental human rights Romania is a party to, and the national laws, the international regulations shall take precedence, unless the Constitution or national laws comprise more favorable provisions. Second, as a member of the EU, the provisions of the constituent treaties of the EU, as well as the other mandatory

community regulations, shall take precedence over the opposite provisions of the national laws, including the Constitution as it results from the jurisprudence of the Court of Justice of the EU, in compliance with the provisions of the accession act.

37. In order to guarantee the supremacy of the Constitution, the Constitutional Court is empowered to adjudicate on the constitutionality of laws and of treaties or other international agreements as well as to decide on objections as to the unconstitutionality of laws and ordinances, brought up before courts of law or commercial arbitration.

38. The hierarchy of norms is also reinforced by the principle of legality that states that an inferior legal norm cannot contradict a superior legal norm. The legal control of all the other normative acts adopted in order to ensure the execution of the law is realized by the administrative law courts.

39. The codification is also a main feature of the Romanian legal system. All the main areas of social life are regulated by a main source of law, namely a code, such as: the Civil Code, the Civil Procedure Code, the Criminal Code, the Criminal Procedure Code, the Fiscal Code, the Fiscal Procedure Code, the Administrative Code, the Forestry Code, the Custom Control Code, and the Aerial Code.

40. The first Romanian Civil Code has been adopted in 1865 after the model of the Napoleonic French Civil Code. Over time there were several attempts to adopt a new Civil Code, but it was not until 2009 that such an endeavor was realized. The new Civil Code[2] was aimed to be a modern codification that reconciles the old traditions of the Civil Code with the new challenges of the recent legislation. Thus, a large part of the rules consecrated by the 1865 Civil Code have been maintained in accordance with the interpretation given by the doctrine and the jurisprudence. However, different solutions have also been adopted apprehended by newer codifications such as the Quebec Civil Code, Italian Civil Code, Suisse Obligations Code as well as by the unification projects existing at the European level, like the principles of European contract law.

II. Position of the Judiciary

41. The judicial power is one of the three independent powers on which Romania, as a state, is built on. In this regard, Article 1, paragraph 4 of the Constitution, provides that Romania is organized based on the principle of the separation and balance of powers—legislative, executive, and judicial—within the framework of constitutional democracy. Furthermore, Article 126, paragraph 1, of the Constitution

2. Law No. 287/2009 concerning the Civil Code, republished in the Official Journal (O.J.) No. 505/15.07.2011. The new Civil Code entered into force on October 1, 2011 according to the dispositions of Law No. 71/2011 for the implementation of the new civil code.

provides that justice shall be administered by the High Court of Cassation and Justice,[3] and the other courts set up by the law, while Article 133, first paragraph, states that the Superior Council of Magistracy shall guarantee the independence of justice.

42. Acting as one of the three powers, the main role of the judiciary is to solve the legal disputes that occur while applying the laws. There are four types of courts: first instance courts, tribunals, courts of appeal and the High Court of Cassation and Justice, the last being the only supreme court in Romania. Usually, for all cases the legal norms provide at least two levels of jurisdiction (first instance and appeal), but in recent years, as a result of a Constitutional Court decision[4] and some new legislations,[5] a three-level jurisdiction (first instance, appeal and appeal on points of law) seems to become the rule. Depending on its object, a case may start at the first instance court or at the tribunal, and, in exceptional cases, the Court of Appeal. The High Court of Cassation and Justice decides as a first instance court only in criminal matters, while in all other domains it decides only on appeals on points of law. Also, its constitutional role is to ensure the unitary interpretation and application of the law.[6] The constitutional control of the laws is not in the competence of regular courts, but of the Constitutional Court, a body outside the judiciary, made of nine judges, appointed for nine-year term by the Parliament and President. In order to be appointed as judge at the Constitutional Court, one does not have to be a judge, but only to have a specific experience in the field of law. Once delivered, a judicial decision can be enforced by a bailiff. The courts keep some competence in the enforcement proceedings as well. For example, no decision can be enforced without a court order and any interested party may file a complaint to court against the acts and deeds of the bailiff.[7]

43. In Romania all judges are professionals. There are two ways to become a judge. As a rule, a law graduate must pass a series of exceedingly difficult entering exams to become student at the National Institute of Magistracy, the organ that trains the future judges and prosecutors.[8] According to the new rules adopted in 2018, once at the National Institute of Magistracy, the students undergo four years of theoretical and practical trainings and then need to pass another series of exams in order to become judge trainees.[9] Then, they seat as judge trainees for two

3. Over time, the High Court of Cassation and Justice had different names. During the communism, it was called the Supreme Tribunal and after the communism, until 2003, the Supreme Court of Justice.
4. Constitutional Court Decision No. 369/2017, published in Monitorul Oficial (M. Of.) No. 582/20 July 2017.
5. *See* Law No. 310/2018, published in Monitorul Oficial No. 1074/18 of December 2018.
6. *See* Art. 126(3) of the Constitution.
7. *See* Arts. 666 and 712 of Civil Procedure Code.
8. According to Art. 15 of Law No. 304/2004 the exam is organized each year and is common for future judges and prosecutors. The distinction between judges and prosecutors is made only after graduating the National Institute of Magistracy when the students can choose one of the two in the limit of the positions offered.
9. *See* Art. 16 of Law No. 304/2004, regarding the status of judges and prosecutors, republished in Monitorul Oficial No. 653/22 July 2005.

years,[10] during which they decide as a regular judge, but having a limited competence to simple cases. After this period and a new series of exams, they become judges. The other way to become a judge is addressed to those who have at least five years of experience in a legal profession (lawyer, public notary, jurisconsult, etc.). They become judges by simply passing an exam organized by the National Institute of Magistracy.[11] The latter modality is considered an exception. It is worth mentioning, in this context, that in order to get to upper courts a judge must fulfill some experience criteria, score "very good" at the last evaluation and pass a new series of exams.[12]

44. Though it is in balance with the other powers, the judiciary is completely independent in fulfilling its role, as the means through which the other powers may intervene within the scope and competence of the judiciary are highly limited. For example, both the Parliament and the Government must respect and enforce a judicial decision and cannot pass legislation in order to escape such an obligation. The only exception in this regard is the right of the President and the Parliament to pardon a convict who committed a crime. The element of balance is kept through instruments that do not interfere with the core of judicial functions. For example, after passing all the exams, the President is the one who appoints the judges, through presidential decree. The Senate validates the elected members in the Supreme Council of Magistracy and the Ministry of Justice administrates the courts' budget and infrastructure (except the High Court of Cassation and Justice). The independence of judiciary is guaranteed by the Supreme Council of Magistracy, a body made of nineteen members, out of which nine judges, five prosecutors, two representatives of civil society appointed by the Senate, the Minister of Justice, the President of the High Court of Cassation and Justice and the General Prosecutor. The judges and prosecutors are elected by their colleagues for a six-year term and are representative for each type of courts. The Council has competence in meters such as disciplinary responsibility of judges and prosecutors, organizing the entering and promotion exams and defending the reputation of judiciary as a whole or of the magistrates.

III. Distinction Between Public and Private Law

45. Roman law has had a major influence over the architecture of Romania's legal system, and these can be noticed in multiple aspects, one of which is the perpetuation of the Ulpian's distinction between public and private law.[13] According to Romanian doctrine, under a general perspective, public law encompasses those norms that regulate the status of public authorities and civil servants, their powers and prerogatives and their relationship with privates, while private law refers to the

10. *See* Art. 22 of Law No. 304/2004.
11. *See* Art. 33 of Law No. 304/2004.
12. *See* Art. 44 of Law No. 304/2004.
13. Regarding the Roman origin of the distinction and its misinterpretation, *see* M. Nicolae, *Drept civil. Teoria Generală. Vol. I. Teoria dreptului civil (Civil Law. General Theory. First Volume. The Theory of Civil Law)*, p. 40, note 90.

norms that regulate the relationship between privates, natural or moral persons.[14] Multiple criteria were proposed as landmarks for distinguishing between public and private law. First, while the public law applies to public authorities and their relationship with individuals, private law applies mainly to privates. Second, the public law protects and promotes the public interests, whereas the private law focuses on the interest of the individuals. Finally, while the public law is characterized by its force, with its ability to unilaterally impose a certain conduct, private law deals with relationships that are based on the free will of the parties.[15] Though well rooted, the distinctions and the main criteria that are based on it are not beyond any debate, as sometimes a clear boundary between the two cannot be drafted.[16] Furthermore, as a scholar underlined, there are branches of law, such as labor law, that contain both public and private norms, whereas there are others, like criminal law, that are neutral, as are meant to protect both private and public interest.[17]

46. In any case, traditionally, some legal branches of law, such as constitutional law, criminal law, administrative law or fiscal law are considered as part of public law, whereas others, such as civil law, commercial law and international private law as part of private law.[18] In this regard, tort law is generally considered as a part of private law, but it is worth mentioning that when the damage is caused by a civil servant, a magistrate or a public authority, the legislator imposed special public law norms, derogatory from the civil rules, which regulate the conditions on which such a damage can be repaired.[19] Even so, the special legislative framework provides only specific rules and, for this reason, when applied, it needs to be complemented with civil tort law.

47. The general distinction between public and private law does not only relate to doctrinal works and structuring criteria for classes in law faculties. It also reflects on the judiciary. Apart from different substantive law that applies on a given case and the authorities that may have attributes in the legal dispute, public and private law often lead to different competence of courts. For example, if usually a private law case falls within the primary competence of first instance courts, in public law cases the competence belongs to the tribunals or courts of appeal. Furthermore, in the same court, often there are different panels or sections for public and private law.

48. Still, deviating considerably from most of European legal systems, in Romania there are no special administrative courts. Administrative litigations are within

---

14. *See*, *e.g.*, I. Deleanu, *Instituţii şi proceduri constituţionale în dreptul român şi în dreptul comparat (Constitutional Institutions and Proceedings in Romanian Comparative Law)*, C.H. Beck, Bucureşti, 2006, pp. 12–13; M. Nicolae, *supra*, p. 44.
15. I. Deleanu, *supra*, pp. 12–13.
16. I. Deleanu, *supra*, pp. 14–16.
17. *See* M. Nicolae, *supra*, pp. 50–51.
18. *See* M. Nicolae, *supra*, pp. 44–48.
19. For the legal norms applicable to civil servants, *see*, *e.g.*, Emergency Governmental Ordinance (O.U.G.) No. 57/2019, Administrative Code.

the competence of regular courts and are mainly decide by Tribunals or Courts of Appeals (as first jurisdictions) in panels or sections that have special competence for such cases.

IV. Sources of Private Law in General and of Tort Law in Particular

49. The regulation of the sources of private law has a prior importance in the civil Romanian system. The first article of the Civil Code states that legislation, customs and general principles of law are the sources of private law.

50. Legislation represents the main source and it includes international and supranational legal acts (such as international treaties regarding human rights or European Union Law) as well as Romanian legal acts (such as the Constitution, Civil Code, organic and ordinary laws—acts of the Parliament and governmental ordinances that comprise civil law norms).

51. Customs represent a source of law in the absence of a written law (as mentioned above) or whenever the latter makes express reference to customs.

52. If there is no written or customary law for a certain situation that should be regulated by the private law, the general principles of law will be applied directly by the judge. Such principles are the principle of property, the principle of equality under the law, the principle of good faith, the principle of guaranteeing and protection of subjective rights and the principle of combination of individual interest with the general interest.[20]

53. This hierarchy of general private law sources makes possible for the judge to analyze all civil claims brought before the court as he cannot dismiss a claim on the ground that there is no law applicable.

54. The Civil Code sets the ground rules concerning tort law. Chapter IV of Book V about civil obligations is dedicated to civil liability. Articles 1.349–1.395 of the Civil Code is dedicated to this chapter that is being organized in six different sections concerning: general dispositions (first section), causes of exoneration (second section), liability for own act (third section), liability for act of others (fourth section), liability for damage caused by animals or things (fifth section), compensation of damage (sixth section).

55. The influence and effect of the European Union's legislation as well as the multiplication of the sources and types of damages led to a constant growth in the number of dedicated laws concerning different form of liabilities. Thus, the special tort legislation started to develop and to represent an important source of tort law. In this category the following may be included: Governmental Ordinance No. 137/ 2000 on the prevention and sanction of all forms of discrimination, Law No. 703/

20. *See* M. Nicolae, *supra*, p. 243.

2001 concerning civil liability for nuclear damage, Law No. 240/2004 of the civil liability of producers for damages generated by defective products, Law No. 95/2006 concerning the reform in the medical system, O.U.G. No. 195/2005 concerning the environmental protection and O.U.G. No. 68/2007 concerning the environmental liability, Law No. 132/2017 concerning the mandatory motor insurance for civil liability for damages caused to third parties by trams' and vehicles' accidents, etc.

§3. Functions of the Law of Torts

56. Romanian legal scholars are unanimously admitting that law of torts plays a number of functions, some of which are directly regulated by civil law norms, while others implicitly result from the general judicial regime of tortious liability. Though there is no consensus among scholars regarding the number, the nature and the precise content of this function, the majority admits that tort liability plays a reparatory function, a deterrent function and an educative function.

I. The Reparatory Function

57. Regarding the reparatory function, Article 1.357(1) Civil Code[21] states that "the one who causes another a damage, by an imputable illicit deed, must repair it," while Article 1.381(1) C.C. provides that "any damage entitles [the victim] to compensation" and finally, Article 1.385(1) C.C. states that, "the damage shall be fully compensated, if the law does not provide otherwise." Materializing the principle of corrective justice, the mentioned norms describe the general framework of the so-called reparative function of tort law.[22]

58. Every individual must respect the subjective rights and legitimate interest of others. Each time one breaches this obligation and interferes with the right or legitimate interest of another, by committing an illicit deed, the tort law provides the victim with the judicial instruments by which to obtain the indemnification of the damage he has suffered.[23] As such, the main roles of tort law are to allow a *restitutio in integrum* for the victim (to place his patrimony to the state it would have

21. *Brevitatis causa*, "C.C."
22. *See* I.I. Neamţ, *Acţiunea colectivă ca mijloc de reparare a prejudiciilor în masă. O analiză din perspectiva dreptului comparat (The Class Action as an Instrument for Repairing Mass Torts. A Comparative Law Analysis)*, Universul Juridic, Bucharest, 2017, p. 187.
23. *Ibid. See also* I.I. Neamţ and L.T. Dăuceanu, *Drept Civil. Obligaţiile. Caiet de seminar. Ediţia a II a. revăzută şi adăugită (Civil Law. Obligations. Seminar Book, 2nd ed., revised and consolidated)*, Universul Juridic, Bucharest, 2019, p. 123; I.I. Neamţ, *Instrumente vechi pentru probleme noi. Prejudiciile în masă faţă-n faţă cu răspunderea civilă (Old Instruments for New Problems. Collective Damages Face to Face with Civil Liability)*, in Revista Română de Drept Privat No. 2/2020, p. 202; C. Jugastru, *Prejudiciul. Repere româneşti în context european (The Damage. Romanian Landmarks in European Context)*, Hamangiu, Bucharest, 2013, p. 12.

been in the absence of the tortious conduct), by removing all the negative consequences[24] and to reinstate the social balance dilapidated by the illicit deed.[25] Therefore, it has been stated that in the core of civil liability lies the idea of repairing a damage[26] and that no civil liability exists without a damage.[27] These doctrinal conclusions are validated by the fact that most of the tort law norms are constructed around the reparatory finality.[28]

59. From this point of view, the tort law is the mechanism by which the negative consequences of tortious conducts are removed, and the subjective rights and legitimate interest are being protected.[29] In direct connection with the analyzed function, it must be mentioned that while the Civil Code, adopted in 2009 and entered into force in 2011, has undoubtedly brought some major reforms in many domains of civil law, it does not provide with a general form of civil liability based on the principle of precaution. In other words, the only form of civil liability is still the one based on the existence of damage.[30]

60. For a *restitutio in integrum* to happen, the victim of the tortious conduct must be entitled to a full restoration of his rights. In this regard, according to Article 1386(1) C.C. the damage shall be repaired in kind by reestablishing the *status quo ante*. As such, if the wrongdoer destroyed an object belonging to the victim, it must repair or replace it with an identical one or if an asset is illicitly held, it must be returned. This is the only true way in which the victim of a tortious conduct can obtain a *restitutio in integrum*, and the negative consequences of the harmful act are

24. *See* L. Pop, *Răspunderea civilă (Civil Liability)*, Alma Maters Timisienis Mirton, 2001, p. 14; F.I. Mangu, *Răspunderea civilă. Constantele răspunderii civile (Civil Liability. The Constants of Civil Liability)*, Universul Juridic, Bucharest, 2014, p. 50. F.I. Mangu, *Funcţiile răspunderii civile în filosofia actualului Cod civil (Functions of Civil Liability in the Philosophy of the Current Civil Code)*, in Analele Ştiinţifice ale Universităţii "AL. I. Cuza" Iaşi, Tomul LIX, Ştiinţe Juridie, 2013, No. 1, p. 218; L.R. Boilă, in F.A. Baias, E. Chelaru, R. Constantinovici, and I. Macovei (coord), *Noul Cod Civil. Comenariu pe Articole. Ediţia 2. Revizuită şi adăugită (New Civil Code. Comment on Articles. 2nd ed., revised and consolidated)*, C.H. Beck, Bucharest, 2014, p. 1551; I.I. Neamţ, *Instrumente vechi* ... , *supra*, p. 202.
25. *See* P. Vasilescu, *Drept civil. Obligaţiile. Ediţia a 2-a revizuită (Civil Law. Obligations. 2nd ed., revised)*, Hamangiu, Bucharest, 2017, p. 585.
26. *See* I.I. Neamţ, *Poate frica faţă de un prejudiu viitor constitui un temei suficient pentru o răspundere civilă delictuală actuală. O privire în cutia Pandorei (Is the Fear of a Future Damage Likely to Be a Sufficient Basis for a Current Tort Liability? An Insight into Pandora's Box)*, in Revista Română de Drept Privat, No. 3/2020, p. 228; L. Pop, *Răspunderea* ... , *supra*, p. 14; L. Pop, *Tratat. Drept civil. Teoria generală a obligaţiilor (Treaty. Civil Law. General Theory of Obligations)*, Chemarea, Iaşi, 1998, p. 164.
27. *See* I. Neamţ, *Acţiunea colectivă* ... , *supra*, p. 188; I.I. Neamţ, *Instrumente vechi* ... , *supra*, p. 203; C. Stătescu and C. Bîrsan, *Drept civil. Teoria generală a obligaţiilor. Ediţia a IX-a, revăzuta şi adăugită (Civil Law. General Theory of Obligations. 9th ed., revised and added)*, Hamangiu, Bucharest, 2008, p. 145; F.I. Mangu, *Răspunderea civilă. Constantele* ... , *supra*, p. 146. *See also* C.A. Cluj, S. I. civ., dec. civ. 714/A/2015, in Curtea de Apel Cluj. Buletinul Jurisprudenţei. Repertoriu annual, Universul Juridic, 2015, p. 85.
28. *See* I. Neamţ, *Acţiunea colectivă* ... , *supra*, p. 188,
29. *See* I.I. Neamţ and L.T. Dăuceanu, *supra*, p. 123; I.I. Neamţ, *Instrumente vechi* ... , *supra*, p. 203; F.I. Mangu, *Funcţiile* ... , *supra*, p. 218.
30. *See* I.I. Neamţ, *Acţiunea colectivă* ... , *supra*, p. 188.

fully averted.[31] The problem is that in-kind reparation is only possible when it comes to pecuniary damages or damages caused to regular objects, considering that only such assets can be replaced without affecting the status quo. Also, sometimes an object cannot be repaired. In such situation, the same Article provides that the victim is entitled to damages. The amount is established by mutual agreement with the wrongdoer or by the court. Furthermore, the victim can choose to be afforded damages even when in-kind remedy is possible.

61. Another issue is related to the situation in which the tortious conduct breached a nonpecuniary subjective right, such as the right to private life, reputation, the right to one's own image or the right of personal integrity. In most of these situations, a real *restitutio in integrum* is not possible as you cannot, for example, repair the sufferance caused by losing a member of the family or the pain caused by an inflicted injury. For these types of damages, the Romanian law provides that the victim can ask for special remedies, such as the injunction of the illicit civil wrong[32] and is entitled to damages. The damages allowed to the victim are not meant to repair the harm he has suffered, but to compensate it through pecuniary means.

II. The Deterrent Function

62. Tortious liability is also considered to play a deterrent function,[33] which, unlike the previous one, has no express normative support,[34] but is thought to emerge from the general judicial regime and mechanism of civil liability.[35] In this regard, according to scholars and jurisprudence, the tortious liability is a specific civil sanction, of pecuniary nature, directed against the wrongdoer.[36] Based on the effects that it is has over the wrongdoer's patrimony, tortious liability acts as an inhibitory and a preventive mechanism when it comes to civil wrongs, because knowing that a damageable deed may lead to tortious liability and the obligation to repair the damage caused, one will restrain from such deeds.[37]

---

31. *See* L. Pop, *Tratat de drept civil. Obligaţiile. Volumul III. Raporturile obligaţionale extracontractuale (Civil Law Treaty. Obligations. 3rd Volume. Extracontractual Legal Relations)*, Universul Juridic, 2020, p. 497; P. Vasilescu, *supra*, p. 586.
32. *See* Arts. 253–255 C.C.
33. *See* L. Pop, *Drept civil român. Teoria generală a obligţiilor (Romanian Civil Law. General Theory of Obligations)*, Lumina Lex, Bucharest, 2000, p. 189; C. Stătescu and C. Bîrsan, *supra*, p. 127; I.I. Neamţ, *Acţiunea colectivă ...*, *supra*, p. 189; F.I. Mangu, *Funcţiile ...*, *supra*, p. 219.
34. *See* I.I. Neamţ, *Acţiunea colectivă ...*, *supra*, p. 189; I.I. Neamţ, *Instrumente vechi ...*, *supra*, p. 208.
35. *See* L. Pop, *Răspunderea ...*, *supra*, p. 13; I.I. Neamţ, *Instrumente vechi ...*, *supra*, p. 208.
36. *See* L. Pop, *Drept civil ...*, p. 170; L. Pop, *Răspunderea ...*, *supra*, p. 13; C. Stătescu and C. Bîrsan, *supra*, pp. 126–127; I.I. Neamţ, *Acţiunea colectivă ...*, *supra*, p. 189; I.I. Neamţ and L.T. Dăuceanu, *supra*, p. 124. It is a sanction and not a punishment as it is meant to be an instrument through which the victim may obtain the redress and not the punishment of the wrongdoer. Furthermore, tortious liability gravitates around the tortfeasor's patrimony and not his person, this being the reason why the obligation to repair the damage is transmitted to successors.
37. *See* L. Pop, *Drept civil ...*, p. 170; C. Stătescu and C. Bîrsan, *supra*, p. 127; I.I. Neamţ, *Acţiunea colectivă ...*, *supra*, p. 189; I.I. Neamţ and L.T. Dăuceanu, *supra*, p. 124; I.I. Neamţ, *Instrumente*

63. From this perspective, the deterrent effect of tortious liability is closely linked to the condition of fault, as in order to foresee the consequences of a certain civil wrong and restrain from committing it, one must have the psychological representation of them.[38] In other words, the civil wrong must be imputable to the wrongdoer as he acted either intentionally or by negligence. Nevertheless, the doctrine has underlined that the deterrent effect also exists in the case of strict liability and the only thing that changes is the way in which it manifests.[39] All the hypotheses of strict liability have as fundament the idea of risk and in most of the cases the risk creator is also the one who must control it or to repair the damage caused if the risk materializes. This perspective, of having to repair a certain damage, will determine the risk controller to take the optimum measures to prevent the risk from materializing.[40]

64. The existence of assurances for civil liability was also considered to have a destructive effect when it comes to deterrence because of the fact the tortfeasor no longer has to pay for the damage caused, the responsibility being transferred to the assurance company. Still, the existence of an assurance does not completely void the deterrent effect of tortious liability. The highly spread "bonus-malus" clause will determine an increasing cost of assurance if the risk materializes, which in turn will have a deterrent effect over the risk controller.[41] Furthermore, in most of the cases, the assurance company will indemnify the victims only to a certain amount.[42] If the damage caused exceeds that limit, the responsibility for the extra amount belongs to the tortfeasor and such a probability will conserve the deterrence, even if an assurance contract was concluded.[43] Moreover, when it comes to companies, the fact that a tortious conduct can have devastating consequences on commercial reputation and credibility, acts as a deterrent for engaging in such conducts, no matter if an assurance contract was concluded or not.[44] Finally, it has been noticed that sometimes

---

vechi ... , supra, p. 208; I.M. Anghel, Fr. Deack, and M.F. Popa, *Răspunerea civilă (Civil Liability)*, Ştiinţifică, Bucharest, 1970, p. 25; F.I. Mangu, *Răspunderea civilă. Constantele ... , supra*, pp. 51–52; F.I. Mangu, *Funcţiile ... , supra*, p. 219.

38. *See* I.F. Mangu, *Răspunderea civilă delictuală obiectivă (Objective Civil Liability)*, Universul Juridic, Bucharest, 2015, p. 10.
39. In Romanian legal doctrine, the term used to describe the situation when no fault is required in order to engage one's liability is "objective liability" and not strict liability, in contrast to "subjective liability" which describes those situations when the liability is based on fault. These notions are used because fault is considered to be a subjective condition, as it refers to one's state of mind in relation to an illicit act. For these reasons, in this monograph, we will use the notions of objective liability and strict liability as synonyms, meant to describe those forms of liability in which no prove of fault is required.
40. *See* I.I. Neamţ, *Acţiunea colectivă ... , supra*, p. 190; F.I. Mangu, *Funcţiile ... , supra*, pp. 223–224.
41. *See* I.I. Neamţ, *Acţiunea colectivă ... , supra*, p. 190; F.I. Mangu, *Răspunderea civilă. Constantele ... , supra*, pp. 52–53; F.I. Mangu, *Funcţiile ... , supra*, pp. 220.
42. Article 2.224(2) C.C. provides that "The insurer can be sued by the injured persons only within the limits of his obligation as set in the assurance contract."
43. *See* I.I. Neamţ, *Acţiunea colectivă ... , supra*, p. 190.
44. *Ibid.*

assurance companies closely watch the compliance of the policyholder with the prevention rules and legal norms in order to prevent the risk, which further strengthens the deterrence when an assurance contract exists.[45]

65. Deterrence is most intense when tortfeasor is bound to repair the damage caused.[46] Having to wear off the negative consequences of the illegal deed, the wrongdoer will internalize the costs of repairing the damage, and this will lead to a strong, concrete, deterrence for future. Occurring only *ex post*, this type of deterrence will influence the behavior of the wrongdoer after he was held liable. There is also a form of abstract deterrence, that influences the behavior of the entire community, which results from the mere existence of the norms that regulate tortious liability. The individual, knowing that if a legal or social norm is breached tortious liability will be engaged, will abstain from acting so or will take the necessary preventive measures. Though it exists as a consequence of the normative framework, this type of deterrence consolidates when the norms are predictably applied, and individuals realize that being held liable is not just an abstract possibility. Whereas concrete deterrence operates *ex post*, abstract deterrence acts *ex ante.*[47]

66. Finally, a distinction can be drawn between under deterrence, over deterrence and optimal deterrence. Under deterrence exists when the tortfeasor does not internalize all the negative consequences of the civil wrong[48] or when it does not prevent the risk, though the expenses for doing so would have been optimal compared to the results. Over deterrence occurs when the tortfeasor is held liable for more than the damage caused. Thus, the deterrence is optimal when the wrongdoer is held liable for the entire damage caused and noting more. Both under and over deterrence have undesirable consequences. While first may encourage the perpetuation of illicit acts, the second leads to an overcharge of the wrongdoer and may discourage innovation and technological development. Therefore, optimal deterrence should be the landmark.[49] By stating the principle of full compensation and not allowing punitive damage, the Romanian legislator tried to achieve an optimal deterrence. Still, the lack of a special procedure for mass torts may sometimes lead to under deterrence or over deterrence, regardless of the substantive legal framework.

---

45. *Ibid.*
46. *See* I.I. Neamţ, *Instrumente vechi ...* , *supra*, p. 209.
47. For further details regarding concrete and abstract deterrence, *see* I.I. Neamţ, *Acţiunea colectivă ...* , *supra*, pp. 191–193.
48. So is the case, for example, when the same illicit deed damages multiple victims but only some are compensated by the tortfeasor.
49. For further details, *see* I.I. Neamţ, *Acţiunea colectivă ...* , *supra*, pp. 193–194; I.I. Neamţ, *Instrumente vechi ...* , *supra*, p. 209.

III. The Educative Function of Law of Tort

67. Like the previously analyzed function, the educative one is not expressly regulated, but it results from the general regime of tortious liability. From this perspective, it was asserted that tortious liability is meant to create and maintain a social order in which all the individuals respect the rights and freedoms of others.[50] If this legal order is breached, the victims are entitled to seek the coercive force of the state in the form of ordering the tortfeasor to repair the damage caused.[51] The very existence of such entitlement shapes the social consciousness in the sense that individuals realize that committing tortious act is undesirable.[52] As such, because of the influence that it has over the human consciousness, civil liability plays an educative function,[53] underlining the behaviors that are socially accepted and the ones that are not, and sanctioning the last.[54]

68. Furthermore, another manifestation of the educative function is considered to be the normative one. Although any breach of legal or social norms may lead to tortious liability, there are a lot of situations in which for regular individuals it is difficult to decide the legal or illegal nature of a given conduct, especially because of the huge number of legal norms and their technicality. Still, each time one alleges of being a victim of a civil wrong, a court shall establish if the conduct brought before it is or not legal. From this perspective, tortious liability plays a certain normative role, establishing *in concreto* which conduct is or not legal.[55]

69. Finally, in a recent paper, a new facet of the educative function of law of torts was underlined. The author has shown that, usually, the victim is the only one entitled to decide if the tortfeasor should be brought before a court or not and to reclaim the indemnification for the damaged caused. Nor the society, nor other individuals and not even the state (except particular situations provided by law) can act on behalf of the victim and ask for the tortfeasor to be held responsible for the damage caused. As so, in relation to the damage suffered, the victim acts like a private prosecutor invested with full discretionary powers. After considering the advantages and disadvantages of every option, the victim may decide to use the law of torts and ask the tortfeasor to pay for the damage caused or to remain passive because either he absolved the wrongdoer or the effort for engaging tortious liability is unreasonable in comparison to eventual benefits.[56] In any case, the victim also carries a social responsibility. If the victim decides to leave unpunished the tortfeasor and to remain passive without a good reason, the victim will implicitly encourage similar conducts, which may lead to other victims in the future and the perpetuation of social tension. When it decides to act, after personally enduring the

50. *See* I.I. Neamţ and I.T. Dăuceanu, *supra*, p. 124; F.I. Mangu, *Răspunderea civilă. Constantele …* , *supra*, p. 54.
51. *See* I.I. Neamţ, *Acţiunea colectivă …* , *supra*, p. 190.
52. *Ibid. See also* F.I. Mangu, *Funcţiile …* , *supra*, p. 219.
53. *See* C. Stătescu and C. Bîrsan, *supra*, p. 127.
54. *See* L. Pop, *Răspunderea …* , *supra*, p. 13.
55. *See* I.I. Neamţ, *Acţiunea colectivă …* , *supra*, p. 191; P. Vasilescu, *supra*, p. 588.
56. *See* I.I. Neamţ, *Acţiunea colectivă …* , *supra*, p. 191.

effect of an illicit deed, the victim, consciously or not, assumes a social role and determines the preventions of similar illicit acts for the future, by engaging the tortious liability of the wrongdoer.[57] The victim may sometimes decide to act not for the personal benefit, but to prevent such deed from happening in the future. While the previous facets of educative function were related to community in general, and tortfeasors in particular, the last opinion focuses on the victims and their role in keeping the social balance, once a tort was committed.

70. As described, the preventive and educative function of tortious liability are highly interconnected, one being just another perspective of the other. This is why, until recent years prevention and education were regarded as parts of the same concept and were analyzed together.[58]

IV. The Relation Between Deterrence and Indemnification

71. Though both deterrence and indemnification are unanimously considered by Romanian legal scholars as fundamental functions of the tortious liability, little attention is paid to the relation between them or, more precisely, their hierarchy in connection to tortious liability. Still, when the aspect was analyzed, the opinions seem, so far, to be opposite.

72. On one hand, some consider that the indemnification, or reparatory, function prevails, several arguments being put forward in this respect.[59] First, it has been emphasized that in the cases of strict liability deterrence is highly diminished, as the sanctioning function of the tortious liability is averted. Second, the damage was considered to be the main landmark of tortious liability because of the fact that the tortfeasor cannot be held liable for more or less them the damage caused to the victim and, in some situations, the law admits that the victim is entitled to indemnification even though no guilt can be attributed to the defendant. Third, another argument was that the characteristic of tortious liability (the right of the victim to ask for indemnification or not, the fact that the compensation allowed to the victim is limited to the damage suffered, the fact that an individual subjective right or legal interest must be breached in order to engage tortious liability, the fact that the form of guilt usually has no significance and the fact that tortious liability is impregnated with a pecuniary characteristic) compete to the conclusion that indemnification is the main function of tortious liability. Finally, that fact that preventive liability (liability without damage, based on the principle of precaution) is only exceptionally admitted was considered to be another argument in favor of indemnification function.

57. *Ibid.*
58. *See* L. Pop, *Răspunderea ...* , *supra*, pp. 13–14; L. Pop, *Drept civil ...* , p. 170; C. Stătescu and C. Bîrsan, *supra*, p. 127.
59. For all these arguments, *see* I.I. Neamţ, *Acţiunea colectivă ...* , *supra*, p. 195; F.I. Mangu, *Răspunderea civilă. Constantele ...* , *supra*, pp. 58–64; F.I. Mangu, *Funcţiile ...* , *supra*, pp. 228–230.

73. On the other hand, there are scholars according to whom deterrence is the prevailing function, arguing that the role of tortious liability is rather to restate the social balance destroyed by the illicit deed and to ensure the compliance of individual with the legal norms, than to repair the damages, the last being only the mean by which such role is fulfilled.[60] As arguments for this conclusion, it was stated that in most of the cases a full indemnification of the victim and a proper fulfillment of reparatory function is an illusion, considering that no amount of money will ever be able to repair the damage caused to a victim who's health was affected or who lost a member of the family as a consequence of the tortious act. Even when the damage is purely pecuniary, the indemnification will not avert the lost time, the stress, the anxiety and the discomfort caused to the victims by the tortious conduct. Furthermore, some damages can never be truly repaired, such as when an illicit pollution leads to the extinction of a plant or animal species.[61] Furthermore, asked to make an *ex ante* decision, any reasonable individual will prefer the prevention to indemnification and if so, the law of tort, must consider this optic. Moreover, the social cost for eliminating the negative consequences of a tortious act are in most of the cases higher than those for preventing it, considering, among others, that even if the victim is fully compensated, the costs for community, such as those with carrying trial, will remain at least partially uncovered.[62] Finally, deterrence is not specific to tortious liability, but is rather an essential and fundamental function of legal norms, which is fulfilled trough a multitude of mechanism, one of which being tortious liability.[63]

V. The Sanctioning Function

74. The sanctioning function of tortious liability is indispensably linked to the idea of guilt. No civil sanction may be applied to an individual without proving his guilt, which means that the wrongdoer could have at least anticipated the consequences of the act, but negligently missed to do so. If when the first Civil Code was enacted, in 1864, most of tortious liability hypothesis were subjective or based on fault,[64] with the new Civil Code, entered into force on October 1, 2011, though the subjective tortious liability remains the rule, there are a lot of exceptions, which may lead to the conclusion that the sanctioning function was at least partially abandoned in favor of indemnification of the victim.

---

60. *See* I.I. Neamţ, *Acţiunea colectivă ... , supra*, p. 195.
61. *Ibid.*, pp. 195–196.
62. Even though in order to file a suit the plaintiff must pay a tax, which in the end will be paid by the losing party, the law provides a lot of exception to this rule and, in any case, in most of the time, the tax is too small to cover all the expenses made by the state with the trial.
63. *See* I.I. Neamţ, *Acţiunea colectivă ... , supra*, p. 196.
64. *See* L. Pop, *Încercare de sinteză a evoluţiei principalelor teorii cu privire la fundamentul răspunderii civile delictuale (Attempt to Summarize the Evolution of the Main Theories Regarding the Fundaments of Tortious Liability)*, în L. Pop, *"Contribuţii la studiul obligaţiilor civile" (Contributions to the Study of Civil Obligations)*, Universul Juridic, Bucharest, 2010, pp. 21–26.

75. It must be underlined that a distinction is drawn between sanction and punishment, in the sense that while first refers to one's patrimony, the second is connected to personal freedoms and liberties.[65] The sanctioning function of tortious liability rests on the idea of obliging the tortfeasor to repair the damage caused to victim within the limits the damage caused. This sanction refers to the tortfeasor's patrimony and not his personality. As such, on one hand the victim will face an eventual insolvency of the tortfeasor, but, on the other hand, if the wrongdoer dies before the damage is repaired, the obligation is transmitted to successors.

76. Romanian law of tort does not provide for punitive damages. No matter the type of tort or the form of fault on which the tortious conduct was committed, the amount of money afforded to the victim must reflect, as accurate as possible, the damage suffered and the tortfeasor cannot be obliged to pay more than the damage caused.[66] From this perspective, tortious liability cannot be used as a legal mechanism for punishing the tortfeasor for the illicit conduct. The only general hypothesis when one can be coerced to pay something similar to punitive damages is regulated within the enforcement proceedings and the debtor obligation is *intuitu personae*. In this regard, Article 906 of Civil Procedure Code provides that if the debtor does not fulfill the obligation within ten days after the bailiff has communicated the court order for starting the enforcement proceedings, he can be obliged to pay per diem penalties.[67] Still, the legal norms only apply in the enforcement proceedings and only when the debtor refuses to voluntary fulfill an *intuitu personae* obligation.[68]

§4. Relationship Between Torts and Criminal Law

77. If the wrongful act represents a crime, civil liability and criminal liability will concur. The victim has an option between demanding compensation separately before a civil court or during the criminal action.

78. The civil action brought before the criminal court will be tried according to the rules of tort law. It is argued that an exception to this rule may intervene whenever the crime represents a failure to perform a contractual obligation. In this case the victim may choose to ground its grief on contractual liability or tortious liability

65. *See* I.I. Neamţ and L.T. Dăuceanu, *supra*, p. 124.
66. Nevertheless, more and more legal scholars underline the need of a regulation in this regard and affirm that punitive damages exist even nowadays in different forms. *See, e.g.*, D. Gîrbovan, *Criterii de stabilire a daunelor morale: caracterul punitiv al daunelor ca satisfacţie pentru victimă. Repere europene şi naţionale (Criteria for Determining Moral Damages: The punitive Characteristic of the Damages Allowed as a Satisfaction for the Victim)*, in Revista Română de Drept Privat, No. 2/2020, pp. 50–73.
67. On the idea that these penalties are not meant to repair a damage but to sanction the debtor who refused to fulfill his obligation, *see* High Court of Cassation and Justice, Decision No. 16/2017, available at http://www.scj.ro/, last checked on Apr. 15, 2020.
68. For a specific hypothesis of enforcement proceedings when punitive damages are available, *see* I.I. Neamţ, *Executarea silită a dreptului de a avea legături personale cu minorul. Iluzie sau realitate? (Enforcement of the Right to Have Personal Connection with the Minor Child. Illusion or Reality?)*, in Revista de Dreptul Familiei, No. 1–2/2019, pp. 377–426.

rules. However, there are authors that challenge this conclusion stating that this exception is no longer an option for the victim.[69]

79. The criminal judgment of acquittal or cessation of the criminal trial has no effect concerning the damage or the fault of the wrongdoer/author. Instead the criminal judgment of conviction has a res judicata effect concerning the existence of the wrongful act and its author.

80. For this reason, a civil action brought before a civil court while the criminal proceedings are pending will most likely be suspended until the criminal judgment is rendered as this situation represents one of the cases in which a civil trial may be suspended by the judge.

§5. Relationship Between Contractual and Delictual or Tortious Responsibility *(Is There a Rule of Non Cumul? What About Precontractual Liability?)*

81. The generally accepted thesis recognizes a unitary character of civil responsibility but with a distinct legal regime between contractual and tortious responsibility.

82. The similarities that led to the conclusion of the unity of civil liability reside in the four general conditions that need to be met: wrongful act, damage, causality and fault.

83. The differences of the legal regime vary and mainly consist in: the specificity of the wrongful act (contractual liability supposes the breach of contract while tortious liability implies the breach of duty *neminem laedere*); the parties' capacity (required only for contractual liability where legal act rules apply); formal notice (required only for contractual liability); disclaimers (usually allowed for contractual liability and exceptionally prohibited while usually prohibited for tortious liability and exceptionally allowed); the extent of compensation of the damage (as a rule only the predictable damage will be compensated on contractual liability ground while on tortious liability ground the predictable and unpredictable damage will be compensated); solidarity (the obligations to compensate the damage issued of contractual liability are usually divisible between debtors and those issued from tortious liability are solidary); fault proof (in contractual liability cases, there is a fault presumption of fault that comes out of proven contractual breach while in tortious liability cases fault must always be proven by the victim).

84. In view of these distinctions it can be stated that contractual liability is applicable whenever there is a breach of contractual obligations assumed by one of the party that creates a damage for the other contractual party. Therefore, the contract

69. R. Dincă, Comparaison de la réforme du droit francais de la responsabilité civile avec le nouveau Code civil roumain. Volume 1 sous la direction Patrice Jourdain, Mireille Bacache, IRJS, 2018.

must be valid in order for a contractual liability ground to be admitted. Damage caused by a null contract will be compensated according to the tortious liability rules.

85. Also, tortious liability will be the applicable ground anytime the damage is caused to a third party or by a third party to the contract. In the latter case, this rule applies as long as the parties did not assume liability for such circumstances.

86. A distinction needs to be made for the wrongful acts committed during the negotiation's phase, namely in the precontractual stage. Thus, if the parties signed a negotiation or preparatory agreement and the damage is caused by a breach to an obligation issued of these agreements, the contractual liability will be applicable; if not, the damage will be compensated according to the tortious liability rules. It has to be mentioned that the Romanian doctrine or jurisprudence do not distinguish in this matter between the positive damage (the parties' situation in case the contract would have been signed) and negative damage (the parties' situation in case they would not have entered the negotiations). Therefore, the damage will be compensated according to the general rules, namely if the victim can prove his certainty and the direct causality. If a ground is contractual liability, predictability of the damage will also be a determinant factor for the compensation.

87. Concerning the victim's option to choose between the tortious liability and contractual liability it needs to be mentioned that the Civil Code has reinforced a strict rule of non cumul. Unless the law provides otherwise, neither of the parties cannot avoid contractual liability rules in favor of other rules more favorable. At the moment, there is no such case provided by the law that allows a victim to choose between the contractual or tortious liability. However, it is argued that an exception is provided by the Criminal Procedure Code that admits only tortious liability for the compensation of damage caused by a criminal act. In this case, if the criminal act also represents a breach of contract, the victim would have the option between tortious liability ground provided by the Criminal Procedure Code and contractual ground provided by the Civil Code.

§6. Protected Interests *(Are All Interests Equally Protected? Are Subjective Rights More Protected than Others?)*

88. One of the main characters of subjective civil rights is that of being granted legal protection when violated in the form of specific actions or liability.

89. The act of violating a subjective civil right of another is normally considered to be a wrongful act that gives rise to a distinct obligational legal relationship issued of tortious liability between the parties. Therefore, if there is damage, the victim can demand compensation on liability ground.

90. However, Article 1359 of the Civil Code expressly grants protection also to the interests by giving rise to the obligation to claim compensation from the author of the wrongful act when the damage was caused by the violation of another person's interest as long as the interest is legit, serious and by its manifestation creates the appearance of a subjective civil right. This is a general disposition and thus it allows any claim that satisfies the conditions required by law even if the interest has never been recognized by it before.

91. In the tortious liability regulation, the Civil Code recognizes two different interests: the commercial secret and the financial support offered benevolently by the victim to a third person.

92. The violation of the commercial secret is being indirectly regulated in Article 1363 where the legislator sets a special exemption cause related to it. Namely, a person can be exonerated of liability for the damage caused by the disclosure of the commercial secret if he or she can prove that it was required by serious circumstances concerning health or public security.

93. The interest of a third party to further receive financial support is also indirectly regulated by Article 1390 that establishes the person entitled to compensation in case of wrongful death. The rule is that it is entitled to compensate for pecuniary loss the person that by law had a right to receive financial support from the deceased. However, the legislator also allows the judge to set a compensation, according to the circumstances, to the person that the victim benevolently aided financially on a regular basis.

Part I. Liability for One's Own Acts

Chapter 1. General Principles

94. The entering into force of the new Civil Code on October 1, 2011 brought major reforms in all branches of civil law, and law of torts made no exception. While some new texts are the result of transforming into law the doctrine and jurisprudence under the previous Civil Code,[70] others represent an absolute novelty in our legal system.[71] In which the last is concerned, doctrine and jurisprudence is still evolving and there are some important aspects on which consensus had not been reached but things are starting to clarify.

95. When it comes to liability for own's act, first thing that can be noticed, by comparison with the old legislation, is the more detailed regulation of this hypothesis.[72] Though no major reforms were enacted in this domain, the legislator did, however, put into law the previous doctrine and jurisprudence. As in the old law, liability for own's act represents the common type of liability, the *jus commune* for all other forms of liability, setting the standard and the terms for reparatory civil liability.[73] For this reason, whenever the law does not state specific rules in regard to other types of liability, the general norms provided in the case of liability for own's act will apply.

96. The legal framework which regulates liability for own's acts is provided by Article 1.349, paragraphs (1) and (2), C.C. and Articles 1.357–1.371 C.C. corroborated with Articles 1.381–1.395 C.C, the last providing the rules generally applicable to indemnification no matter the type of tortious liability.[74] The main rules for engaging own's liability are provided by Article 1.349, paragraphs (1) and (2) C.C. and Article 1.357 C.C., first stating that "(1) Any individual has the duty to respect the rules of conduct provided by law or local custom and not to damage, by action

70. The previous Civil Code entered into force in 1864 and was French inspired.
71. So is the case, for example, of Art. 1.368 C.C. which provides that the one who lacked discernment at the time of the deed may still be held liable in certain conditions that will be later addressed.
72. For the synthetic regulation of the previous law of torts, *see* L. Pop, in L. Pop, I.Fl. Popa, and S.I. Vidu, *Tratat elementar de drept civil. Obligaţiile conform noului Cod civil (Basic Treaty on Civil Law. Obligations According to the New Civil Code)*, Universul Juridic, Bucharest, 2012, p. 405.
73. *See* P. Vasilescu, *supra*, p. 591.
74. *See* L. Pop, *Tratat elementar ... , supra*, p. 411 and L. Pop, in L. Pop, I.Fl. Popa, and S.I. Vidu, *Curs de drept civil. Obligaţiile (Civil Law Course. Obligations)*, Universul Juridic, Bucharest, 2015, p. 329.

or inaction, the rights and legitimate interest of others. Whoever, acting with discernment, breaches this duty is liable for all the damages caused and is obliged to fully repair them"[75] and the second that "(1) The one who causes a damage to another by an illicit deed committed with guilt, is bound to repair it. (2) The wrongdoer is liable for the smallest fault."

97. Doctrine and jurisprudence unanimously hold that the above-mentioned norms provide the terms for liability for own's act and for any other type of liability, if the law does not otherwise provide.[76] Referring to the above-mentioned norms, the terms that need to be met in order to engage tortious liability for own's fault are: the illicit act, the damage, the causal relation between illicit act and damage and the guilt. Some of these conditions, such as the damage and the *nexum* are common to all types of tortious liability, while others, such as guilt, is only specific to some. In case of a trial, all these terms must be proven by the victim, though some presumptions are provided by law to ease the task.

98. When it comes to the fundaments, under the previous Civil Code, liability was generally based on fault and no liability could be engaged without the victim proving that the defender could have at least foreseen the consequences of the illicit deed but decided to act.[77] This gave civil liability a strong moral component, as one could not be held liable if innocent and liability was seen as a sanction for committing an illicit act, which consisted in obliging the wrongdoer to repair the damage caused.[78] The social transformations that occurred after the old Civil Code was enacted, especially those related to technological and economic development, have soon tested the boundaries of the subjective perspective on civil liability, often proven to be unfitted for the new realities. No matter the form, a liability based on fault implied that the victim had to prove the psychological attitude of the defender toward the illicit deed and its consequences. When the damage resulted from a multitude of facts and circumstances or when machines were involved, such a task was often impossible,[79] which meant that the innocent victim had to endure the damages suffered and no one could be held liable. Obviously, this type of situation could not be accepted, and a solution had to be found. The first step was to adopt a French theory which meant that in some situations, such as liability for acts of others or

---

75. The title of Art. 1.349 C.C. is "răspunderea delictuală" which literally translates as "delictual liability." The legal doctrine has emphasized that the term is not accurate in today's context, as, reflecting the idea of guilt, it does not cover all the hypothesis. For this reason, considering also the EU Law, the notion of "extracontractual liability" was proposed. *See* L. Pop, *Tratat elementar* ... , *supra*, p. 407.
76. For example, *see* L. Pop, *Tratat elementar* ... , *supra*, p. 411; L. Pop, *Curs de drept civil* ... , *supra*, p. 329 and also Înalta Curte de Casaţie şi Justiţie (The High Court of Cassation and Justice), Second Panel, Decision No. 2483/2014, available at www.scj.ro, last checked on Nov. 4, 2019.
77. *See* I.I. Neamţ, *Acţiunea colectivă* ... , *supra*, p. 22; I.I. Neamţ and L.T. Dăuceanu, *supra*, p. 124; L. Pop, *Drept civil* ... , *supra*, p. 311; L. Pop, *Tratat elementar* ... , *supra*, pp. 394–396; L. Pop, *Curs de drept civil* ... , *supra*, pp. 310–311; F.I. Mangu, *Răspunderea civilă. Constantele* ... , *supra*, pp. 72–73.
78. *See* I.I. Neamţ, *Acţiunea colectivă* ... , *supra*, p. 22; L. Pop, *Tratat elementar* ... , *supra*, p. 396; C. Stătescu and C. Bîrsan, *supra*, p. 126; F.I. Mangu, *Răspunderea civilă. Constantele* ... , *supra*, p. 74.
79. *See* P. Vasilescu, *supra*, p. 577; F.I. Mangu, *Răspunderea civilă. Constantele* ... , *supra*.

liability for things and animals, the fault was presumed.[80] The liability was still subjective, based on fault, but the victim no longer had to prove the fault. If the defendant wanted to avoid liability, he had to prove that it was impossible to foresee the consequences of the illicit conduct.[81] Still, this perspective has proven to be artificial, as in some situations it was obvious that no fault could be reasonably ascertained.

99. This meant that the very fundament of civil liability needed to be reconsidered. First emerging in German legal doctrine and then promoted by scholars from other systems, such as the French one, the objective or strict liability was never unanimously accepted by Romanian legal doctrine and jurisprudence.[82] Still, different versions of this theory were proposed by relevant legal scholars as solutions for subjective liability and did not remain without impact in practice. Among these, the most important was the theory of risk, with its forms: the theory of risk-profit, the risk of activity theory and risk of authority theory.

100. According to the *risk theory*, as developed in German law and then assumed by Romanian legal scholars, human acts should be divided into common and dangerous, the last including activities such as the surveillance of animals, the use of agents, the use of machines and technological installations.[83] While for the first one can be held liable only if acting with fault, for the second liability one can be engaged no matter the fault, as the tortfeasor assumed the risk of liability when it engaged in a dangerous act.[84] From this perspective, civil liability is no longer seen as a sanction, but as an instrument for ensuring *restitutio in integrum* for the victim. The attention is shifted from sanctioning the tortfeasor to repairing the damage.[85] The fault is no longer presumed, but it becomes irrelevant, the liability of the one that is in charge of exercising the supervision, direction and control of the dangerous activity being engaged no matter the fault.[86]

101. The *risk-profit theory* (*ubi emolumentum, ibi onus*) states that the one who takes advantages from a certain activity must also assume the associated risks and compensate eventual damages caused.[87] This theory was intensely criticized on the

80. *See* F.I. Mangu, *Răspunderea civilă. Constantele ...*, *supra*, p. 72.
81. *See* I.I. Neamţ, *Acţiunea colectivă ...*, *supra*, p. 23; L. Pop, *Drept civil ...*, *supra*, p. 182; L. Pop, *Tratat elementar ...*, *supra*, p. 396; L. Pop, *Curs de drept civil ...*, *supra*, p. 312.
82. *See* L. Pop, *Tratat elementar ...*, *supra*, p. 397; L. Pop, *Curs de drept civil ...*, *supra*, p. 312.
83. *See* L. Pop, *Curs de drept civil ...*, *supra*, p. 313; F.I. Mangu, *Răspunderea civilă. Constantele ...*, *supra*, p. 75.
84. *See* I.I. Neamţ and L.T. Dăuceanu, *supra*, p. 124; L. Pop, *Tratat elementar ...*, *supra*, pp. 397–398; L. Pop, *Curs de drept civil ...*, *supra*, p. 313; F.I. Mangu, *Răspunderea civilă. Constantele ...*, *supra*, p. 75. For an evolutive perspective over risk as a fundament of civil liability, *see* P. Vasilescu, *supra*, pp. 578–582; F.I. Mangu, *Răspunderea civilă. Constantele ...*, *supra*, pp. 74–78.
85. *See* I.I. Neamţ and L.T. Dăuceanu, *supra*, p. 124; L. Pop, *Tratat elementar ...*, *supra*, pp. 397–398; L. Pop, *Curs de drept civil ...*, *supra*, p. 313.
86. *See* I.I. Neamţ, *Acţiunea colectivă ...*, *supra*, p. 23.
87. *See* I.I. Neamţ and L.T. Dăuceanu, *supra*, p. 124; L. Pop, *Tratat elementar ...*, *supra*, p. 398; L. Pop, *Curs de drept civil ...*, *supra*, p. 313; P. Vasilescu, *supra*, p. 580; F.I. Mangu, *Răspunderea civilă. Constantele ...*, *supra*, p. 75.

grounds that it only refers to profit producing activities whereas there are a lot of dangerous activities that do not fall within this category.[88]

102. The *risk of activity theory* was meant to elude the criticism that followed the risk-profit theory by giving the notion of "risk" a broader meaning. According to this theory, whenever one initiates, organizes, conducts, directs or controls a dangerous activity he implicitly assumes the risk of damaging another and is obliged to repair it no matter the fault.[89] This theory was considered particularly suitable for explaining the liability for the damages caused by animals or things.[90]

103. The *risk of authority theory* states that where the authority is, there should also be the liability.[91] Whenever one uses an agent to fulfill a duty, an extra risk is created. The fact that the principal is the one under whose orders and instructions the agent works leads to the conclusion that he should also be held responsible for the damages caused by the agent. In other words, the one who exercises the authority should also be held liable if the one over whom the authority is exercised creates a damage, no matter if a fault could be or not identify.[92] This theory was especially suitable for explaining the liability of the employer for the acts of the employee where no fault of the first could establish.

104. Though it was intensely presented by the legal doctrine and had some support in jurisprudence, especially in the final years of the old Civil Code, the risk theory met its opponents who strongly emphasized that the fault cannot be completely neglected.[93]

105. Following the French legal doctrine, the *mixed theories* also received some support. The mixed theory basically states that fault and risk coexist and, depending on the circumstances, each could explain the liability.[94] The problem was that the theory proved to be incapable in clearly delimitating the subjective liability, based on fault, and by strict liability, based on risk.[95] Among the forms of mixed theories lies the *guaranty* one, according to which a difference should be made between corporal damage and material damage, first being repaired without the need to prove any fault, while the last required the proof of fault.[96] This theory had no direct

---

88. *See* I.I. Neamţ and L.T. Dăuceanu, *supra*, p. 124; L. Pop, *Tratat elementar ...*, *supra*, p. 398; L. Pop, *Curs de drept civil ...*, *supra*, p. 313.
89. *See* I.I. Neamţ and L.T. Dăuceanu, *supra*, p. 125; L. Pop, *Tratat elementar ...*, *supra*, p. 398; L. Pop, *Curs de drept civil ...*, *supra*, pp. 313–314; F.I. Mangu, *Răspunderea civilă. Constantele ...*, *supra*, pp. 75–76.
90. *See* L. Pop, *Curs de drept civil ...*, *supra*, p. 314.
91. *See* I.I. Neamţ and L.T. Dăuceanu, *supra*, p. 125; P. Vasilescu, *supra*, p. 581; F.I. Mangu, *Răspunderea civilă. Constantele ...*, *supra*, p. 76.
92. *See* I.I. Neamţ and L.T. Dăuceanu, *supra*, p. 125; L. Pop, *Tratat elementar ...*, *supra*, p. 399; L. Pop, *Curs de drept civil ...*, *supra*, p. 314.
93. *See* L. Pop, *Tratat elementar ...*, *supra*, p. 400; P. Vasilescu, *supra*, p. 582.
94. *See* F.I. Mangu, *Răspunderea civilă. Constantele ...*, *supra*, pp. 78–80.
95. *See* L. Pop, *Tratat elementar ...*, *supra*, pp. 400–401; L. Pop, *Curs de drept civil ...*, *supra*, p. 315.
96. The theory was issued by French professor Boris Starck. For further details, *see* P. Vasilescu, *supra*, pp. 582–584; F.I. Mangu, *Răspunderea civilă. Constantele ...*, *supra*, pp. 80–81.

impact in Romania, but, instead, the concept of guaranty as a base for liability was given another interpretation and meaning in order to explain the mechanism and fundaments of fault.[97]

106. Over time, though the evolution was not linear, a clear step was made toward strict liability. In general, the fault remain the fundament of liability, but doctrine and jurisprudence started to admit, in the last few decades, the existence of multiple hypothesis in which liability was objective or strict, such as the liability for the deeds of the agent, the liability for the damages caused by things, animals or the ruin of an edifice[98] and there were discussions on the liability of parents for the deeds of their children.[99] In most of these cases, strict liability was based on the idea of guaranty (having usually as support the risk of activity), but the concept of guaranty was given a totally different meaning than the one first established in the French doctrine. In case of liability for the acts of others, the guaranty was seen as similar with fidejussion, guaranteeing the solvability of the wrongdoer by offering the victim one more patrimony from which to cover the damage caused by the tortfeasor. For the other types of strict liability, it was considered as a guaranty of the legal guardian for the "behavior" of the thing, animal or edifice.[100]

107. The new Civil Code followed this optic. The fault remains, as a general matter, a condition for engaging tortious liability, being expressly provided by Article 1.357 C.C. in the case of liability for own's acts, which, as previously shown, represents the *jus commune*. Nevertheless, no such condition is stipulated for other types of liability, such as the liability for the damages caused by minors or incapables (Article 1.372 C.C.), the liability of the principal for the acts of the agent (Article 1.373 C.C.), the liability for the damages caused by animals (Article 1.375 C.C.), the liability for the damages caused by things (Article 1.376 C.C.) and the liability for damages caused the ruin of the edifice (Article 1.378 C.C.), which lead the majority of legal scholars to conclude that all this represents hypothesis of strict liability, based on the obligation of guarantee, having as support the risk of activity or the risk of authority.[101] For some hypotheses, such as liability of the principal for the acts of the agent, the opinion is not unanimous, some legal scholars still consider that the liability is subjective, based on fault, but the fault is presumed by law.

---

97. *See* L. Pop, *Curs de drept civil ... , supra*, pp. 315–316; F.I. Mangu, *Răspunderea civilă. Constantele ... , supra*, p. 82.
98. Both the old (Art. 1.002) and the new (Art. 1.378) Civil Code provide a special form of liability for the damages caused by things: the damages caused by the ruin of an edifice. This form of liability can be used only when the damages result from the partial or total collapse of a building or construction as a result of bad maintenance or construction defect and only the owner can be held liable.
99. *See* L. Pop, *Tratat elementar ... , supra*, p. 403; L. Pop, *Curs de drept civil ... , supra*, p. 317; C. Stătescu and C. Bîrsan, *supra*, pp. 253–254, 279, 283, 299–303; F.I. Mangu, *Răspunderea civilă. Constantele ... , supra*, p. 81.
100. *See* L. Pop, *Tratat elementar ... , supra*, p. 404; L. Pop, *Curs de drept civil ... , supra*, p. 318; C. Stătescu and C. Bîrsan, *supra*, pp. 253–254, 279, 283, 299–303.
101. *See* I.I. Neamţ and L.T. Dăuceanu, *supra*, p. 125; L. Pop, *Tratat elementar ... , supra*, p. 404; L. Pop, *Curs de drept civil ... , supra*, p. 319.

§1. Unlawfulness and Fault

108. As previously shown, in Romanian law the illicit deed and the fault represent two different conditions for engaging civil liability, each with its own particularities and legal regime.[102] While the illicit deed represents a materialization of the tortfeasor's will,[103] the fault refers to the same individual's mental attitude toward the act and its consequences.[104] The fact that the illicit deed and fault represent two different conditions of tortious liability results undoubtedly from Article 1.357(1) C.C. which provides that the one who causes a damage to another by "an illicit deed committed with guilt," is bound to repair it.[105] The illicit deed is considered to be an objective condition, together with damage and causation, whereas fault is categorized as the only subjective condition.[106] Because illicit deed and fault represent two different conditions, it is not enough for the victim to prove that the defendant has committed a certain act and that the act is against the law or the social norms; but, furthermore, it also has to be proven that the act is imputable to the defendant. Of course, the latter condition must be proven only in those cases where civil liability is based on fault, such as liability for own's act. From this point of view, an act can be unlawful, but if no fault can be attributed to the tortfeasor, the conditions for engaging civil liability are not fulfilled.[107] Also, the fact that the defender acted consciously is irrelevant if his deed does not constitute a breach of a legal or social norm.

109. The particularities of fault will be analyzed in the next paragraph and on this point the attention we will address only toward the illicit deed and its particularities.

110. The tortious conduct was defined as a human conduit that breaches imperative legal or social norms and infringes the subjective rights and liberties of another, committed without the intention of producing legal effects, but which produce such

102. *See* L. Pop, *Tratat de drept civil. Obligațiile. Volumul III ...*, *supra*, pp. 223–226; F.I. Mangu, *Răspunderea civilă. Constantele ...*, *supra*, p. 118.
103. *See* P. Vasilescu, *supra*, p. 635; F.I. Mangu, *Răspunderea civilă. Constantele ...*, *supra*, p. 119.
104. *See* I.I. Neamţ and L.T. Dăuceanu, *supra*, p. 130; L. Pop, *Tratat elementar ...*, *supra*, pp. 424–425; C. Stătescu and C. Bîrsan, *supra*, p. 144.
105. The previous Civil Code did not expressly mention that the damageable act must be illicit. This led some scholars, following French legal doctrine, to consider that the unlawfulness of the act is a component of the fault and that fault had two components: an objective one—the breach of a legal norm, and a subjective one—the mental attitude of the wrongdoer toward the act and its consequences. *See*, *e.g.*, M.B. Cantacuzino, *Elementele dreptului civil (The Elements of Civil Law)*, Cartea Românească, Bucharest, 1921, p. 427. This optic was soon abandoned, and legal doctrine unanimously admitted that the two represent different conditions. *See*, *e.g.*, C. Stătescu and C. Bîrsan, *supra*, pp. 176–178.
106. *See* L. Pop, *Tratat de drept civil. Obligațiile. Volumul III ...*, *supra*, p. 234; C. Stătescu and C. Bîrsan, *supra*, pp. 176–177; F.I. Mangu, *Răspunderea civilă. Constantele ...*, *supra*, p. 119; L.R. Boilă, *supra*, p. 1500.
107. *See* L. Pop, *Tratat elementar ...*, *supra*, pp. 424–425; C. Stătescu and C. Bîrsan, *supra*, p. 177.

effects under the law.[108] The tort, or illicit conduct, as a distinct condition for tortious liability, is provided by a multitude of legal norms, among which Article 1.357(1) C.C. states that the one who causes a damage to another "by an licit deed" committed with guilt, is bound to repair it, or Article 1.359 C.C. according to which "the author of an illicit deed" is bound to repair the damage caused, even when the latter results from the breach of a legal interest.

111. Considering the definition, not any human conduit, even when it damages another, may lead to tortious liability. For this to happen, it must fulfill certain conditions: it has to be materialized, it must consist of an action or inaction, it must breach a legal or social norm and it must breach a subjective right or interest of the victim.

112. The illicit deed represents, as previously mentioned, *a materialization of the decision* adopted by the tortfeasor.[109] Thus, civil liability cannot be engaged if the illicit deed remained a simple intention, a mere psychological projection of the wrongdoer,[110] even if the victim suffered in the end the same damages as those imagined by the wrongdoer, but as a consequence of another circumstance.[111] In another words, the illicit deed represents the mean by which the will of the wrongdoer becomes reality.

113. The unlawful act or conduct may consist in *an action or inaction.*[112] There are a lot of ways in which subjective rights or interest may be infringed. In most of the cases, the law provides what we can and cannot do, and, in exceptional cases, obliges us to adopt a certain conduct. Usually, if one acts according to the law, no civil liability is engaged. Instead, if the law prohibits a certain action, and one decides nevertheless to act, a typical tort is being committed.[113]

114. Considering that the civil law rarely creates an obligation to act, most often the tort will be commissive, taking the shape of an action by which a duty to abstain provided by law or social norms is breached.[114] There are a lot of actions that may fall within this category, among which: a physical manifestation of the tortfeasor in the exterior, such as a movement of the limbs or body (e.g., when the tortfeasor punches the victim), a mimic (e.g., when the tortfeasor mimics disgust each time it meets the victim and this creates the victim a state of anxiety), a gesture (as when the wrongdoer uses the fingers to show the victim obscene gestures) or even words

---

108. *See* L. Pop, *Tratat elementar ..., supra*, p. 423; P. Vasilescu, *supra*, p. 643; F.I. Mangu, *Răspunderea civilă. Constantele ..., supra*, p. 119.
109. *See* L. Pop, *Tratat elementar ..., supra*, p. 424; F.I. Mangu, *Răspunderea civilă. Constantele ..., supra*, p. 119. *See also* C.A. Cluj, S.I. civ., dec. civ. 714/A/2015, in *supra*, p. 86.
110. *See* P. Vasilescu, *supra*, p. 635.
111. *See* I.I. Neamţ and L.T. Dăuceanu, *supra*, p. 130.
112. The condition is provided by Art. 1.349, paras. (1) and (2), C.C. which states that "Any individual has the duty to respect the rules of conduct provided by law or local custom and not to damage, *by action or inaction*, the rights and legitimate interest of others. Whoever, acting with discernment, breaches this duty is liable for all the damages caused and is obliged to fully repair them."
113. *See* L. Pop, *Tratat de drept civil. Obligaţiile. Volumul III ..., supra*, pp. 239–240.
114. *See* P. Vasilescu, *supra*, p. 643; F.I. Mangu, *Răspunderea civilă. Constantele ..., supra*, p. 116.

(when words are used to slender somebody).[115] In other words, the tortious action implies a certain dynamic and alteration of the environment. It requires the tortfeasor to do something, to get out of passivity. When this aspect is being analyzed, the fact that the action was voluntary or involuntary plays no importance, as such aspects are relevant only when fault or other circumstances that avert the illicit nature of the fact are being assessed. Thus, from this perspective, it does not matter that, for example, the wrongdoer was pushed and when falling destroyed an asset of the victim or caused another type of damage.

115. As a general matter, an inaction does not have an illicit nature, the individual having the freedom to stay passive in relationship with others. Still, though it represents the exception, in those particular situations in which the law prescribes a duty to act and one does not perform accordingly, the tort may take the shape of an abstention, an inaction.[116] It must be underlined that in order to be considered a tort, the obligation must be provided by a legal or social norm. If one breaches a contractual obligation, the contractual liability is incident and not the tortious liability.

116. Another condition for considering unlawful a certain conduct is its *contrariety with a legal or social norm.* In other words, the action or inaction must come against an obligation prescribed by a legal or social norm. This condition is expressly provided by Article 1.349, paragraphs (1) and (2) C.C. which states that individuals have the duty to respect the rules of conduct provided "by law or local custom." The mere fact that an act causes a damage is not enough to lead to tortious liability, as long as no obligation to act or to abstain, provided by a legal or social norm, was breached.[117] Regarding the legal norms, they can be of any kind, contained in laws or secondary legislation.[118] The only condition is to be imperative and not dispositive. If the norm is dispositive, a contrary conduct cannot be seen as illegal, as the individual has, by definition, the option to conform with the norm or not. Furthermore, in given circumstances, one can be held liable even if the damage was caused by exercising a subjective right, but this will be later addressed.[119]

117. Problems may exist when it comes to local custom. According to Article 1 C.C. the custom may be regarded as a source of law and it is incident whenever the

115. *See* I.I. Neamţ and L.T. Dăuceanu, *supra*, p. 130; L. Pop, *Tratat elementar ... , supra*, p. 426; L. Pop, *Curs de drept civil ... , supra*, p. 338.

116. *See* I.I. Neamţ and L.T. Dăuceanu, *supra*, p. 130; L. Pop, *Tratat elementar ... , supra*, p. 426; L. Pop, *Curs de drept civil ... , supra*, p. 339; C. Stătescu and C. Bîrsan, *supra*, p. 178; P. Vasilescu, *supra*, p. 643; F.I. Mangu, *Răspunderea civilă. Constantele ... , supra*, p. 117. The legal doctrine has never the lass concluded that the number of torts that take the shape an abstention are increasing as more and more security obligations are enacted by the legislator. *See* L. Pop, *Tratat elementar ... , supra*, p. 427; L. Pop, *Curs de drept civil ... , supra*, p. 339. *See also* High Court of Cassation and Justice, Commercial Section, Decision No. 3996/2006, available at www.scj.ro, last checked on Apr. 16, 2020.

117. *See* L. Pop, *Tratat de drept civil. Obligaţiile. Volumul III ... , supra*, p. 82; P. Vasilescu, *supra*, p. 643.

118. P. Vasilescu, *supra*, p. 644.

119. For further details, *see* I.I. Neamţ, *Poate frica ... , supra*, pp. 258–259.

law does not regulate a specific situation. When a legal regulation exists, custom may be used only if the law refers to it. Also, the custom must be in accordance with the law and moral rules. Finally, the one who refers to custom must prove its existence and content. Transferring these rules to tortious liability, we may conclude that a given conduct is tortious whenever it is contrary to an obligation which is provided by law. If no legal norm was breached, the victim may appeal to local custom, but for doing so it must prove the existence of the custom and the fact that it provided an obligation which was breached by the wrongdoer.[120] Any type of proof may be used, including witness testimony.[121] In any case, if the act was allowed by a legal norm, local custom cannot be used in order to engage civil liability. The wrongdoer may defend by arguing that the custom is against the law or moral norms or that, in any case, it is not applicable to the given situation.

118. Finally, in order to be considered unlawful, the act must *violate the subjective rights or interests of the victim.* This condition, together with the previous one, gives the act its illicit nature. Furthermore, the fact that the victim's rights or obligations were violated leads to the existence of damage. Without such violation no damage may exist and without a damage there is no tortious liability.[122] Still, the nature of infringed right plays no importance. It can be any type of subjective right, from property rights to personal integrity or private life and honor. On the other hand, not any personal interest falls within the protection of tortious liability. In this regard, Article 1.359 C.C. provides that "The tortfeasor must repair the damage caused even when it resulted from a violation of another's interest, as long as the interest is legitimate, serious, and, by the way it manifests, it creates the appearance of a subjective right." In other words, in order to entitle the victim to indemnification, the violated interest must be in accordance with the law (as no illegal interest can be protected), it must be serious (which means that it must be exercised for a sufficient period of time) and it must appear to others as a subjective right.[123] The classical example is the one in which someone who was killed as a result of the tortious act, used to provide regular maintenance for one, without a legal obligation. In this case, the tortfeasor can be obliged to pay for the damage caused by violating the legitimate interest of the maintenance creditor.[124]

119. There are situations in which a damage is the result of multiple actions or when multiple tortfeasors act together. In such cases, according to Article 1.382

120. For further details, *see* L. Pop, *Tratat de drept civil. Obligațiile. Volumul III ...*, *supra*, pp. 236–237.
121. *See* Arts. 252 and 255 Civil Procedure Code.
122. *See* I.I. Neamț, *Poate frica ...*, *supra*, p. 228.
123. *See* C. Stătescu and C. Bîrsan, *supra*, pp. 146–147; F.I. Mangu, *Răspunderea civilă. Constantele ...*, *supra*, pp. 147–148. For an analysis of the legitimate interest in the context of tortious liability, *see* L. Pop, *Tratat de drept civil. Obligațiile. Volumul III ...*, *supra*, pp. 212–217; P. Vasilescu, *supra*, pp. 595, 646–647.
124. *See*, *e.g.*, Supreme Tribunal, criminal section, Decision No. 2722/16 May 1970, in Revista Română de Drept (Romanian Law Review), No. 3/1971, p. 130. For further examples, *see* L. Pop, *Tratat de drept civil. Obligațiile. Volumul III ...*, *supra*, pp. 213–214.

C.C. all who contributed to the damage will be held joint and several liable. Furthermore, Article 1.369 C.C. provides that the instigator, the accomplice, the fence, the one who took any advantages from the damage caused to the victim and the one who, by any mean, delayed or prevented the call to trial of the tortfeasor, can be held joint and several liable together with the last. The two norms allow the conclusion that any kind of contribution to the damage or obstacle to bringing the tortfeasor to justice leads to joint and several liability.

120. The way in which victim acted or behaved is also revenant, as Article 1.371(1) C.C. provides that if the victim contributed, intentionally or by negligence, to the causation of damage or its augmentation, or did not avoid it, in whole or in part, though he could have, the tortfeasor can be held liable only for the rest of the damage. Therefore, the victim of a tort must abstain from any conduit that may contribute to the damage or amplify it and must take any reasonable effort to prevent or reduce the damage. If not, the tortfeasor can end up being exonerated, in whole or in part, of the obligation to repair the damage.

§2. The Concept of Fault

121. Liability for own's acts is, in Romanian law, the typical form of subjective liability, based on fault.[125] Because of this, the victim must prove, in addition to the existence of an illicit deed, a damage and causation, the fact that the deed is imputable to the tortfeasor. The condition of fault is expressly stipulated by Article 1.357 C.C. which states that the damageable act must be committed with fault and that even the smallest fault leads to liability.

122. Considering its characteristics, liability may be defined as the mental attitude of the tortfeasor toward the act and its consequences.[126] It thus results that fault is a mental process with two main components, one intellective and one volitional.[127] The intellectual component of fault consists in the image of the tortfeasor over the illicit act; his prefiguration, or the possibility to foresee, the damageable consequences of the civil wrong and its illicit nature.[128] Therefore, to comply with the condition of fault, the victim must prove that the tortfeasor could have at least prefigure the negative consequences of the illicit deed and that he decided to act even though aware that a legal or social norm will be breached. Also, the tortfeasor may defend arguing that the consequences of the deed were unforeseeable or that he acted under an *error in jus*. After the tortfeasor prefigured to what the deed my

125. *See* L. Pop, *Tratat elementar ...*, *supra*, p. 446; L. Pop, *Curs de drept civil ...*, *supra*, p. 351; F.I. Mangu, *Răspunderea civilă. Constantele ...*, *supra*, p. 114.
126. *See* I.I. Neamţ and L.T. Dăuceanu, *supra*, p. 141; P. Vasilescu, *supra*, p. 634; C. Stătescu and C. Bîrsan, *supra*, p. 196. *See also* C.A. Cluj, S. I. civ., dec. civ. 714/A/2015, in *supra*, p. 87.
127. *See* L. Pop, *Tratat de drept civil. Obligaţiile. Volumul III ...*, *supra*, p. 300.
128. *See* I.I. Neamţ and L.T. Dăuceanu, *supra*, p. 141; L. Pop, *Tratat de drept civil. Obligaţiile. Volumul III ...*, *supra*, pp. 300–301; L. Pop, *Tratat elementar ...*, *supra*, p. 448; L. Pop, *Curs de drept civil ...*, *supra*, p. 352; C. Stătescu and C. Bîrsan, *supra*, p. 196; F.I. Mangu, *Răspunderea civilă. Constantele ...*, *supra*, p. 221; L.R. Boilă, *supra*, p. 1502.

lead to, the volitional component intervenes, which consists in deliberating whether to act or not, and making a decision. Thus, after imagining the possible outcomes of the act, the individual must analyze the pros and cons and decide.[129] For this, the tortfeasor must be able to decide consciously and freely and to choose to abstain from committing the act.[130] If the intellectual component is inherent no matter the type of fault, the volitional one will only exist in those cases were the tortfeasor actually has a prefiguration of the consequences, but not when he acted with negligence, not foreseeing the damageable consequences, though he should and could have. In the latter case, as the tortfeasor did not foresee the consequences, the volitional component will not exist, considering that no deliberation and decision-making may exist on such hypothesis.

123. The previous Civil Code did not pay much attention to classifications of fault or its form.[131] This aspect was partially solved by the new Civil Code. Though it does not provide with a specific definition of fault in the domain of tortious liability, nor with specific forms, the new Civil Code nevertheless regulates in general terms the problem of fault to the entire field of civil law and those rules also apply when it comes to tortious liability. On this line, Article 16(1) C.C. states that if the law does not otherwise provide one may be held liable only for the acts committed with intention and negligence. Thus, fault has two different manifestations: intention and negligence. The concept of intention and negligence are described by the following two paragraphs.

124. According to Article 16(2) C.C., an act is committed with *intention* if the tortfeasor foresees the result of his deed and either aims such result or, though it does not aim it, accepts the possibility that the deed can cause such results. As such, intention has two components: the foreseeability of the result and the fact that the tortfeasor acts willing for that result to occur or at least accepts that it may happen so. Because of this, the legal doctrine underlined that intention takes to forms: direct intention, when the tortfeasor foresees the result, is aware of its illicit nature and wants for that result to happen; and indirect intention, when the tortfeasor prefigures the result and though he does not aim it, he accepts that by deciding to act that result may occur.[132]

125. Article 16(3), first thesis, C.C. provides that an illicit deed is committed with *negligence* when the tortfeasor either foresees the result but does not accept it,

129. *See* I.I. Neamţ and L.T. Dăuceanu, *supra*, p. 141; L. Pop, *Tratat de drept civil. Obligaţiile. Volumul III …* , *supra*, p. 301; L. Pop, *Tratat elementar …* , *supra*, p. 448; L. Pop, *Curs de drept civil …* , *supra*, p. 352; C. Stătescu and C. Bîrsan, *supra*, p. 196; L.R. Boilă, *supra*, p. 1503.

130. *See* L. Pop, *Tratat elementar …* , *supra*, p. 448; L. Pop, *Curs de drept civil …* , *supra*, p. 352; C. Stătescu and C. Bîrsan, *supra*, pp. 196–197; F.I. Mangu, *Răspunderea civilă. Constantele …* , *supra*, p. 222.

131. For further details, *see* P. Vasilescu, *supra*, p. 635.

132. *See* I.I. Neamţ and L.T. Dăuceanu, *supra*, p. 141; L. Pop, *Tratat de drept civil. Obligaţiile. Volumul III …* , *supra*, pp. 302–303; L. Pop, *Tratat elementar …* , *supra*, p. 449; L. Pop, *Curs de drept civil …* , *supra*, p. 352; P. Vasilescu, *supra*, p. 636; F.I. Mangu, *Răspunderea civilă. Constantele …* , *supra*, p. 224.

considering without basis that it will not occur, or does not foresee the result of the deed, though it should have. Given the norm, the legal doctrine classified the negligence in imprudence, when the tortfeasor has foreseen the result but appreciated that it will not occur and negligence when the tortfeasor did not foresee the result though he could and should have.[133] It must be underlined that in case of imprudence the tortfeasor must fundament its conclusion that the prefigured result will not occur on objective grounds and not on a mere personal belief or wish. In other words, there must exist some objective elements or circumstances that have, from an abstract point of view, the capacity of preventing the result, but which failed to do so because they were misevaluated or for other reasons. The second form of negligence is the only form of fault that lacks the volitional component and is based on the idea that the tortfeasor did not foresee the result because of his own lack of diligence, which cannot be reflected on the victim.

126. Following the Roman Law, negligence was also classified by the legal doctrine in gross negligence (*culpa lata*), ordinary negligence (*culpa levis*) and slight negligence (*culpa levissima*).[134] Gross fault has an express legal support, being defined by Article 16(3), final sentence, C.C. as the situation in which the tortfeasor acts with a negligence or imprudence that even the most devoid person would not manifest toward his own interests. For the rest, the legal doctrine stated that ordinary negligence arises from the failure to act with the same level of diligence and care as a *bonus paeter familias*, while slight negligence is the negligence or imprudence that could have been avoided only by an individual acting with a maximum diligence and with an extraordinary foreseeability.[135]

127. When analyzing the condition, the judge must observe that the tortfeasor acted with intention or by negligence at the time when the tort was committed. If at the time of the deed the tortfeasor acted faultless because, for example, he lacked discernment, no liability will be engaged even if previously he decided to commit the same deed. To this conclusion there is one notable exception, when an *actio libera in causa* hypothesis is incident. In this situation, Article 1.367(2) C.C. states that the one who lacks discernment and caused a damage shall be held liable if the temporary mental disorder was personally caused by the use of alcohol, drugs or other substances. Thus, if at the time of the deed one cannot foresee the results and consequences of the action or inaction because he has willingly deprive himself from such possibility by using substances that effect the mental capacity, this cannot be successfully invoke as a defense in order to escape liability. The legal doctrine

133. *See* I.I. Neamţ and L.T. Dăuceanu, *supra*, p. 141; L. Pop, *Tratat de drept civil. Obligaţiile. Volumul III ...*, *supra*, p. 303; L. Pop, *Tratat elementar ...*, *supra*, p. 450; L. Pop, *Curs de drept civil ...*, *supra*, p. 353; P. Vasilescu, *supra*, p. 637; F.I. Mangu, *Răspunderea civilă. Constantele ...*, *supra*, p. 224.

134. *See* L. Pop, *Tratat de drept civil. Obligaţiile. Volumul III ...*, *supra*, p. 305.

135. *See* I.I. Neamţ and L.T. Dăuceanu, *supra*, p. 142; L. Pop, *Tratat elementar ...*, *supra*, p. 451; L. Pop, *Curs de drept civil ...*, *supra*, pp. 353–354; P. Vasilescu, *supra*, pp. 637–638; F.I. Mangu, *Răspunderea civilă. Constantele ...*, *supra*, pp. 225–226.

stated that the norm is a manifestation of the principle *nemo auditur propriam turpitudinem allegans* and that in such cases the liability is based on the previous fault, when the tortfeasor still had discernment.[136]

128. Though the tortfeasor must be liable for the act, the form of liability plays little importance in the architecture of tortious liability, since once any type of fault is proven, the damage must be fully repaired.[137] In Romanian law, the limits of tortious liability are set by the dimension of damage and not the form of fault[138] and there are no special rules depending on the type of fault with which the tort was committed. Nevertheless, the type of fault is not completely irrelevant, as there are specific situations in which it may influence the existence and the amplitude of liability. For example, in case of joint and several liability, the tortfeasor who, by himself, repaired the entire damage may regress against the other tortfeasors in accordance with Articles 1.382–1.383 C.C. In the regress action, the extent of liability will be determined considering the participation of each tortfeasor at the damage endured by victim. If the level of participation cannot be established, the liability of each will be determined considering the type of fault, as Article 1.383 C.C. provides.[139] Furthermore, an exception clause referring to the pecuniary damage caused to assets is valid only if the tort was committed with *culpa levis* or *culpa levissima.*[140] Finally, if the damage was caused while the tortfeasor was giving the victim a disinterested help, liability can be engaged only if intention or gross negligence can be upheld.[141]

§3. Duty of Care

129. The standard for duty of care plays a significant importance when the intellectual component of fault is being analyzed, as it is directly connected to the diligence one must manifest when assessing whether to act or not and the capacity to foresee the consequences of a certain act. Furthermore, the later depends on elements such as the tortfeasor's intellectual capacity, the level of knowledge and information available. The question is what landmark should be considered when the intellectual component of the fault is addressed by the court.

130. The problem was quite controversial under the old Civil Code, as multiple opinions were advanced, but was dealt with by the new legislation.[142] In this regard, Article 1.358 C.C. provides that "for assessing the fault, the circumstances, independent by the tortfeasor, in which the damage occurred will be taken into account

136. *See* L. Pop, *Tratat elementar ...* , *supra*, p. 455.
137. *See* P. Vasilescu, *supra*, p. 639.
138. *See* I.I. Neamţ and L.T. Dăuceanu, *supra*, pp. 140–141.
139. The final thesis of the article states that if the extent of liability cannot be established in this manner either, each will be held equally liable.
140. *See* Art. 1.355, second paragraph, C.C.
141. *See* Art. 1.354 C.C. The same applies when the victim was using for free a thing, animal or edifice that caused the damage.
142. *See* L. Pop, *Tratat de drept civil. Obligaţiile. Volumul III ...* , *supra*, pp. 307–311.

and, if applicable, the fact that the damage was caused by a professional in the operation of an enterprise." According to the norm, when assessing the fault, the personal circumstances of the tortfeasor, such as age, sex, and education will not be considered, but only circumstances related to the act, such as the time, environment or behavior of others. This allows the conclusion that fault is being analyzed by an objective criterion, meaning a reasonably diligent individual found in the same circumstance.[143] The criterion was qualified by the legal doctrine as being both dynamic and variable. It is dynamic because the exigencies are constantly higher due to the fact that as the society evolves and the level of knowledge increases, so is the level of education and diligence of the human standard taken as landmark. It is also variable, as it considers the objective circumstances in which the tort was committed.[144]

131. Furthermore, when the damage was caused by a professional in the operation of an enterprise, the duty of care is higher, as the professional is bound to know all the norms and safety measures that regulate the field in which it operates and cannot invoke the contrary. Nevertheless, the damages must be the result in which the professional operated the enterprise, otherwise being said, the result in which he exercised his professional duties.[145] If the damage is caused outside this limit, the regular standard of care applies.

§4. Capacity

132. Being a form of subjective liability, liability for own's act requires the proof of fault. As previously shown, all types of fault imply an intellectual component which consists in the ability of the tortfeasor to foresee the consequences of the projected deed and its illicit nature. Such ability cannot exist without discernment, without the capacity of the tortfeasor to have a clear image over reality and discern between what is allowed by law and what is not.[146] If the discernment lacks, no fault and, implicitly, tortious liability, can be upheld.[147] In this regard, Article 1.349(2) C.C. expressively provides that, in order to be held liable for the damage caused by breaching a legal or moral norm and violating the subjective rights or legitimate

---

143. *See* I.I. Neamţ and L.T. Dăuceanu, *supra*, p. 141; L. Pop, *Tratat de drept civil. Obligaţiile. Volumul III …* , *supra*, p 310; L. Pop, *Tratat elementar …* , *supra*, p. 453; L. Pop, *Curs de drept civil …* , *supra*, pp. 355–356; P. Vasilescu, *supra*, p. 639; F.I. Mangu, *Răspunderea civilă. Constantele …* , *supra*, p. 231. For the opinion that the criterion for assessing the liability is intermediate, neither objective nor subjective, *see* L.R. Boilă, *supra*, p. 1505.
144. *See* L. Pop, *Tratat de drept civil. Obligaţiile. Volumul III …* , *supra*, p. 311; L. Pop, *Tratat elementar …* , *supra*, p. 454.
145. *See* L. Pop, *Tratat de drept civil. Obligaţiile. Volumul III …* , *supra*, p. 131.
146. *See* L. Pop, *Tratat elementar …* , *supra*, p. 454; L. Pop, *Curs de drept civil …* , *supra*, p. 356; F.I. Mangu, *Răspunderea civilă. Constantele …* , *supra*, p. 239.
147. Nevertheless, the conclusion is only valid in the case of subjective liability, meaning in those cases where liability is based on fault. On the contrary, in case of strict (or objective) liability, the discernment is relevant because the liability is based on other grounds and, thus, it can be engaged even if the defendant lacked the discernment at the time of the damageable act—*see* P. Vasilescu, *supra*, p. 610.

interest of another, one must act with discernment. Furthermore, according to Article 1.367(1) C.C. "the one who caused a damage shall not be held liable if at the time of the damageable act was, event temporary, in a state of mental disorder which made it impossible to foresee the consequences of the did."

133. The existence of discernment was associated by legal doctrine with tortious capacity.[148] Despite this being a relatively unanimous accepted optic by the doctrine on tortious liability, some reserve may still be manifested. Discernment is a matter of fact as it depends on factual circumstances such as age, health or substances consumed. On the other hand, capacity is a legal state, depending not on factual circumstances, but on the objective conditions prescribed by law. Of course, between the two there is a close connection, as the existence of capacity leads to a relative presumption that the discernment also exists but, evens so, discernment and tortious capacity should not be considered synonyms, as they have a different judicial nature. Furthermore, a distinction must be drawn between tortious capacity and legal capacity. While first relates to tortious liability for the damageable acts, the second refers to the capacity of independently concluding a contract and fulfilling the assumed contractual obligations.[149]

134. The condition of discernment must be met no matter the age, the sex or the psychical or psychological condition of the wrongdoer and the discernment must exist at the time of tortious deed.[150] If the wrongdoer lacked discernment before or after committing the illicit deed, the liability can be engaged. Furthermore, the fact the damage occurred after the illicit deed was committed and when the tortfeasor no longer had discernment does not avert the liability, as long as at the time of the deed the mental capacity of the tortfeasor was not affected.

135. Only the complete lack of discernment may exempt the tortfeasor from liability, whereas a diminished discernment does not influence the incidence of tortious liability or its limits.[151] The tortfeasor may still be held fully liable for the illegal act even if his discernment was partially altered.[152]

136. The discernment may be altered by several factors such as the consumption of substances like alcohol or drugs, mental health or age. In order to ease the proof, the legislature stipulated a series of presumptions. In this regard, Article

---

148. *See* L. Pop, *Tratat de drept civil. Obligaţiile. Volumul III ...*, *supra*, p. 312; L. Pop, *Tratat elementar ...*, *supra*, p. 454; L. Pop, *Curs de drept civil ...*, *supra*, p. 356; L.R. Boilă, *supra*, p. 1486. For the idea that capacity is a distinct condition for engaging tortious liability, *see* P. Vasilescu, *supra*, pp. 628–629. On the contrary, for the opinion that capacity can be seen as an element of fault, *see* C. Stătescu and C. Bîrsan, *supra*, p. 145.

149. *See* L. Pop, *Tratat elementar ...*, *supra*, p. 454; L. Pop, *Curs de drept civil ...*, *supra*, p. 356; F.I. Mangu, *Răspunderea civilă. Constantele ...*, *supra*, p. 240 L.R. Boilă, *supra*, p. 1513.

150. *See* I.I. Neamţ and L.T. Dăuceanu, *supra*, p. 143; L. Pop, *Tratat elementar ...*, *supra*, p. 454; L. Pop, *Curs de drept civil ...*, *supra*, p. 356; L.R. Boilă, *supra*, p. 1513.

151. *See* I.I. Neamţ and L.T. Dăuceanu, *supra*, p. 143; L. Pop, *Tratat elementar ...*, *supra*, p. 455; L. Pop, *Curs de drept civil ...*, *supra*, p. 356; F.I. Mangu, *Răspunderea civilă. Constantele ...*, *supra*, p. 242.

152. *See* L.R. Boilă, *supra*, p. 1515.

1.366, first paragraph, C.C. provides that "The minor who has not yet reached the age of 14 years or the legally incapacitated is not liable for any damage caused, unless the existence of discernment at the time of the damageable act is proven." The second paragraph of the same Article state that "The minor who has reached 14 years is liable for the damage caused, unless it is proven that he lacked discernment at the time of the damageable act."

137. The two legal norms provide two different presumptions.[153] First, if the individual is under 14 years of age or was legally incapacitated the presumption is that he acted without the discernment and cannot be held liable for the damage. Second, if the individual turned 14 and was not declared legally incapacitated he is presumed to have had discernment at the time of the damageable act.[154] The two presumptions configure the architecture of tortious capacity. If the tortfeasor is at least 14 years and was not declared legally incapacitated he has tortious capacity and is presumed to have discernment. The presumptions are, nevertheless, relative, as the victim or the tortfeasor may prove the contrary, that the underaged or the legally incapacitated had discernment or that the 14 years old had not.[155]

138. Though fault and its complement, discernment, are imperative conditions for engaging liability for own's fault, in exceptional circumstances one can be held liable even if at the time of the illicit act one had no discernment and did not imputably create this state by voluntarily consuming alcohol or other substances that affect the mental capacity. In this regard, Article 1.368, first paragraph, C.C. provides that the lack of discernment does not exempt the author of the damageable act from paying an indemnification to the victim when the liability of the one who had the obligation to overlook the author cannot be engaged. The mentioned norm provides a subsidiary obligation to indemnify the victim, based on the principle of equity,[156] which becomes available when neither the liability of the tortfeasor can be engaged on common rules, because of the lack of discernment, nor the liability of the one who was in charge of overseeing the author of the illicit deed can be engaged.[157] For the hypothesis to be incident, the author must be either minor or

153. *See* L. Pop, *Tratat de drept civil. Obligaţiile. Volumul III* ... , *supra*, p. 313; P. Vasilescu, *supra*, pp. 629–630; F.I. Mangu, *Răspunderea civilă. Constantele* ... , *supra*, p. 249.

154. *See* I.I. Neamţ and L.T. Dăuceanu, *supra*, p. 143; L. Pop, *Tratat elementar* ... , *supra*, pp. 444–455; L. Pop, *Curs de drept civil* ... , *supra*, p. 356.

155. *See* I.I. Neamţ and L.T. Dăuceanu, *supra*, p. 143; L. Pop, *Tratat elementar* ... , *supra*, p. 455; L. Pop, *Curs de drept civil* ... , *supra*, p. 356; F.I. Mangu, *Răspunderea civilă. Constantele* ... , *supra*, p. 250.

156. *See* L. Pop, *Tratat de drept civil. Obligaţiile. Volumul III* ... , *supra*, pp. 314–332.

157. *See* I.I. Neamţ and L.T. Dăuceanu, *supra*, p. 144. Other legal scholars have argued that the norm does not instate a form of tortious liability, but a distinct and autonomous legal relationship within which the debtor must indemnify the creditor based on the principle of equity. *See* A. Tamba, *Fundamentul obligatiei de reparare a prejudiciului de către persoana lipsită de discernământ (The Fundament of the Obligation to Repair the Damage by the Person Who Lacked Discernment)* in Dreptul, No. 11/2011, pp. 152–154. For the same opinion, *see also* F.I. Mangu, *Răspunderea civilă. Constantele* ... , *supra*, pp. 61, 264. Still, the most important legal scholar in the field of tortious liability underlined that as long as the obligation results from the fact that a damage was caused by committing an illicit act, a tortious liability intervenes with the particularity that it is not based on fault but on the principle of equity-*see* L. Pop, *Tratat elementar* ... , *supra*, p. 457; L. Pop, *Curs*

legally incapacitated.[158] The lack of discernment nevertheless influences the extent of liability, as the second paragraph of the same norm provides that the compensation shall be determined in an equitable quantum, considering the patrimonial status of the parties.[159] Thus, the victim may end up not being fully indemnifiable for the loss if such a solution would seem inequitable.[160] The legal doctrine has expressed the opinion that the norm is ill formulated as only the patrimonial status of the doer should be considered, and not the victim's.[161]

---

de drept civil ... , *supra*, p. 358. For similar opinions, *see* L.R. Boilă, *Considerații referitoare la răspunderea delictuală a persoanei lipsite de discernământ reglementată prin art. 1368 din actualul Cod civil (Reflections on the Tortious Liability of the Person Who Lacks Discernment Regulated by Article 1368 from the Current Civil Code)*, in Dreptul, No. 5/2014, pp. 87–110 and S.V. Gherdan, *Răspunderea delictuală subsidiară (Subsidiary Civil Liability)*, in P.R. No. 6/2012, pp. 1–40.

158. *See* L. Pop, *Tratat elementar* ... , *supra*, p. 457; L. Pop, *Curs de drept civil* ... , *supra*, p. 357. For the opinion that the norm is applicable each time the doer was under the authority of another, including an agent, *see* F.I. Mangu, *Răspunderea civilă. Constantele* ... , *supra*, p. 259.
159. For a court decision in which the accent was put on the need to provide an equitable relief to the victim and not the patrimonial status of the parties, *see* Craiova Court of Appeal, criminal section, Decision No. 1535/2018, available at rolii.ro, last checked on Jan. 18, 2020.
160. For further details, *see* P. Vasilescu, *supra*, pp. 631–632.
161. *See* L. Pop, *Tratat elementar* ... , *supra*, p. 457; L. Pop, *Curs de drept civil* ... , *supra*, pp. 357–358.

Chapter 2. Specific Cases of Liability *(Are All Tortfeasors Subject to the Same Rules?)*

§1. Liability of Professionals

I. In General *(Is There a Higher Standard of Care?)*

139. In the case of tortious liability, as in the case of contractual liability, one of the criteria set by law for the judge in order to appreciate upon the fault of the author of the damage is the quality of professional. According to Article 1358 of the Civil Code regarding the tortious liability, the damage caused while accomplishing the activities concerning the professional duties represents an objective circumstance that influences the appreciation of fault.

140. Similarly, Article 1481 concerning the Civil Code establishes that the standard of duty concerning the fulfillment of an obligation inherent of professional activity will be set by taking into account the fact that the debtor is a professional.

141. Thus, both in the case of tortious liability and contractual liability professionals must meet a higher standard of care. Because most cases of professional civil liability suppose the breach of a professional duty, some authors suggested that professional liability is a third type of civil liability as it does not meet the criteria to be considered neither tortious, nor contractual. However, for the time being this approach remains isolate.

142. Various applications of this general rules can be met in the special legislation concerning different categories of professionals. This extended liability in the case of the professionals was accompanied also by the introduction of mandatory or compulsory professional insurances in order for the professional to be able to cover the damage without ruining himself and to ensure the actual full compensation of the victim.

II. Medical Practitioners

143. In Romania the liability of medical practitioners is regulated by Law No. 95/2006 concerning the reform in the health domain.[162] It states that medical practitioners will be held liable on civil grounds for the damage that they have caused: (i) by mistake, including negligence, recklessness and insufficient medical knowledge in the exercise of the profession, by individual acts as part of prevention, diagnostic or treatment procedures; (ii) by disregarding the regulations concerning confidentiality, informed consent of the patient and medical assistance and (iii) by disregarding the limits of competence, except in emergencies when the competent health professionals are not available.

162. Published in the O.J. No. 372 of 28.04.2006, Art. 653.

144. Another important aspect is that this law imposes a compulsory professional liability insurance for medical practitioners, which reinforces the idea of liability for one's own act.

145. The tortious or contractual liability of medical practitioners represents an object of legal debate. For tortious liability the main arguments that are advanced consist on one hand on the fact that health and body cannot make the object of a contract and on the other hand on the idea that there is no consent of the patient regarding choice of the medical practitioner.

146. These arguments have been rejected by proponents of the contractual nature of physician liability on the ground that the patient's consent is always required before any medical treatment is provided. Thus, between the medical practitioner and the patient an *intuitu personae* agreement is formed the moment the patient gives his consent.

147. A different approach on the nature of the medical practitioner's liability has been made starting from the private or public nature of the health establishment providing the care for the patient. Thus, if the doctor has an employment contract with a public health establishment, there is a tortious liability of the medical practitioner because there is no contract between the doctor and the patient since the patient cannot choose his doctor. On the contrary, if the medical practitioner has an employment contract with a private health establishment, the nature of the liability contractual since the patient is at liberty to choose.

148. The regulation by law of the medical practitioner's liability has also given way to the idea that there is a third type of liability, namely a legal or professional liability resulting from special legislation. The main argument is that the law itself expressly establishes the situations which give rise to civil liability independently of the general rules of liability.

149. However the jurisprudence seems to embrace the tortious nature of the medical practitioner's liability since most of the compensations awarded for pecuniary or nonpecuniary losses were on a tortious ground founded.

150. In a claim seeking compensation for this kind of cases, the challenge for the victim usually consists in proving the medical practitioner's fault and the causation between the wrongful act and the damage.

151. In order to establish the fault of the medical practitioner, normally a medical expertise is needed. In case the conclusions of the medical expertise conflict, the judge has to refer them to a superior medical commission. The territorial medical college may intervene in the process in order to sustain the interests of the medical practitioner. The medical college is also the public institution that can engage the disciplinary liability of the medical practitioner in the discipline commission. Such a decision, especially in the case in which it has been validated or invalidated by court judges may constitute a decisive means of proof.

152. Concerning the causation, it must be noted that the damage cannot be linked directly to the act of the medical practitioner as the evolution of the disease or the consequences due to a different course of intervention are not easily predictable given the particularities of each human being. However, the Civil Code alleviates this condition as it gives right to compensation even in the cases of a loss of chance to obtain a gain or avoid a loss. To compensate this type of damage, the victim must prove that the chance was reel and serious. The compensation however will not be awarded fully but proportionally to the chances of the victim.

III. Legal Practitioners

153. Professional liability of legal practitioners concerns the damage caused to the client that result from the exercise of the profession in noncompliance with the provisions of the law regulating the organization and profession of legal practitioners,[163] of their statute and of the deontological rules. Legal practitioners that infringe these rules can face penal, disciplinary and/or civil liability.

154. In this scope, the legal practitioners have a legal obligation to conclude an insurance policy for professional liability. The Statute of the Legal Practitioners' Profession establishes also a minimum value of the insured risk: an insured risk of at least EUR 3,000 per year for a trainee legal practitioner and an insured risk of at least EUR 6,000 per year for a legal practitioner. The insurance for professional liability must be concluded yearly for a period of a year.

155. Due to the legal assistance contract concluded between the client and the legal practitioner, the civil liability will have a contractual nature. The client and the legal practitioner may set limits of the legal practitioner's liability in the contract of legal assistance that they conclude. However, the clauses of total exemption of liability are considered unwritten, namely they will not produce any effect.

156. The conditions that need to be met in order to hold liable a legal practitioner are the following: nonperformance of a deontological rule, damage, causation and fault of the practitioner. Concerning the last condition, it needs to be mentioned that once it can be proven a nonperformance of a deontological rule, the fault of the legal practitioner is presumed. This leads some authors to the conclusion that the professional liability is a form of strict liability.

157. When the object of the contract is legal assistance in front of a court, the obligation to win the trial is considered to be an obligation of means and not of result. Therefore, if the client loses the trial the legal practitioners' liability cannot be automatically engaged as the nonattainment of the result does not necessarily constitute a wrongful act. If the client wants to hold the legal practitioner liable for

163. Law No. 51/1995 for the organization and exercise of the legal profession, published in O.J. No. 440/2018. Or service is governed by general contractual liability rules and does not fall under the category of strict liability cases.

the damage caused by the loss of the trial, he would have to prove that the legal practitioner breached the standard of care normally applied to the given situation, namely that he breached a deontological rule prescribed by the law or the statute. Given the fact that he is a professional, the standard of care will be appreciated accordingly.

158. Another specificity of this type of liability is that in most of the cases, due to the fact that the outcome is not entirely dependent on the legal practitioner's activity, the compensation of the damage suffered by the client cannot be fully. When it cannot be proven that the damage has been entirely caused by the wrongful act of the legal practitioner, the compensation can be awarded only proportionately to the chances of a favorable outcome of the client. It is the case of compensation for the loss of a chance.

IV. Builders and Architects

159. Builders and architects can be liable on both contractual and tortious grounds depending on the relationship to the party claiming the compensation.

160. Traditionally, this type of liability has been regulated by the Civil Code dedicated to the service agreement, namely by the liability for defects. This liability concerns the parties to the service agreement implying as consequence a contractual liability ground of the builder and the architect toward the beneficiary. If the beneficiary sells the construction, this warranty will not accompany the construction once it is sold or donated, unless all the parties involved agree otherwise. However, the seller will have its own contractual obligation to warrant against the hidden defects of the construction toward the buyer.

161. If the damage does not concern the other party of the agreement, the ground for compensation will be tortious liability. Concerning the wrongful act that can be imputed to the builder or the architect, there is a special legislation regarding this area that needs to be mentioned.

162. Thus, in order to ensure protection of the person's safety and goods, of the society and the environment, the legislator adopted in 1995 Law No. 10/1995 concerning the quality in constructions.[164] By this act, it sets some fundamental requirements that need to be met throughout the life of the constructions such as: (a) mechanical strength and stability; (b) fire safety; (c) hygiene, health and environment; (d) safety and accessibility in operation; (e) protection against noise; (f) energy saving and thermal insulation; (g) sustainable use of natural resources. In order to ensure these requirements, the legislator imposes certain obligations to all the factors involved: investors, administrators, users, contractors (builders included), consultants, supervisors, researchers, designers, certified project verifiers, certified technical experts, certified energy auditors for buildings, authorized

164. Published in the O.J. No. 765/2016.

technical managers, authorized site managers, manufacturers/manufacturers of construction products, their legal representatives, importers, distributors of construction products, bodies evaluating and verifying the consistency of the performance of construction products, European technical assessment bodies in construction, bodies approving construction technical approvals in construction, analysis and testing laboratories in construction, universities technical and research institutes in the field of constructions and professional associations in the field.

163. In this sense, the builder has the following main obligations: (a) notifying the investors on the nonconformities and discrepancies found in the projects, in order to solve them; (b) the beginning of the execution of the construction only if they are authorized in accordance with the law and only on the basis and in accordance with projects verified by certified specialists; (c) ensuring the quality level corresponding to the requirements through its own quality system designed and carried out by its own staff, with authorized technical executives; (d) convening the factors that must participate in the verification of the works reached in decisive phases of the execution and ensuring the necessary conditions for their performance, in order to obtain the agreement to continue the works; (e) solving the nonconformities, defects and inconsistencies appeared in the execution phases, only on the basis of the solutions established by the designer with the investor's consent; (f) the use in the execution of the works only of the products and procedures provided in the project, certified or for which there are technical approvals, which lead to the fulfillment of the requirements, as well as the management of the control samples; replacement of the products and processes provided in the project with others that meet the specified conditions and only on the basis of the solutions established by the designers with the consent of the investor; (g) observance of the projects and of the execution details for the achievement of the quality level corresponding to the requirements; (h) notification, within twenty-four hours, of the State Inspectorate for Constructions in case of technical accidents during the execution of works; (i) submission to the reception only of the constructions that correspond to the quality requirements and for which he handed over to the investor the documents necessary for the elaboration of the technical book of the construction; (j) carrying out, within the established deadlines, the measures ordered by the control documents or by the documents of reception of the construction works; (k) remedying, at its own expense, the qualitative defects arising from its fault, both during the execution period and during the guarantee period established according to the law; (l) restoring the temporarily occupied lands to their initial state, at the end of the execution of the works; (m) establishing the responsibilities of all participants in the production process—liability factors, collaborators, subcontractors—in accordance with its own quality assurance system adopted and with the legal provisions in force.[165]

164. If the builder fails to perform one of these obligations and as a result it causes a pecuniary or nonpecuniary damage to a third party, the victim can claim

165. Article 25 of Law No. 10/1995.

compensation on tortious liability grounds. Given the fact that these obligations derive from the professional activity of the builder the standard of care will be appreciated accordingly.

V. Others *(Notaries, Tax Advisers and Accountants, Banks ...)*

165. According to the public notaries law[166] the civil liability of the notary public can be engaged under the conditions of the civil law, for the violation of his professional obligations, but only when he has caused the damage in a bad faith action. This form of guilt alleviates the liability of public notaries as only a characterized form of guilt may be able to trigger the liability. Moreover, this form of guilt is not characterized by the Civil Code, which only refers to intent and negligence. However, it can be argued that a bad faith action represents damage that results with intention or gross negligence.

166. The Civil Code also dedicates a special article concerning the public notaries' liability. In case of annulment of a contract concluded in authentic form for a cause of nullity whose existence results from the text of the contract, the injured party may request the notary public to repair the damages suffered, according to tort liability rules for his own deed. It might be argued that this article extends the limit established in the public notaries' law as it refers to the general rules of tortious liability for one's own act including negligence. However, it is difficult to imagine a situation in which the existence of an annulment cause that results from the text of the contract does not represent gross negligence and can be therefore qualified as bad faith.

167. Also, as a form of protection of this category of professionals, the civil liability of the public notary can be established only by court decision.

168. Public notaries have an obligation to conclude a professional insurance for civil liability risks through the insurance company set within the National Union of Public Notaries from Romania, the unique professional organization established by law. The public notaries must conclude the insurance contract before they start their activity. The minimum limit of the guaranteed amount of civil liability and the level of the amount of the contribution shall be determined annually by the Council of the National Union.

169. Concerning the liability of tax advisers, the legislator chose not to interfere. Thus, general rules concerning the conditions of tortious liability and reparation of damage apply. However, in order to guarantee the payment of the damage, for the exercise of the tax consultancy activity, the legislator established a mandatory professional liability insurance.[167]

---

166. Law of public notaries and notarial activity, No. 36/1995, published in O.J. No. 237/2018.
167. Ordinance No. 71/2001 on the organization and exercise of the tax consultancy activity published in O.J. No. 538/2001.

170. The limits of the civil liability of accounting experts and certified accountants are established by the service contracts concluded in accordance with the law, depending on the domestic and international customs of the accounting profession. As in the case of tax advisers, general rules of tortious liability apply but in order to guarantee the payment of the damage they have to subscribe a professional liability insurance.[168]

§2. LIABILITY OF PUBLIC AUTHORITIES *(CONDITIONS; ALSO AGAINST THEIR ORGANS? IS COMPENSATION IN KIND POSSIBLE?)*

171. The right of a person aggrieved by a public authority is a constitutional right. Article 52 of the Constitution states that: "Any person aggrieved in his/her legitimate rights or interests by a public authority, by means of an administrative act or by the failure of a public authority to solve his/her application within the lawful time limit, is entitled to the acknowledgement of his/her claimed right or legitimate interest, the annulment of the act and reparation for the damage."

172. The nature of the public authorities' liability has been strongly argued between the civil law and public law authors. While the civil law authors sustain its tortious nature, the public law authors argue that it is a special public law liability.

173. However, a close overlook in the special legislation, Law No. 554/2004 on the administrative contentious[169] seems to favor the tortious nature of this type of liability. Article 8 of this law, restates the constitutional principle above mentioned. Article 28 expressly states that the provisions of this law shall be supplemented with the provisions of the Civil Code and those of the Code of Civil Procedure, so far as they are not incompatible with the specifics of power relations between public authorities, on the one hand, and persons injured in their rights or interests and legitimate, on the other hand. This reference reinforces the idea that the Civil Code represents the common law, namely that its provisions are applicable to other branches of law, whenever there is not a specific disposition or they are insufficient. Thus, given the fact that there are no special provisions establishing a special liability system for the public authorities, the nature of the public authorities' liability is going to be a civil liability, namely a tortious liability as long as the contractual liability rules do not apply.

174. It has also been stated that the liability of public authorities is a form of strict liability. The main argument advanced is that Article 8 of Law No. 554/2004 gives right to compensation does not mention fault whereas Article 16 of the same Law that recognizes the person's possibility to claim compensation against the natural person responsible for the damage expressly mentions the idea of fault. This argument can be challenged on the idea that one of the general principles of the

168. Article 13 of Ordinance No. 65/1994 on the organization of accounting expertise and certified accountants published in O.J. No. 13/2008.
169. Published in O.J. No. 1154/2004.

Civil Code is that the rule in our system is that tortious liability derives from fault and strict liability infers only in the cases in which there are legal provisions that establish this type of liability, which is not the case for Article 8 of Law No. 554/2004.

175. Consequently, in order to demand reparations for the damage caused by a public authority all four general conditions of liability need to be met: wrongful act, damage, causation and fault.

176. As it results from the legal provisions, a specificity is met in this case of liability in the wrongful act that could be claimed by the victim: an illegal unilateral administrative act, failing to resolve the request within a time limit, an unjustified refusal to resolve a request or refusal to carry out a certain necessary administrative operation for the exercise or protection of the right or legitimate interest of the victim.

177. Moreover, in the administrative contentious, the victim cannot demand only the reparation of the damage. This type of claim must always be subsequent to the demand of annulment in whole or in part of the act or of the demand to solve the request of the person or to find that the denial to solve the request is illegal.

178. The defendant in this type of claims is first of all the public authority that issued the illegal act or refused to take action. However, if compensation is demanded, the action can also be brought against the person that contributed to the development, issuance, adoption or conclusion of the act or is guilty of denial to solve the request. If the action is admitted, the person can be obliged to pay compensation solidary with the public authority.

179. The court, if it admits the action, may annul, in whole or in part, the administrative act, oblige the public authority to issue an administrative act, issue another document or carry out a certain administrative operation. It will also decide upon the compensation for pecuniary and nonpecuniary damage caused, upon the rules governed by the Civil Code. If the claimant demanded it and it is still possible, it can also establish the restoring of the claimant's situation before the illegal act. For example, it can grant demolishing of a building built with an illegal permit and reinstatement on an employer's position.

§3. ABUSE OF RIGHTS *(I.E., INJURY CAUSED IN THE EXERCISE OF LEGAL RIGHTS; ABUSE OF LEGAL PROCEDURE)*

180. The principle of good faith is enshrined in the main sources of legislation in the Romanian legal system: Constitution, Civil Code, Civil Procedural Code, etc. A consequence of this general principle is that all rights need to be exercised in good faith.

181. Exercising a subjective civil right (in good faith) represents one of the main nonliability clauses regulated by the Civil Code. According to Article 1353 of the Civil Code the person who causes damage through the exercise of his rights cannot be held liable, unless there is an abuse of right.

182. Therefore, the abuse of a subjective civil right turns a licit form of action into an illicit form. In its general provisions, the Civil Code defines the abuse of rights. It states that no right can be exercised on the purpose of injuring or harming another or in an excessive and unreasonable manner, contrary to good faith. This definition reflects the legislator's choice to prevail a subjective criteria despite an objective one which was used in the prior legislation.[170] Thus, there is an abuse of rights either when the right is exercised with the intent to damage a third party or when it is contrary to good faith. On one side, this approach was valued as it reflects the diversity of opinions expressed in the jurisprudence and doctrine on the other, it has been criticized for being ambiguous and outdated.

183. In a slightly different approach, the civil procedure code adopts a mixed criterion: "(1) The procedural rights must be exercised in good faith, according to the purpose for which they were recognized by law and without violating the procedural rights of another party. (2) The party who exercises his procedural rights abusively is liable for the material and moral damages caused. He may also be required by law to pay a court fine."[171] The subjective element consists in violating the good faith obligation whilst the objective element consists in altering the purpose for which the right was recognized by the law. The abuse of procedural right will have to be ascertained by a judge. The victim will be entitled to material and moral damages to compensate for its loss. The author may as well face specific sanctions such as fine, reject of the demand and annulment of the claim.

184. Some authors affirmed that given the need to preclude the consequences of an abuse of rights, this type of liability should be strict and not take into consideration the fault of the author. It has also been argued that this subjective condition would be superfluous because of the subjective criteria that define the abuse of right. However, in the actual frame of the Civil Code, this solution cannot be admitted as cases of strict liability are defined by law and abuse of rights is not one of them.

§4. Injury to Reputation and Privacy *(Of Natural and Juristic Persons)*

185. The Civil Code has a section dedicated to the protection of nonpecuniary rights (Title V of the First Book on persons) which includes the following system of sanctions: nonpecuniary remedial measures, pecuniary remedial measures, provisional measures and defensive measures.

170. Article 3, para. 2 of the Decree No. 31/1954.
171. Article 12.

186. Article 252 is entitled to protection of human personality and it states that every natural person has the right to the protection of intrinsic values of the human being, such as life, health, physical and mental integrity, dignity, privacy, freedom of conscience, scientific, artistic, literary or technical creation. Reputation is not expressly mentioned by Article 252, but in accordance with the jurisprudence of the European Court of Human Rights it is considered to be one of the main elements of privacy and it is englobed in the protection offered to it. Although this Article is dedicated to the protection of natural persons' rights, Article 257 grants a similar protection to nonpecuniary rights of a juristic person. Thus, the provisions of this title shall apply by similarity to the nonpecuniary rights of a juristic person.

187. The specific means of defense include: (i) the prohibition of committing the illicit deed, if it is imminent; (ii) cessation of the violation and prohibition for the future, if it still lasts; and (iii) finding that the act was committed unlawfully, if the disturbance which it caused persists. However, in case of violation of nonpecuniary rights by exercising the right to free expression, like in the case of reputation, the prohibition of committing the illicit deed is not allowed. In order for these actions to be admitted by the judge, the fault of the author is not a condition that needs to be met. They are considered to be more efficient in preventing and protecting these human being values than penal punishment or compensation.

188. At the same time, the person who has suffered a violation of such rights may request the court to oblige the perpetrator to comply with any measures deemed necessary by the court to reach the restoration of the right, such as: ordering the author, at his own expense, to publish the conviction or any other measures necessary for the cessation of the wrongful act or for the reparation of the damage caused.

189. If the damage has not yet been produced, but there is an imminent or current unlawful action that risks to produce a damage difficult to repair, the potential victim can ask the court to take some provisional measures to impede it such as to order the prohibition of the violation or its temporary cessation or taking the necessary measures to ensure the preservation of evidence.

190. In the same time, the victim of an injury to reputation or privacy can demand compensation or pecuniary reparation for the pecuniary or nonpecuniary damage, if the damage is imputable to the author of the injury. Although some of the authors claimed that this type of liability is autonomous and represents a strict form of liability, the jurisprudence and the majority of the doctrine appreciates that as long as the law refers to the imputable character of the action, fault of the author of the injury represents a condition that needs to be met in order to obtain compensation on tortious ground. In other words, it is still a form of subjective tortious liability in which the general rules apply.

191. Concerning the proof of nonpecuniary damage resulted from injury to reputation what represents a specificity is that the jurisprudence established that the proof of the injury suffices, the damage and the causation being presumed from the simple existence of the injury and the circumstances in which it has been committed,[172] the direct proof of the moral damage being impossible to produce.

§5. Interference by a Third Person with Contractual Relations

192. There are two types of situations that may arise when a third person may interfere and affect the performance of contractual obligations between two or more contractual parties.

193. First, it can be the case in which the debtor decides to subcontract and uses the third party in order to perform its contractual obligations. In this case, if the damage results from the third person's fault, Article 1519 of the Civil Code states that the debtor is liable toward the creditor of the obligation for all the damage caused by the third person, unless the parties agree otherwise.

194. Therefore, the liability of the debtor toward the creditor will be contractual and it will be governed by the limits set in the contract or established by the law. The existence of the third party will not influence the extent of the compensation and neither the conditions that need to be met in order to be obtained by the creditor. Depending on the limits set in the contract between the debtor and the third party, the third party will always be liable toward the debtor for the damage caused to the other party of the contract and the debtor will be able to retrieve the compensation paid to his creditor from the third person.

195. Normally, besides the situations in which the law prescribes it, the creditor does not have a direct action against the third person. However, there are some situations in which the recognizes the right of a third party to the contract to have an action against one of the parties to the contract. It is the case for example for the payment of the rent, in case of sublease: the lessor that wants to retrieve the rent has an action against the sublease in the limit of the rent established in the sublease.

196. Second, the third person's interference could be the result of fortuitous causes and not of a contract concluded with one of the parties. In this case, if the third person's action meets the conditions to be considered a fortuitous case or force majeure, the debtor will be exempted of contractual liability toward the creditor. The creditor however will have a right of compensation on tortious grounds against the third party if the interference is imputable to the third party.

172. High Court of Cassation and Justice, Decision No. 153/27 January 2016, available at www.scj.ro, last checked on Apr. 8, 2021.

§6. OTHERS

197. Another specific case of liability in the Romanian system concerns the damage caused by judicial error. The right of compensation for the aggrieved person has a constitutional dimension as it is enshrined in Article 52 of the Romanian Constitution. According to this article, "The State shall bear patrimony liability for any prejudice caused as a result of judicial errors. The State liability shall be assessed according to the law and shall not eliminate the liability of the magistrates having exercised their mandate in ill will or grave negligence."

198. Thus, the liability toward the victim lies exclusively in the State, through the Ministry of Public Finance. In other words, it is a special and direct liability of the State for the damage occurred as a result of a judicial error committed in the act of public service.

199. This liability represents a guarantee obligation of the State for the risk of judicial activity. As a consequence, it is a form of strict liability, so the victim will have to prove the damage, the judicial error and the causation between the damage and the judicial error in order to be compensated.

200. The notion of judicial error is defined and circumscribes to the law. According to Article 96 of Law No. 303/2004[173] a judicial error may concern a procedural act or a final judgment. A procedural act represents a judicial error when it was ordered within the process to perform a procedural act with obvious violation of the legal provisions of material and procedural law, it seriously violated the rights, freedoms and legitimate interests of the person and it caused an injury that could not be remedied by an ordinary or extraordinary remedy. Whereas a final judgment represents a judicial error if it has been given manifestly contrary to the law or to the facts resulting from the evidence in question, it has seriously affected the rights, freedoms and legitimate interests of the person and caused an injury which could not be remedied by an ordinary or extraordinary appeal. As the law prescribes,[174] other judicial errors may be regulated by the Civil or Criminal Procedure Code or other special laws.

201. The Criminal Procedure Code regulates a specific procedure concerning the compensation for pecuniary damage or nonpecuniary damage in case of judicial error or in case of unlawful deprivation of liberty or in other cases. It also establishes the conditions in which the aggrieved person is entitled to compensation.

202. In the article dedicated to establishing the right to compensation for damage in case of judicial error,[175] this notion concerns the annulment of the conviction for a new or recently discovered fact which proves that a judicial error has occurred, namely a final judgment of acquittal has been pronounced after the person has been

173. Published in the O.J. No. 826/2005, republished version.
174. Article 96, para. 4.
175. Article 538 of the Criminal Procedure Code.

definitely convicted. However, the aggrieved person will not be entitled to seek compensation from the State for the damage suffered if, through false statements or in any other way, they have determined the conviction, except in cases where they have been obliged to do so. The aggrieved person also loses the right to compensation if the nondiscovery of the unknown or recently discovered fact that led to the acquittal is in whole or in part attributable to his imputable conduct.

203. In the case of illegal deprivation of liberty, the Criminal Procedure Code demands that it must be established, either by order of the prosecutor or by the final conclusion of the judge of rights and freedoms or of the preliminary chamber judge, as well as by the final conclusion or final decision of the court invested with the trial.[176]

204. Concerning evaluation of damage, the legal criteria takes into account the duration of the illegal deprivation of liberty and the consequences produced on the person, on the family of the person deprived of liberty or wrongfully convicted. The reparation consists in the payment of a sum of money or in the constitution of a life annuity or in the obligation that, at the expense of the state, the illegally detained or arrested person be entrusted to an institute of social and medical assistance. When choosing the type of repair and its extent, the situation of the person entitled to repair the damage and the nature of the damage caused shall be taken into account.

205. The aggrieved person has no direct right to demand compensation from the magistrate that produced the judicial error. However, this does not imply a lack of liability of the author of the wrongful act as there is a civil liability of the magistrate in relation to the State.

206. The State has a right to recourse against the magistrate if the judicial error was caused as a result of exercising the office in bad faith or gross negligence. Within two months from the communication of the final decision pronounced in the action against the State for judicial error, the Ministry of Public Finance shall notify the Judicial Inspection in order to verify whether the judicial error was caused by a judge or prosecutor as a result of exercising the function in bad faith or gross negligence.[177] The State shall exercise the recourse action against the judge or prosecutor if, following the consultative report of the Judicial Inspection and of its own assessment, considers that the judicial error was caused as a result of the exercise of the function of judge or prosecutor in bad faith or gross negligence. The term for exercising the recourse action is six months from the date of communication of the report of the Judicial Inspection. The magistrates' liability subsists even in the case when they no longer perform the function.

176. Article 539 of the Criminal Procedure Code.

177. According to the procedure provided in Art. 741 of Law No. 317/2004 concerning the Superior Council of Magistracy published in O.J. No. 628/2012.

Part II. Liability for Acts of Others

Chapter 1. Vicarious Liability

207. There are plenty of situations in which the one who caused a damage by breaching the law or social norms and violating the subjective rights or legal interest of the victim cannot be held liable because he is minor, legally incapacitated or, though the conditions for engaging tortious liability are met, including fault, he is insolvable and a judicial decision which states the obligation to pay an indemnification would be useless. In this type of situations, without any other legal mechanism emplaced, the innocent victim would have to face alone the negative consequences of the tortious conduct.[178]

208. In order to prevent such inequity, the Romanian civil legislation provides a substitutive form of civil liability[179] that may be engaged against the one who had the duty to overlook the author of the damageable act (in case of minors and those that were legally incapacitated) or exercised supervision, direction and control over the doer (in case of subordination relations).[180] In this regard, Article 1.349(3) C.C. states that "when the law so provides, one can be made to repair the damage caused by another … ."

209. Thus, unlike other forms of liability, such as criminal liability or disciplinary liability, tortious liability is not purely personal, as, in some circumstances, it can also be engaged for the acts of others, as long as between the doer and the one made to repair the damage a special relationship exists.[181] This possibility rests on the idea that tortious liability is not mainly a punishment directed against the tortfeasor, but a mechanism by which the victim of a tortious conduct may obtain a remedy for the loss. Nevertheless, civil liability for the acts of others may only be engaged when the law so provides, which means that personal liability remains the rule.[182]

---

178. *See* I.I. Neamţ and L.T. Dăuceanu, *supra*, p. 157; I.F. Mangu, *Răspunderea civilă delictuală …* , *supra*, p. 11.
179. As the legal doctrine underlined, this are exception from the rule, which is liability for own's act, and thus they must be narrowly interpreted. *See* P. Vasilescu, *supra*, pp. 662–663.
180. *See* I.I. Neamţ and L.T. Dăuceanu, *supra*, p. 157.
181. *Ibid. See also* I.F. Mangu, *Răspunderea civilă delictuală …* , *supra*, pp. 13–15.
182. *See* L. Pop, *Tratat de drept civil. Obligaţiile. Volumul III …* , *supra*, p. 382; F.I. Mangu, *Răspunderea civilă. Constantele …* , *supra*, p. 111; I.F. Mangu, *Răspunderea civilă delictuală …* , *supra*, p. 12.

§1. EMPLOYEE/EMPLOYER

210. The Romanian law of torts does not expressly regulate the specific hypothesis of liability of the employer for the illicit deeds of the employee, but a broader one, that of liability of the principal for the deed of the auxiliaries, which also includes the liability of the employer.[183] In this regard, Article 1373, first paragraph, C.C. provides that "The principal is obliged to repair the damage caused by his auxiliaries whenever the illicit deed caused by them is related to their duties or with the purpose of the assigned jobs." The norm is meant to offer an extra protection to the victim in those cases in which the wrongdoer did not acted independently, but under the authority of another.[184] If such norm would not exist, the victim could obtain relief only from the wrongdoer, based on liability for own's act, and the liability of the one under who's authority the wrongdoer acted could have been engaged on the same ground only if the victim would prove a direct contribution to the illicit act or that at least he acted as an accomplice or instigator, which, in many situation, would have been an extremely difficult task. In order to overcome such an obstacle, Article 1.373 C.C. allows the victim to directly engage the liability of the one under whose authority the tortfeasor has acted, without having to prove any contribution to the illicit deed.[185] Because the victim does not have to prove any contribution of the authority holder to the deed, the tortious liability is one for the acts of others as he is directly liable for the deed of tortfeasor.

211. The second paragraph of Article 1.373 C.C. states that it shall be considered as principal whoever, under the provision of a contract or based on law, has the power of direction, surveillance and control over the one who performs certain functions or tasks in his interest or the interest of another. Though the terms are usually used for the parties of an agency contract, and as it results from the previously mentioned norm the given relation is substantially broader, for the purpose of this monograph we will use the notion of an agent or auxiliary to name the authority holder (principal) and the one act under the authority of the principal (agent/auxiliary). The relation between the two will be later analyzed.

212. In order to engage the tortious liability of the principal the legal doctrine unanimously holds that at least *three common conditions* must be met: the existence of an illegal deed, the damage and the causation.[186] When analyzing the *illicit deed*, the conduct of the agent is considered. In another words, though the liability of the principal is meant to be engaged, it is not his conduct the one that matters, but the one of the agent's. As in the case of tortious liability for own's acts, the illicit deed may consist in an action or inaction and must breach a legal or social norm and violate the subjective rights or legal interest of the victim. It must be further underlined that the liability of the principal may be engaged on this basis only as long as the

183. *See* L. Pop, *Tratat de drept civil. Obligaţiile. Volumul III* ... , *supra*, p. 382.
184. *See* I.F. Mangu, *Răspunderea civilă delictuală* ... , *supra*, p. 115.
185. *See* I.I. Neamţ and L.T. Dăuceanu, *supra*, p. 160.
186. *See* L. Pop, *Tratat de drept civil. Obligaţiile. Volumul III* ... , *supra*, p. 376.

damage was created outside a contractual relationship with the victim.[187] If a contract was concluded between the principal and the victim, and the agent damaged the victim when acting on behalf of the principal for executing the contractual obligations, the liability is contractual not tortious, and may be engaged on a different legal ground.[188]

213. When it comes to *damage*, there are no differences between liability for own's act and the liability of the principal for the acts of the agent. The damage can be pecuniary or nonpecuniary and all the particularities, that will be later addressed, are applicable. Finally, a *causal link* must exist between the damage endured by the victim and the illicit deed of the agent.

214. If the doctrine is unanimous regarding the previously mentioned conditions, not the same can be stated about the condition of *fault.*[189] Some underline that the condition of fault must also be met in relation to the agent,[190] considering that the law did not expressly avert it, as it deed in other cases (such as such as liability for the acts of minor or legally incapable or liability for the acts of things and animal), but the victim does not have to prove it as it is presumed by law.[191] According to this opinion, the liability of the principal is ancillary to the liability of the agent and so it cannot be engaged as long as the agent is not liable.[192] Other legal scholars consider that no fault must be proven by the victim as the legal norm does not provide with such a condition, as it does in the case of liability for own's act.[193] According to the latter, the liability of the principal is independent and autonomous in relation to the liability of the agent and no conditionality exists between the two. The victim must prove the fault of the agent only if it decides to sue him as well, alone or together with the principal.[194] In this optic, the liability of the principal is based on a legal obligation to guarantee to others that the activity he performs by associating an agent will not cause them any damage, and this guarantee is based on the risk of activity or the risk of authority and the principle of equity.[195] It is thus considered that by using agents to fulfill duties or functions in persona interest or the interest of others, the principal creates for the third parties an extra risk of being

---

187. *Ibid.*; L. Pop, *Tratat elementar ... , supra*, p. 475; L. Pop, *Curs de drept civil ... , supra*, p. 367; I.F. Mangu, *Răspunderea civilă delictuală ... , supra*, p. 117.
188. In such situations the victim may engage the contractual liability of the principal according to Art. 1519 C.C. which provides that "Unless the parties agree otherwise, the debtor is liable for the damages caused by the fault of the ones used for execution of the contractual obligations."
189. For an overview regarding this debate, *see* I.F. Mangu, *Răspunderea civilă delictuală ... , supra*, pp. 118–123.
190. *See* G. Durac, in C.S. Ricu et al., *Noul Cod civil. Comentarii, doctrină, jurisprudenţă. Vol. II. Art. 953-1649 (New Civil Code. Comments, Doctrine and Jurisprudence. 2nd Volume. Articles 953-1649)*, Hamangiu, Bucharest, 2012, p. 704.
191. *See* C. Stătescu and C. Bîrsan, *supra*, pp. 253–254.
192. *See* I.F. Mangu, *Răspunderea civilă delictuală ... , supra*, p. 120.
193. *See* L. Pop, *Tratat de drept civil. Obligaţiile. Volumul III ... , supra*, p. 379.
194. *See* L. Pop, *Tratat elementar ... , supra*, pp. 478–480; L. Pop, *Curs de drept civil ... , supra*, p. 368; P. Vasilescu, *supra*, p. 581, 674; I.F. Mangu, *Răspunderea civilă delictuală ... , supra*, pp. 27–28; L.R. Boilă, *supra*, p. 1525.
195. For a wide analysis of the fundaments, *see* L. Pop, *Tratat de drept civil. Obligaţiile. Volumul III ... , supra*, pp. 391–400.

damaged, which is assumed by the principal when it decides to act.[196] To conclude, even though it is closely linked to the personal liability of the tortfeasor, as the latter's deed damages the victim and puts into action the legal mechanism for repairing the damage, the liability of the principal is autonomous and independent, being based not on fault, but on an obligation to guarantee the third parties that no damage shall be caused by using agents, which is based on the risk of activity and the risk of authority. It is not a simple guarantee of solvability, such as fidejussion, as the liability of the principal is personal and independent.[197]

215. Alongside the three common conditions, in order to engage the liability of the principal, the victim must also prove that *two specific conditions* are met: the existence of a subordinance relationship between the principal and the agent and that the illicit deed is related to the duties and the jobs that were assigned to the agent.

216. The existence of a *subordination relationship* between the principal and agent lies at the very heart of this tortious liability hypothesis and it is the central element that defines it. The particularities of the subordination relation result from the second paragraph of Article 1.373 C.C., which provides that the principal must have the authority to direct, surveillance and control the acts of the agent. The agent acts under the authority of the principal, and the principal has the power to influence the actions of the agent by passing mandatory orders and instructions.[198] It is enough for such power to exist, even if it is not exercised by the principal, and no direct contact between the principal and auxiliary is required.[199] As the existence of a subordination relationship between the principal and auxiliary is essential for this type of tortious liability, if the agent is independent and acts independently only him can be held liable based on liability for own's act.[200]

217. The subordination relationship has a legal nature and it result either from a contract or the law.[201] Most often it rests on an employment contract and the employer stands for the principal, while the employee represents the auxiliary.[202]

196. *See* L. Pop, *Tratat elementar ...* , *supra*, pp. 486–487; L. Pop, *Curs de drept civil ...* , *supra*, p. 371.
197. *See* L. Pop, *Tratat de drept civil. Obligaţiile. Volumul III ...* , *supra*, p. 400; L. Pop, *Tratat elementar ...* , *supra*, p. 487; L. Pop, *Curs de drept civil ...* , *supra*, p. 372; P. Vasilescu, *supra*, p. 675.
198. *See* L. Pop, *Tratat de drept civil. Obligaţiile. Volumul III ...* , *supra*, pp. 381–382.
199. *See* L. Pop, *Tratat elementar ...* , *supra*, p. 481; L. Pop, *Curs de drept civil ...* , *supra*, p. 369; I.F. Mangu, *Răspunderea civilă delictuală ...* , *supra*, p. 125.
200. *See* P. Vasilescu, *supra*, p. 671. For example, if the damage was caused by a lawyer, the victim cannot engage the tortious liability of the client as the client does not have the power to direct, control and surveil his lawyer, the latter being independent in fulfilling the duties.
201. For the idea that event factual circumstances may lead to a subordination relationship, *see* P. Vasilescu, *supra*, p. 671.
202. *See* P. Vasilescu, *supra*, p. 670; C. Stătescu and C. Bîrsan, *supra*, p. 245; I.F. Mangu, *Răspunderea civilă delictuală ...* , *supra*, p. 126; L.R. Boilă, *supra*, p. 1525. This is because the employment contract leads to a legal relationship in which the employee is under the authority of the employer and the later in entitled to direct, control and surveil the activity of the first by passing mandatory decision and instructions.

Nevertheless, other contracts or legal acts, such as building contract, company contract or an act of incorporation may as well lead to such a relationship.[203] Though most often it will be based on a contract, there are cases when the subordination relations results outside the contract. So is the case when the agent was sentenced to community service, and while acting so, damaged the victim. Even if no contract exists, the law provides the public authority, where the community service is rendered, with the power to direct, control and surveillance of the agent, just as in the case of an employment contract.[204] Considering the type of relationship that must exist, the legal doctrine is unanimously in holding that while the principal can be a natural or a legal entity, the agent must, in all circumstance, be a natural person, as no direction, control and surveillance, in the meaning of Article 1.373 C.C., may be expert on a legal entity.[205]

218. The second specific condition refers the circumstances in which the tort was committed and the relation between the tortious activity and the authority of the principal in relation to the agent. First paragraph of Article 1.373 C.C. states that the tortious deed must be *related to the agent's duties or the purpose of the jobs assigned.* As such, a *nexum* must exist between the tortious conduct and the activities, duties and jobs that were assigned to the agent by the principal or at least with their purpose. This is because the principal cannot be held liable for the deeds of the agent that fall outside the domains in which the authority can be expert. The tortious liability of the principal is thus resumed to those deeds of the agent he could have influenced by properly exercising the authority. Considering the second paragraph of Article 1.373 C.C., the duties or functions can be performed for the principal or for another, but under the direction, surveillance and control of the principal. It is thus unimportant who is the beneficiary of the agent's activities. What it matters is that in relation to those activities, the principal exercised or could have exercised authority over the auxiliary. The condition will be undoubtedly fulfilled when the illicit deed was committed with the complete observance of the duties and functions entrusted, the auxiliary acting just as the principal asked him too.[206] Furthermore, even if acted outside his duties or functions, but the illicit deed is related to them or their purpose, the principal can still be held liable.[207] The principal can

203. *See* I.I. Neamţ and L.T. Dăuceanu, *supra*, p. 161; L. Pop, *Tratat de drept civil. Obligaţiile. Volumul III* ... , *supra*, p. 384; P. Vasilescu, *supra*, p. 670.

204. *See* I.I. Neamţ and L.T. Dăuceanu, *supra*, p. 161; L. Pop, *Tratat de drept civil. Obligaţiile. Volumul III* ... , *supra*, p. 385.

205. *See* I.I. Neamţ and L.T. Dăuceanu, *supra*, p. 161; L. Pop, *Tratat elementar* ... , *supra*, p. 483; L. Pop, *Curs de drept civil* ... , *supra*, p. 36; P. Vasilescu, *supra*, p. 670.

206. *See* I.I. Neamţ and L.T. Dăuceanu, *supra*, p. 161; L. Pop, *Tratat elementar* ... , *supra*, p. 483; L. Pop, *Curs de drept civil* ... , *supra*, p. 370; I.F. Mangu, *Răspunderea civilă delictuală* ... , *supra*, p 147.

207. The relation between the deed of the agent and his duties and functions may be of place (the deed was committed in the same place as where the agent performs his obligations toward the principal), of time (the deed is committed during working time) or of means (an item entrusted by the principal for fulfilling the duties or functions was used to commit the illicit deed). *See* L. Pop, *Curs de drept civil* ... , *supra*, p. 370; I.F. Mangu, *Răspunderea civilă delictuală* ... , *supra*, pp. 148–149.

also be held liable when the agent acts outside his duties and functions but for a neutral observer it looked as he acted within. Still, in the later hypothesis, the principal is exonerated as long as the victim knew or could have known that the agent acted outside his duties and functions.[208]

219. If previously mentioned conditions are met, the principal may be held liable for the illicit deed committed by the agent and may be obliged to repair the damage caused to the victim. Nevertheless, the victim may still choose to sue the agent and not the principal, as the liability of the principal does not avert the liability of the agent.[209] In such case, the agent shall be held liable according to the conditions provided by law for liability for own's acts and the victim must also prove the fault of the agent. For a fault to be attributed to the agent, the illicit deed must be placed outside his duties and function. If the agent acted according to the orders and instructions coming from the principal and they were not manifestly illegal, he cannot be held liable. In such case, the victim can act direct only against the principal.[210] If the victim chooses to sue both the principal and the agent, they will be held joint and several liable. Joint and several liability will also be incident if the damage was caused by multiple agents acting for the same principal or for different principals, in which case all agents and principals may be held liable.

220. The tortious liability of the principal is meant to offer an extra guarantee to the victim that the damaged caused by the tortfeasor shall be repaired.[211] Nevertheless, it must be remembered that the one guilty for inflicting the damage is the agent and he should be, in the end, held liable for the damage.[212] This is the reason why, if the principal repaired the damage caused by the agent, Article 1.384, first paragraph, C.C. provides that the one who was held liable for the acts of other may regress against the author of the damage except when he is not liable for the damage caused. As such, if the victim acted only against the principal or against the agent and the principal and the latter has repaired the damage in whole or in part, the principal is entitled to regress against the agent and to ask the refund of what he was made to pay. The agent shall be obliged based on the liability for own's act, which means that in the regress action the principal must also prove the fault of the agent.[213] Still, the agent will be held liable only if he acted outside his duties or functions or their purpose. If the agent acted within such limits and by doing so inflicted a damage to the victim, he cannot be held liable, the damage resulting from the way in which the principal used his authority to control, direct or supervised the

208. *See* Art. 1373(3) C.C. For further details, *see* I.I. Neamţ and L.T. Dăuceanu, *supra*, p. 161; L. Pop, *Tratat de drept civil. Obligaţiile. Volumul III ...*, *supra*, p. 390; L. Pop, *Tratat elementar ...*, *supra*, pp. 483–484; C. Stătescu and C. Bîrsan, *supra*, p. 262; L.R. Boilă, *supra*, p. 526.
209. *See* L. Pop, *Tratat de drept civil. Obligaţiile. Volumul III ...*, *supra*, p. 400; P. Vasilescu, *supra*, pp. 675–676.
210. *See* L. Pop, *Curs de drept civil ...*, *supra*, p. 373.
211. *See* I.F. Mangu, *Răspunderea civilă delictuală ...*, *supra*, p. 160.
212. *See* I.I. Neamţ and L.T. Dăuceanu, *supra*, p. 163.
213. *Ibid. See* also L. Pop, *Tratat elementar ...*, *supra*, p. 488; L. Pop, *Curs de drept civil ...*, *supra*, p. 373 and High Court of Cassation and Justice, Decision No. 3595/2003 in V. Terzea, in V. Terzea, *Noul Cod civil. Ediţia a II a. Vol. II (The New Civil Code. 2nd ed., 2nd Vol.)*, p. 400.

agent. A different solution would allow the principal to invoke his own fault and to make the agent liable for a damageable deed which was just a materialization of the orders and instructions coming from the principal.[214] If the damage is partially the result of acting outside the orders and instructions and partially the result of the orders and instructions, both principal and agent can be held liable proportionally with the fault of the agent.[215]

221. If the damage is the result of deed committed by multiple agents who acted under the authority of different principals, the principal who repaired the damage may regress against the agents who contributed to the damageable deed and their principals. Nevertheless, the action is limited to what exceeds the part of damage for which his agent is liable and cannot exceed the part of damage for which the ones against whom the action was directed are responsible for.[216] As such, if in relation to the victim the liability will be joint and several whenever multiple individuals can be held liable, in the regress action the liability becomes divisible, each being liable only for the part of damage for which is responsible. In any case, the one who regresses against another may not recover the part corresponding to his contribution to the damage.[217]

222. Considering that a subordination relationship may also exist between a minor agent and a principal,[218] a conflict of liabilities may exist between the liability of the principal and the liability of the one who is responsible for the illicit acts of the minor. In order to solve this conflict, Article 1.374(2), first thesis, C.C. states that no other person than the principal shall be held liable for the damage caused by a minor who acted as an agent. Thus, if the conditions for engaging tortious liability of the principal are met, the victim may not decide to act against another individual who, otherwise, may be held liable for the acts of the minor. Still, if these conditions are not met, as for example the agent acted outside the orders and instructions and the victim knew or could have known this aspect, the action may be directed against others, most often the parents. One exception, nevertheless, exists. According to the final thesis of the same paragraph, if the principal is also the parent of the minor agent, the victim is allowed to choose between the liability of the principal and the liability of the parent.

§2. INDEPENDENT CONTRACTORS

223. Romanian law does not provide for specific norms when it comes to the liability for the damages caused by independent contractors. Thus, in such cases the

214. *See* I.I. Neamţ and L.T. Dăuceanu, *supra*, p. 163; L. Pop, *Tratat elementar ...* , *supra*, p. 488; L. Pop, *Curs de drept civil ...* , *supra*, p. 370.
215. *See* L. Pop, *Tratat elementar ...* , *supra*, p. 488; L. Pop, *Curs de drept civil ...* , *supra*, p. 370; I.F. Mangu, *Răspunderea civilă delictuală ...* , *supra*, p. 170.
216. *See* Art. 1.384(3) C.C.
217. *See* Art. 1.384(4) C.C.
218. For example, according to Art. 13, first paragraph, of Romanian Labor Code, one can become employee starting to the age of 16.

victim must be able to prove that either the conditions of liability for own's act or those for the liability of the principal for the acts of agents are met.

224. By default, an independent contractor is not an employee. Still, this does not mean that the hiring party cannot be held liable on the same grounds as an employer, as in most of the cases, though partially independent, the contractor must nevertheless act according to the orders and instructions coming from the hiring party or stated in the contract. The independence most often refers to the fact that the hiring party cannot pass orders and instructions outside the limits set in the contract and cannot disciplinarily sanction the contractor, but it can still ask him to fulfill the obligations assumed. For example, when a contract was concluded with a construction worker and the last assumed the obligation to construct a house according to the plans and orders delivered by the beneficiary, at least some degree of authority is kept by the beneficiary and if the victim may prove that this authority was sufficient to expert direction, control and surveillance over the contractor, the liability of the beneficiary can be engaged based on the liability of the principal for the acts of the agent. Thus, as long as a certain level of subordination exists and the hiring party can still control, direct and surveil the activity of the independent contractor, the liability of the principal for the acts of the agent may be engaged.

225. Still, the conclusion is valid only as long as the contractor is a natural person. If the contractor is a legal entity and the damage was caused by one of the employees of the contractor, no direct subordination relationship exists between the wrongdoer and the beneficiary and for that reason the last cannot be consider principal in relation to the wrongdoer and cannot be held liable.

226. Furthermore, the damage must result outside a contractual relation between the victim and the beneficiary. If the independent contractor was hired in order to fulfill a contractual obligation that the beneficiary had in relation to the victim, the contractual liability of the hiring party can be engaged. In such case, Article 1.519 C.C. provides that the victim must also prove the fault of the doer, but no subordination relationship must be proven to exist between the hiring party and the independent contractor.

227. In any case, the hiring party may be held liable based on the liability for own's acts for failure to choose a proper contractor or to take the necessary safety measure prescribed by law or local custom, if the victim is able to prove a faulty illicit deed.

§3. Liability of the Legal Entities for Acts of Their Organs

228. Legal entities such as companies, association or foundations are, by, their very nature, an abstraction, an intellectual construction with no physical reflection in the real world. They only exist because the law says so. Thus, they cannot decide for themselves and they cannot do or abstain from anything. Instead, the legal entities express their will, exercise their rights and fulfill their obligations through their governing bodies.[219] In relation to the third parties no distinction can be drawn between the legal entity and its governing body.[220] The legal entities exist and manifest in accordance with the decisions made by their governing bodies and the decision of the governing body is the decision of the entity itself.

229. For this reason, if the decision or the act of the governing body damages someone outside the legal entity, the legal entity may be held liable. Still, it is not a liability for the acts of others, but a *personal liability*. It is a liability for its own acts, as the acts of the governing body are the acts of the entity itself.[221] For this, Article 219, first paragraph, C.C. provides that the legal or illegal acts of the governing bodies oblige the legal entity itself, as long as they are related to the attributes or the purpose of entrusted functions.

230. If the legal conditions are met, the legal entity can be held liable for its own acts, committed by its leadership, or for the damages caused by its agents, things, animals or edifices.[222] In other words, the legal entity may be held liable for the same reasons as a natural person. Nevertheless, the liability of the legal entities implies certain particularities that distinguish it from the liability of the natural person.

231. As in any other hypothesis of liability, the tortious liability of legal entity may be engaged only if certain *conditions* are fulfilled. Still, the legal doctrine had not yet reached a unanimous agreement on what these conditions are. It is generally accepted that the victim must prove the existence of a damage, of an illicit deed and the causation.[223] While the conditions of damage and causation do not imply any particularities, by comparison to the liability of a natural person, the condition of the *illicit deed* is characterized by the fact that, though it was not committed by the legal entity, but by its governing bodies, the tortious liability is still personal, for its own acts.[224] Such illicit acts may take the form of business decisions regarding the development of dangerous activities that breach the security norms: the use of dangerous technologies and machines; the breach of competition norms; the productions of dangerous goods; the breach of good faith in negotiation; the decision to use production technologies which pollute over the legal standard, and so on.[225]

---

219. In this regard, Art. 209, first paragraph, C.C. provides that "the legal entity exercises its rights and fulfils its obligations through its administrative board ... ." *See also* L. Pop, *Tratat de drept civil. Obligaţiile. Volumul III ...*, *supra*, p. 337.
220. *See* F.I. Mangu, *Răspunderea civilă. Constantele ...*, *supra*, p. 273.
221. *See* I.I. Neamţ and L.T. Dăuceanu, *supra*, pp. 144–145; L. Pop, *Tratat de drept civil. Obligaţiile. Volumul III ...*, *supra*, p. 338; L. Pop, *Tratat elementar ...*, *supra*, pp. 458–460; L. Pop, *Curs de drept civil ...*, *supra*, p. 359; P. Vasilescu, *supra*, p. 633; C. Stătescu and C. Bîrsan, *supra*, p. 211; F.I. Mangu, *Răspunderea civilă. Constantele ...*, *supra*, p. 274.
222. *See* L. Pop, *Tratat elementar ...*, *supra*, p. 458; C. Stătescu and C. Bîrsan, *supra*, p. 211.
223. *See* I.I. Neamţ and L.T. Dăuceanu, *supra*, pp. 144–145; L. Pop, *Tratat de drept civil. Obligaţiile. Volumul III ...*, *supra*, pp. 338–339; L. Pop, *Tratat elementar ...*, *supra*, p. 460; L. Pop, *Curs de drept civil ...*, *supra*, p. 359.
224. *See* L. Pop, *Tratat de drept civil. Obligaţiile. Volumul III ...*, *supra*, p. 339; L. Pop, *Tratat elementar ...*, *supra*, p. 460; L. Pop, *Curs de drept civil ...*, *supra*, p. 359.
225. *See* L. Pop, *Tratat elementar ...*, *supra*, p. 460; L. Pop, *Curs de drept civil ...*, *supra*, p. 359.

232. If regarding the three above-mentioned conditions there are no divergences among legal scholars, the situation is substantially different when it comes to *fault*. Some legal scholars affirm that the tortious liability of the legal entity is subjective, based on fault, considering that the law of torts does not provide an exception in this matter, as it does in other cases, such as the tortious liability for goods or animals.[226] Another argument would be that at least two other legal norms, which play as common rules in the field of liability, provide fault as a condition for engaging liability, if the law does not otherwise provide. In this regard, as previously shown, Article 16, first paragraph, C.C., states that if the law does not otherwise provide, one shall be held liable only if the illicit deed was committed with intention or by negligence. Furthermore, Article 1.349(2) C.C. provides that the one who breached a legal or social norm and by doing so violated a subjective right or legitimate interest of another is obligated to repair the damage caused if he acted with discernment. As we saw, discernment is closely linked to fault. If we accept the idea that the tortious liability of legal entities is subjective, then the condition of fault must be analyzed considering the natural persons that form the governing body which made the decision that lead to the illicit deed, considering that the will of the legal entities, thus including the capacity to foresee the consequences and the illicit nature of a deed or to deliberate and make a decision, is express through its governing bodies.[227]

233. On the other hand, there are very important legal scholars that see tortious liability of the legal entities as a form of strict liability, in which fault is irrelevant. They argue that the fault of the natural persons that form the governing body cannot be transposed to the judicial entity[228] and that in most of the cases the victim is not required to even prove the identity of the ones that form the leadership of the legal entity[229] and without knowing their identity to fault can be proven.

234. Another argument may also be brought. When it regulated the tortious liability for own's act and contractual liability for the acts of others, the law expressly provides the condition of fault. By contrary, the law expressly stipulates that in some circumstances, such as liability for things or animals, no prove of fault is required. Then there are cases when the law does not provide either way, such as the liability of the legal entities. In those cases it either accepted that the norms regulating a specific form of liability are incomplete and shall be completed with the

226. *See* C. Stătescu and C. Bîrsan, *supra*, p. 213.

227. *See* I.I. Neamţ and L.T. Dăuceanu, *supra*, p. 145.

228. *See* L. Pop, *Tratat de drept civil. Obligaţiile. Volumul III ...* , *supra*, p. 339; L. Pop, *Tratat elementar ...* , *supra*, p. 460; F.I. Mangu, *Răspunderea civilă. Constantele ...* , *supra*, p. 280. Though seductive, we cannot subscribe to this argument. If we accept that the will of the legal entities is expressed through the natural persons that form the governing bodies, then any particularity of that will also belong to the legal entity. In relation to third parties, what the natural persons that form the governing bodies do and think cannot be dissociated from the legal entity itself. Furthermore, in other fields of law, such as criminal law, it is unanimously accepted that legal entities may commit a faulty deed and fault is analyzed by considering the natural persons that form the leadership of the entity.

229. *See* L. Pop, *Tratat de drept civil. Obligaţiile. Volumul III ...* , *supra*, p. 339; L. Pop, *Curs de drept civil ...* , *supra*, p. 360.

provisions of Articles 16 C.C. and 1.349 C.C. or qualify those norms as special and derogatory, in which case no addition is possible. From our standing point, the last optic is the correct one.

235. The general regime of tortious liability is provided by Article 1.349 C.C. and the legal scholars seem to be unanimous in admitting that this regime further completes with liability for own's act. All the other types of tortious liability are special and specific as for each the law provides a special set of conditions. Being special forms of liability, they derogate from the regular rules, and therefore no further conditions shall be added than those especially provided by the law. If the law would have intended for the special forms of liability to complete with the common rules, then it would have provided only for those extra rules and expressly state which rules from the common regime do not apply. But this is not the case, as the norms regulating the special forms of liability expressly refer to common conditions, such as the illicit deed, damage or causation, which would not be necessary if those norms would complete with the common ones, as the last already provide for such conditions, and no reference is made to what common rules do not apply. It is, nevertheless, true, that sometimes, as we have previously stated, the norms regulating the special forms of liability do complete with the general or common one, but not in the sense that, by doing so, an extra condition may be added. Rather, whenever the special norms do not define a condition or a term, that condition and term shall have the meaning given by the common norms. As such, considering that the special norms regulating the tortious liability of legal entities do not provide the condition of fault, the liability may be considered objective or strict.

236. In any case, if the strict liability theory is accepted, the legal doctrine underlined that the liability of the legal entity is based on the obligation to guarantee to the third parties that their governing bodies shall not inflict any damage. The support of the previously mentioned obligation to guarantee is the risk of activity which the legal entities create for society by their very existence and by developing the activities for which they were incorporated or created.[230]

237. Alongside the common conditions, an extra, specific condition must be met, as it results from Article 219 C.C.: the illicit deed must be committed in relation to the duties or the purpose of functions that were entrusted the governing bodies. The natural persons that form the governing bodies of the legal entity can also express and act outside this quality. For instance, if a director punches a neighbor during a fight on the line between their proprieties, it is obvious that no liability of the legal entity may be engaged, as the natural person who also stands as a governing body, the director, did not act in the last quality.[231] As a general matter, the tortious liability of the legal entity may be engaged only by those activities, acts and decisions that circumscribe and define its will of and that are related to its interest, legal or not, or its field of activity.

230. *See* L. Pop, *Tratat elementar ...* , *supra*, pp. 460–461; L. Pop, *Curs de drept civil ...* , *supra*, p. 360.
231. *See* F.I. Mangu, *Răspunderea civilă. Constantele ...* , *supra*, p. 283.

238. Trying to draw a demarcation line between what leads to the liability of the legal entity and what not, the legal doctrine claimed that the tortious liability may be engaged whenever the illicit deed was committed by the governing body while strictly fulfilling its duties or in order to achieve the purpose of the entrusted functions.[232] The legal entity may still be held liable event if the act does not fall precisely within the duties or the purpose of functions that were entrusted the governing bodies, as long as between the tortious act and those duties or function a sufficiently strong connection exists and the illicit deed was committed in the interest of the legal entity, or at least an appearance exists that is was committed in the interest of the legal entity.[233] The tortious liability of the legal entity shall not be engaged if the victim knew that the natural persons that form the governing bodies acted abusively, in personal interest, or outside their duties or the purpose of their functions. Nor shall the liability be engaged if there is no connection between the illicit deed and the duties or the purpose of the functions entrusted to the governing bodies.[234]

239. The personal tortious liability of the legal entity may be engaged only if the illicit deed was committed by the governing bodies. If the illicit deed was not committed by a governing body, but, for example, by an employee, its liability could be engaged on different ground, respectively as the liability of the principal for the acts of the auxiliaries, if the conditions are met.[235] Nevertheless, no strict meaning must be given to the notion of "governing bodies." The notion does not relate to the governing bodies provided by law or by status of incorporation, but it refers to the body or natural person which is entrusted de jure or de facto the power to decide for the legal entity. As such, it may be considered governing bodies' event those that lead de facto the legal entity (even if there is no support for this power in law or act of incorporation) or the body to which this power was transferred by power of attorney or in another way. In other words, what matters is not the competence of the governing body to make decision for the legal entity or their legality, but the fact it makes the decision for the legal entity and this is accepted as a practice.

---

232. *See* I.I. Neamţ and L.T. Dăuceanu, *supra*, p. 145; L. Pop, *Tratat elementar ... , supra*, p. 461; L. Pop, *Curs de drept civil ... , supra*, p. 360.
233. *See* L. Pop, *Tratat de drept civil. Obligaţiile. Volumul III ... , supra*, p. 340; L. Pop, *Tratat elementar ... , supra*, p. 461; L. Pop, *Curs de drept civil ... , supra*, p. 360; F.I. Mangu, *Răspunderea civilă. Constantele ... , supra*, p. 287. For the opinion that the tortious act must in all circumstances be committed in the personal interest of the legal entity, *see* C. Stătescu and C. Bîrsan, *supra*, p. 213. If all the above-mentioned conditions are met, the legal entity can be held liable whether it is a private legal entity or a public legal entity. In this regard, Art. 221 C.C. states that if the law does not otherwise provide, public legal entities shall be held liable in the same conditions as private legal entities.
234. *See* L. Pop, *Tratat de drept civil. Obligaţiile. Volumul III ... , supra*, p. 340; L. Pop, *Tratat elementar ... , supra*, pp. 461–462; L. Pop, *Curs de drept civil ... , supra*, pp. 360–361.
235. *See* I.I. Neamţ and L.T. Dăuceanu, *supra*, p. 145; L. Pop, *Tratat elementar ... , supra*, p. 461; L. Pop, *Curs de drept civil ... , supra*, p. 360; C. Stătescu and C. Bîrsan, *supra*, p. 212; F.I. Mangu, *Răspunderea civilă. Constantele ... , supra*, p. 274.

240. Even though the acts of the governing body represent the acts of the legal entity and the latter may be held liable on the ground of liability for own's act for the decisions and acts of the governing bodies, this does not mean that the natural persons that committed the illegal deed are exonerated. The second paragraph of Article 219 C.C. provides that the illicit deeds also lead to personal and joint and several liability of the ones who committed them, both to the legal entity and the victim. As so, the victim may choose to sue the legal entity, the tortfeasor or both the legal entity and the tortfeasor, in which case the two will be held jointly and several liable.[236] If the legal entity repairs the damage, it can regress against the natural persons that form the governing body who's act or decision lead to damage.[237] The element of particularity lies in the fact that while the general norms provide that in the regress action the liability is divisible among the wrongdoers, in this specific case the law provides a case of joint a severe liability. In other words, if the act was committed by multiple natural personal acting as a collective governing body, they shall be held joint and several liable not just for the damage caused to the victim, but also in an eventual regress action of the legal entity. Nevertheless, if one of the natural persons repaired the damage, this time in an eventual regress action, the liability is no longer joint, but divisible, each being held liable according to the contribution to the damage or, if this cannot be established, depending on the type of fault.[238]

236. *See* C. Stătescu and C. Bîrsan, *supra*, p. 214; F.I. Mangu, *Răspunderea civilă. Constantele* ... , *supra*, p. 290.
237. For further details, *see* F.I. Mangu, *Răspunderea civilă. Constantele* ... , *supra*, pp. 292–312.
238. For further details, *see* I.I. Neamţ and L.T. Dăuceanu, *supra*, p. 145; L. Pop, *Tratat elementar* ... , *supra*, pp. 462–463; L. Pop, *Curs de drept civil* ... , *supra*, p. 361.

Chapter 2. Liability of Parents, Teachers and Instructors *(For Children, Minors, Students, Etc.)*

241. The Romanian Civil Code places the liability for the torts of minors in the person who has an obligation to supervise the minor. This obligation may arise from the law, a contract or a court order and it can hold liable a natural persona or an artificial person.

242. The third person's liability will arise even if the minor that caused the damage is not liable for its own act.

243. Normally the duty to supervise the minor is bestowed upon the parents who have legal parental authority over the child. Parental authority implies that both parents have the right and duty to raise the child by taking care of his health, his physical, psychological and intellectual development as well as of his education, teaching and professional training. Thus, the parents' obligation to supervise his child derives from the larger duty to exercise parental authority. When parents are not able or are not considered worthy to exercise the parental authority the law establishes that the rights and duties concerning the child and its assets will be transferred to a tutor appointed by court order.

244. The parents or the tutors may exempt themselves only if they prove that the wrongdoing is the result of a different cause than that of how they fulfilled their parental duties. It has been argued that given the content of parental duties the parents or tutors possibility to exempt themselves is illusory, placing their liability on the round of strict liabilities.

245. Other people who may be held liable beside the parents are: nannies, teachers in public schools or kindergarten, private schools, hospitals, craftsmen or any sport instructor that teach minors, foster parents, etc. Basically the liability lies in any third person that had the obligation to supervise the minor according to the contract, law or court order at the moment the damage had been produced. If the conditions are met in order to hold liable this third person, the parents' liability ceases. However, in this case the person held liable may prove he could not prevent the wrongful act in order to exempt himself. Thus parents' liability is general and subsidiary in relation to the liability of other people that have the obligation to supervise the minor.

246. Moreover, the parents' liability ceases if the conditions for vicarious liability are met. In this case, no other person than the employer can be held liable for the minor's wrongful act committed under their authority. However, if the employer is the parent of the minor, the victim has an option to ground its claim either on parents' liability or on the vicarious liability.

247. In order to establish this type of liability the victim needs to prove the general conditions of liability in the person of the minor—the damage, the wrongful act of the minor and the causation between the two as well as two special conditions—the minority (0–18 years) and the existence of the obligation to supervise the minor in the person held liable at the moment of the wrongful act. The existence of the minor's discernment when he acted is irrelevant. Therefore, the liability of a third person for minors is autonomous and direct leaving the victim the possibility to obtain damages regardless of its option to file a claim against the minor.

248. The payment of damages entitles the person held liable to demand damages against the minor, author of the wrongful act. However, in this case the right of recourse is conditioned to the minor's discernment when he acted as the ground of this claim is liability for one's own act.

Chapter 3. Liability for Things and Animals

249. There are situations in which the damage is not the result of a human conduct but more of the way in which an animal or thing "behaved." Still, most of the animals and things belong to someone, who, when deciding to become the legal supervisor of the animal or thing, assumes that it creates an extra risk for society which, if it materializes, may lead to liability.[239] In this regard, as a general rule, Article 1349(3) C.C. provides that in cases specifically provided by law, one may also be obliged to repair the damage caused by the things and animals that are under his guard or by the ruin of the edifice. What can be immediately noticed is that by comparison to tortious liability for own's acts, tortious liability for things, animals and the ruin of edifice is more of an exception, as it can be engage only in those specific cases provided by law.[240]

250. The Romanian law of torts addresses distinctly the liability of the damages caused by things and the liability for the damages caused by animals. Also, two extra, specific hypotheses, were regulated: the tortious liability for the damages caused by the ruin of edifice and the liability for the damage caused by the falling or throwing of a thing from a building. As the four present some particularities, they will be further distinctly analyzed.

§1. Tortious Liability for Animals

251. The tortious liability for the damages caused by animals is regulated by Article 1.375 C.C. which provides that "The owner of an animal or the one that uses it, shall be held liable, no matter of fault, for the damage caused by that animal, even when it escaped from his guard." The Article further completes with Article 1.377 C.C. which defines the notion of "guard" and Article 1.380 C.C. which provides when one can be exonerated.

252. Regarding the one *who may be held liable*, from the above-mentioned norm it results that when the damage was caused by an animal, the victim may sue the legal guardian of the animal in order to ask for redress. Article 1.377 C.C. provides that the legal guardianship of the animal belongs to the owner or to the one who, under a legal or contractual provision or even only as a matter of fact, independently exercises control and surveillance of the animal and uses it in personal interest.[241] As such, the law presumes that the legal guardianship belongs to the owner of the animal, as the ownership also implies the obligation to oversee and control

239. *See* I.I. Neamţ and L.T. Dăuceanu, *supra*, p. 166.
240. *See* Art. 1.349, first and second paragraphs, C.C. which state that the tortious liability for own's act shall be engaged whenever a damage was caused by an illicit deed that violated the subjective rights or legitimate interest of the victim and the tortfeasor acted with discernment.
241. For an extensive analysis of the legal guardianship of animals and things, *see* L. Pop, *Tratat de drept civil. Obligaţiile. Volumul III* ... , *supra*, pp. 417–430; L. Pop, *Tratat elementar* ... , *supra*, pp. 495–501; L. Pop, *Curs de drept civil* ... , *supra*, pp. 377–380.

the animal.[242] In case of joint ownership, all owners shall be held jointly liable.[243] Nonetheless, the presumption is relative, as it can be overturned by the owner showing that at the time of the illicit act the legal guardianship belonged to another.[244] When it does not belong to the owner, the legal guardianship may have its cause in a legal provision (when the law provides that another person than the owner is the legal guardian) a contract (when the legal guardianship was transmitted by contract to another) or in a de facto situation. The last hypothesis refers to situations when one exercises control and surveillance of the animal without a legal right, such as when the animal was stolen from the legal guardian. In this case, the legal guardianship is transferred to the thief and so is the liability for the damages caused by the animal. Thus, it is not necessary to have a legal basis for becoming legal guardian. Considering that the norm is meant to protect the victim and it does not deal with the legal status of the animal, but with the damage caused by it, even an illegal action, such as stilling the animal, may lead to legal guardianship in the meaning of Article 1.375 C.C.[245]

253. In order to lead to liability, the oversee and control of the animal must be exercised independently and in the interest of the guardian. If the oversee and control are exercised in the interest of another, the last shall be held liable for the damage caused by the animal. For example, if during the day the animal is cared of by an animal caretaker or in an animal hotel, the liability still belongs to the owner, as the caretaker and the hotel do not act in their interest, but in the interest of the owner. Thus, a distinction must be drawn between physical (or material) guardianship and legal guardianship.[246] While the physical guardianship belongs to the animal caretaker or the hotel, the legal guardianship belongs to the owner, in this scenario. The difference between the two lies in the way in which the oversee and control are exercised. In the case of legal guardianship, the oversee and control are exercised independently and in the interest of the guardian, while in the case of physical guardianship the oversee and control are exercised under the authority and in the interest of the legal guardian.[247] The liability of the material guardian may be engaged by the victim only on the basis of liability for own's acts, which implies also the proof of fault.[248]

---

242. *See* L. Pop, *Tratat elementar ...* , *supra*, pp. 509–510; L. Pop, *Curs de drept civil ...* , *supra*, p. 385; C. Stătescu and C. Bîrsan, *supra*, p. 278; I.F. Mangu, *Răspunderea civilă delictuală ...* , *supra*, pp. 217–218; L.R. Boilă, *supra*, p. 1531.
243. *See* L. Pop, *Tratat elementar ...* , *supra*, p. 497; C. Stătescu and C. Bîrsan, *supra*, p. 279; I.F. Mangu, *Răspunderea civilă delictuală ...* , *supra*, p. 218; L.R. Boilă, *supra*, p. 153. Still, if just one of the owners acted as legal guardian, either because all the owners decide so or because one usurped the rights of others, only he/she shall be held liable.
244. *See* I.I. Neamţ and L.T. Dăuceanu, *supra*, p. 164.
245. *Ibid.*
246. *See* L. Pop, *Tratat de drept civil. Obligaţiile. Volumul III ...* , *supra*, p. 419; L. Pop, *Tratat elementar ...* , *supra*, p. 510; C. Stătescu and C. Bîrsan, *supra*, p. 278; I.F. Mangu, *Răspunderea civilă delictuală ...* , *supra*, pp. 208–209.
247. *See* L. Pop, *Tratat de drept civil. Obligaţiile. Volumul III ...* , *supra*, p. 419; L. Pop, *Tratat elementar ...* , *supra*, p. 510; I.F. Mangu, *Răspunderea civilă delictuală ...* , *supra*, p. 208.
248. *See* L. Pop, *Tratat de drept civil. Obligaţiile. Volumul III ...* , *supra*, p. 419.

254. Furthermore, it must also be considered that the legal guardianship itself can be, in certain circumstances, divided.[249] One such example is when the animal is leased to another, in which case both the lessor and the lessee are legal guardians of the animal, as both, to a given point, exercise independently and in self-interest the oversee and the control of the animal. If these happen, the liability depends on what caused the damage.[250] If the damage was caused by the way in which the animal was used, by its behavior, the lessee shall be held liable. In any other case, the liability belongs to the lessor.[251]

255. Another problem relates to the *animals for which one can be held liable*. In a very broad meaning, the notion of animal defines any living body, besides human, but not all the animals may lead to tortious liability. For example, if a wild bear creates a damage, no one can be held liable on common norms referring to tortious liability.[252] The kind of animals for which one can be held liable result from the definition of legal guardianship. As Article 1.377 C.C. provide, one can be held liable only for the animals that are overseen and controlled.[253] Falling into this category are not only the domestic animals but also the wild animals that are held in captivity (such as the animals from the zoos, circus, rehabilitation centers) or semi-captivity (such as the animals from hunting grounds or protected areas).[254] For the wild animal, special rules were adopted, which derogate, at least partially, from the common ones provided by Civil Code.[255]

256. In order to engage tortious liability for the damage caused by the animal, some general and special conditions must be fulfilled. As for the *general conditions,* there must exist a damageable deed of the animal, a damage infringed to the victim and a nexum between the behavior of the animal and the damage. There is also a special condition: the animal must be under the legal guardianship of the one against whom the victim acted.[256]

257. In this specific hypothesis the damaged is not caused by a human conduct, but by an *animal "behavior."* The causational deed must be broadly understood as encompassing not only actions or inactions but also deeds that are related to the

249. *See* L. Pop, *Tratat de drept civil. Obligațiile. Volumul III ...*, *supra*, pp. 424–425; L. Pop, *Tratat elementar ...*, *supra*, p. 498; L. Pop, *Curs de drept civil ...*, *supra*, p. 379; I.F. Mangu, *Răspunderea civilă delictuală ...*, *supra*, p. 228.
250. *See* L. Pop, *Tratat elementar ...*, *supra*, p. 499; L. Pop, *Curs de drept civil ...*, *supra*, p. 379.
251. *See* I.I. Neamţ and L.T. Dăuceanu, *supra*, pp. 164–165; I.F. Mangu, *Răspunderea civilă delictuală ...*, *supra*, pp. 228–229.
252. In such cases, the liability may be engaged on special norms which regulate the administration of wild fauna, which implicitly refer to liability for own's act. *See* Art. 3 of Law No. 407/2006 published in Monitorul Oficial No. 944 from November 22, 2006.
253. *See* First Instance Court of Craiova, Civil Sentence No. 10907/2011, in V. Terzea, *supra*, p. 373.
254. *See* I.I. Neamţ and L.T. Dăuceanu, *supra*, p. 165; L. Pop, *Tratat elementar ...*, *supra*, p. 510; L. Pop, *Curs de drept civil ...*, *supra*, p. 385; P. Vasilescu, *supra*, p. 688; C. Stătescu and C. Bîrsan, *supra*, p. 276; I.F. Mangu, *Răspunderea civilă delictuală ...*, *supra*, pp. 186–187. *See also* Supreme Tribunal, Decision No. 996/1982, in V. Terzea, *supra*, p. 374.
255. *See* Law No. 407/2006 referring to hunting and the protection of wildlife.
256. *See* I.I. Neamţ and L.T. Dăuceanu, *supra*, pp. 165–166.

being of the animal, such as a disease. For example, if the animal suffers from a disease and transfers it to an animal of the victim, the condition is met. The animal "behavior" must, as in the case of liability for own's act, come against a legal or social norm and violate the subjective rights or legal interest of the victim.[257] There are no specific elements when it comes to the *damage*. Tortious liability can be engaged for the same kind of damages and under the same condition as in the other forms of liability, including tortious liability for own's acts. No major particularities exist when it comes to *causation* either. The only specific element is that the causation must exist between the animal behavior and the damage suffered by the victim and not between a human behavior and the damage.[258]

258. Referring to the *specific condition*, the victim of the animal damageable behavior must sue the one under whose legal guardianship the animal was at the time of the deed. If the legal guardian abandoned the animal before the damageable deed was committed this will not avert the liability, as long as the animal did not acquire a new legal guardian.[259] Thus, the legal guardianship maintains even if the animal is abandoned until a new legal guardianship is emplaced. Furthermore, it is irrelevant that at time of the deed the legal guardian could not exercise the control because the animal escaped or for other similar reasons, as the obligation to repair the damages subsists even in such situations.

259. The liability for the damages caused by the animals is strict and *no fault* must be proven by the victim, as Article 1.375 C.C. expressly provides. Thus, the fact that no fault can be attributed to the legal guardian is irrelevant, as the liability is not based on fault, but on the obligation of guarantee that the "behavior of the animal" shall not inflict any damage to others, which is related to the risk of activity.[260] As fault is irrelevant, it does not matter that at the time of the deed the legal guardian had no discernment.[261]

260. In this case of strict liability, Article 1.380 C.C. provides that legal guardian may be *exonerated* only if it is proven that the damage is entirely the consequence of a victim's deed or of a third's party deed or that that is the result of a force majeure. If the legal guardian repaired the damage and at the time of the damageable deed the animal deed was under the material guardianship of another, the legal guardian may regress against the material guardian and engage the liability for his own acts[262] or, if a contractual obligation was breached, his contractual liability. In either case, in the regress action, the legal guardian must also prove the fault of the material guardian as both hypotheses of liability are subjective.

257. *See* I.F. Mangu, *Răspunderea civilă delictuală ...* , *supra*, pp. 189–190.
258. For an analysis of this condition, *ibid.*, pp. 190–202.
259. *See* L. Pop, *Tratat elementar ...* , *supra*, p. 497.
260. *See* L. Pop, *Tratat elementar ...* , *supra*, p. 511; L. Pop, *Curs de drept civil ...* , *supra*, p. 386.
261. *See* I.I. Neamţ and L.T. Dăuceanu, *supra*, p. 166; L. Pop, *Tratat elementar ...* , *supra*, pp. 499–501; L. Pop, *Curs de drept civil ...* , *supra*, p. 380; I. Lulă, *Observaţii asupra pazei juridice şi capacităţii delictuale (Observations Regarding Legal Guardianship and Tortious Capacity)*, in Dreptul No. 3/1996, pp. 18–27; I.F. Mangu, *Răspunderea civilă delictuală ...* , *supra*, p. 212.
262. *See* L. Pop, *Tratat elementar ...* , *supra*, p. 512; L. Pop, *Curs de drept civil ...* , *supra*, p. 387.

§2. Tortious Liability for Things

261. The tortious liability for the damages caused by things follows a similar pattern as tortious liability caused by animals. In this regard, Article 1.376, first paragraph, C.C. states that the legal guardian of a thing shall repair the damage caused by that thing, no matter the fault.[263]

262. Thus, if the damage was caused by a thing, the victim may sue the *legal guardian* in order to obtain the reparation of damage. The concept of legal guardianship is identical as the one used in the case of tortious liability for the damage caused by animals, considering that Article 1.377 C.C. provides a unique definition of legal guardianship for both hypotheses. Therefore, it shall be considered legal guardian the one who under the law, provisions of a contract or as a matter of fact, independently exercises control and surveillance of the thing and uses it in personal interest.[264] The owner is presumed to be the legal guardian, but the presumption may be overturned by proving that the legal guardianship belongs to someone else.[265] If the presumption is overturned by the owner, it further operates in relation to other right holders, such as the usufructuary, the fiduciary or the retentor.[266] It is possible for the legal guardian to be an illegal possessor, as long as it exercises an independent control and surveillance of the thing and the thing is used for personal interest.[267]

263. As in the case of tortious liability for the damages caused by animals, the legal guardship must be differentiated from material guardianship. While in the case of legal guardship the guardian independently and in his own interest exercise control and surveillance of the thing, the material guardian control and oversees the thing in accordance with the orders and instructions coming from the legal guardian and in the latter's interest.[268] The material guardian may be held liable by both the victim and the legal guardian only on the bases of liability for own's fault. Finally, the legal guardship may be devised by partially transferring it on to another trough a contract,[269] in which case the owner or possessor shall be held liable for the damages caused by the thing's substance, while the other party shall be held liable for the damages caused by the thing's "behavior" or the way in which is used or

263. The nature of thing is irrelevant. It can be movable or immovable, physical or immaterial, including electricity. In this regard, *see*, *e.g.*, High Court of Cassation and Justice, Decision No. 2725/2003, in V. Terzea, *supra*, p. 376.

264. *See* P. Vasilescu, *supra*, p. 678; C. Stătescu and C. Bîrsan, *supra*, p. 288.

265. *See* L. Pop, *Tratat de drept civil. Obligaţiile. Volumul III* ... , *supra*, p. 420, 423; C. Stătescu and C. Bîrsan, *supra*, p. 290.

266. *See* L. Pop, *Tratat elementar* ... , *supra*, p. 498; P. Vasilescu, *supra*, p. 679.

267. *See* L. Pop, *Tratat de drept civil. Obligaţiile. Volumul III* ... , *supra*, pp. 428–430.

268. *See* L. Pop, *Tratat elementar* ... , *supra*, p. 496; L. Pop, *Curs de drept civil* ... , *supra*, p. 377; C. Stătescu and C. Bîrsan, *supra*, pp. 288–289.

269. *See* Supreme Tribunal, Decision No. 528/1982, in V. Terzea, *supra*, p. 385.

kept.[270] Considering that sometimes it is hard to distinguish what caused the damage it is better for the victim to sue both the legal guardian of the substance or structure and the legal guardian of the use or conservation. If the damage is both the result of the structure or substance and of the way in which the thing was used, two can be held jointly and several liable.[271]

264. Generally, anyone who suffered a damage as a consequence of the way in which a thing "behaved" is entitled to ask for repairmen from the legal guardian. Still, there are some particularities. First, the liability cannot be engaged on this legal ground by the one who acquired, even if temporary, the legal guardianship of the thing, before the damage was caused, nor by the legal guardian against the material guardian.[272] Still, the material guardian may engage the liability of the legal guardian on this legal ground.[273] Second, if a contract was concluded between the legal guardian and the victim, and the thing was the object of the contract or it was used in order to fulfill the obligations of the legal guardian, only contractual liability may be engaged.[274] Finally, if the victim used the thing without the approval of the legal guardian, the latter's liability cannot be engaged for the damages caused by the thing.[275]

265. Regarding the conditions that must be met, they are similar with those provided for tortious liability for the damages caused by animals. There are three general conditions—the damageable deed, the damage and the causation—and one specific condition—for the thing to be under someone's legal guardianship.[276] The common conditions do not present any major particularities. The *illicit deed* is characterized by the fact that it does not consist in a human activity, but the breach of a legal or social norm and the violation of the victim's subjective rights or interest results from the way in which a thing behaved or its internal vices. The damage may be caused by any material thing, as long as it is suitable to be placed under a legal guardianship or it result from a thing found under the legal guardianship.[277] The *damages* present no particularities. It may be a pecuniary or nonpecuniary damage, present or future, corporal or material, etc. Regarding the causation, one particularity must be underlined. The *causal link* must exist between the "behavior" of the thing and the damage suffered by the victim, which implies a certain causal autonomy of the thing as it does not have to be a mere tool used by the tortfeasor

270. *See* L. Pop, *Tratat elementar ...* , *supra*, pp. 498–499; L. Pop, *Curs de drept civil ...* , *supra*, p. 379; C. Stătescu and C. Bîrsan, *supra*, p. 292.
271. *See* L. Pop, *Tratat elementar ...* , *supra*, p. 499.
272. If the damage was caused because of the way in which the thing was guarded, the legal guardian may sue the material guardian, but only on the bases of liability for own's thing, which means that the fault must be also proven.
273. *See* L. Pop, *Tratat elementar ...* , *supra*, pp. 499–500; L. Pop, *Curs de drept civil ...* , *supra*, p. 380–381; C. Stătescu and C. Bîrsan, *supra*, p. 296.
274. *See* L. Pop, *Tratat elementar ...* , *supra*, p. 500; C. Stătescu and C. Bîrsan, *supra*, p. 296.
275. *See* L. Pop, *Tratat elementar ...* , *supra*, p. 505.
276. *See* I.I. Neamţ and L.T. Dăuceanu, *supra*, pp. 166–167; L. Pop, *Tratat elementar ...* , *supra*, p. 508; L. Pop, *Curs de drept civil ...* , *supra*, p. 383.
277. *See* I.F. Mangu, *Răspunderea civilă delictuală ...* , *supra*, pp. 180–185.

to commit a crime. If the thing was just an instrument used by the tortfeasor to commit the crime, then the liability may be engaged in the form of liability for own's acts, and not liability for the damages caused by things.[278] Finally, the special condition implies that at the time of the illicit deed the thing was under the *legal guardianship* of the defendant, with all the above-mentioned distinctions. Therefore, this form of tortious liability cannot be used if no legal guardianship was exercised over the thing, such as the case of *res nullius*.

266. *Fault* is not a condition for engaging tortious liability for the damages caused by things, as Article 1.376 C.C. expressly provides. Thus, this is a strict liability hypothesis. According to the legal doctrine, the liability is based on the obligation of one to guarantee that, by expending his activity through the use of things, no damage shall be inflicted to others, which supports on the risk of activity theory.[279] Though one exception does exist, and it is provided by Article 1.354 C.C., which states that the victims is not entitled to damage repairment if damage was caused by a thing that was freely used, unless it is proven that the legal guardian acted with the intention to inflict the damage or by gross negligence.

267. The victim must prove all the above-mentioned conditions, but if it manages to do so, the legal guardian is bound to repair the damages and may defend only by proving that the damage is entirely victim's fault or the result of a third party deed which meets the characteristic of force majeure or a force majeure hypothesis.[280]

§3. Tortious Liability for the Damages Caused by the Ruin of Edifice

268. Though the decision is debatable, the new Civil Code kept as a distinct form of tortious liability the hypothesis in which the damage was caused "by the ruin of edifice."[281] In this regard, Article 1.378 C.C. provides that the owner of an edifice or construction of any kind is obliged to repair the damage caused by their running or by detachment of parts as a result of lack of maintenance or a construction vice.

---

278. *See* I.I. Neamţ and L.T. Dăuceanu, *supra*, pp. 166–167; L. Pop, *Tratat elementar ...* , *supra*, p. 508.

279. *See* I.I. Neamţ and L.T. Dăuceanu, *supra*, p. 167; L. Pop, *Tratat elementar ...* , *supra*, p. 507; L. Pop, *Curs de drept civil ...* , *supra*, pp. 382–383.

280. *See* I.I. Neamţ and L.T. Dăuceanu, *supra*, p. 167; L. Pop, *Tratat elementar ...* , *supra*, p. 508; L. Pop, *Curs de drept civil ...* , *supra*, p. 384; P. Vasilescu, *supra*, p. 685.

281. The decision is debatable because the norm is quite useless as long as the wider tortious liability for the damages caused by things may be used in the same conditions. For a critical perspective regarding this aspect, *see* L.R. Boilă, *Răspunderea civilă delictuală pentru ruina edificiului (Tortious Liability for the Ruin of Edifice)*, in Dreptul, No. 11/2010, pp. 131–132. Still, as long as the specific conditions for engaging this form of tortious liability are met, the victim may not choose to use another form of tortious liability, such as the one for the damages caused by things, because *specialia generalibus derogant*. For further details, *see* L. Pop, *Tratat elementar ...* , *supra*, pp. 512–513.

269. Considering the norm, only the legal owner of the construction or edifice may be held liable even if at the time of the deed they were used by another.[282] In case of joint ownership, all the owners shall be held jointly liable no matter if only one or some of them used the construction or the edifice.[283]

270. The notions of "edifice" or "construction of any kind" refers to any human made construction attained by assembling or durably incorporating materials into soil or another construction so that it becomes an immobile by its nature. The construction may be overground or underground and it may have any destination (house, factory, barn, dam, tunnel, a mine, etc.) as long as it is a human made and not a natural structure.[284] A temporary construction, such as a tent, a shack or a scaffold does not fall within the domain of the norm.[285]

271. In order to engage the owner's liability on this legal ground, the victim must prove several conditions. First, the damage must be caused by *the ruining or by detachment of parts* from a construction or edifice which is the result of lack of maintenance or a construction vice. The construction vice may refer to an architectural error, the poor quality of construction materials or a construction error. In any case, the ruining or detachment may not have a voluntary nature.[286] Thus, if for example the damage was caused during a demolition, the hypothesis is not met. Then, a *damage* must be caused to the victim, which it may be of any nature. Finally, a *causal link* must exist between the ruining or detachment of parts and the damage suffered by the victim. No fault must be proven by the victim, as in this case the tortious liability is objected, based on the idea of guarantee as an obligation associated to property right.[287] Nevertheless, the exception provided by Article 1.354 C.C. also applies in this case. As such, the victim is not entitled to damage repairment if the damage was caused by an edifice that was freely used, unless it is proven that the owner acted with the intention to inflict the damage or by gross negligence.

---

282. *See* L. Pop, *Tratat de drept civil. Obligaţiile. Volumul III ... , supra*, p. 455; P. Vasilescu, *supra*, pp. 689–690.
283. *See* I.I. Neamţ and L.T. Dăuceanu, *supra*, p. 168; L. Pop, *Tratat de drept civil. Obligaţiile. Volumul III ... , supra*, p. 456; L. Pop, *Tratat elementar ... , supra*, pp. 512–513; L. Pop, *Curs de drept civil ... , supra*, pp. 387–388; P. Vasilescu, *supra*, p. 690.
284. *See* I.I. Neamţ and L.T. Dăuceanu, *supra*, p. 168; L. Pop, *Tratat de drept civil. Obligaţiile. Volumul III ... , supra*, p. 454; L. Pop, *Tratat elementar ... , supra*, p. 513; L. Pop, *Curs de drept civil ... , supra*, p. 387; P. Vasilescu, *supra*, p. 690; C. Stătescu and C. Bîrsan, *supra*, p. 281; I.F. Mangu, *Răspunderea civilă delictuală ... , supra*, p. 228.
285. *See* P. Vasilescu, *supra*, p. 690. For the opposite opinion, *see* I.F. Mangu, *Răspunderea civilă delictuală ... , supra*, p. 282.
286. *See* I.I. Neamţ and L.T. Dăuceanu, *supra*, p. 168; L. Pop, *Tratat de drept civil. Obligaţiile. Volumul III ... , supra*, p. 458; L. Pop, *Tratat elementar ... , supra*, p. 514; L. Pop, *Curs de drept civil ... , supra*, p. 388; C. Stătescu and C. Bîrsan, *supra*, p. 281.
287. *See* I.I. Neamţ and L.T. Dăuceanu, *supra*, p. 168; L. Pop, *Tratat elementar ... , supra*, p. 515; L. Pop, *Curs de drept civil ... , supra*, p. 389 P. Vasilescu, *supra*, p. 691.

272. If these conditions are fulfilled, the victim may ask the owner to repair the damage and the latter can defend only by proving that the damage is entirely victim's fault or the result of a third party deed which meets the characteristic of force majeure or a force majeure hypothesis.[288] Nevertheless, after repairing the damage the owner may then regress either against the one who is liable for the construction vice, such as the construction company, the architect, the engineer or against the one who should have assured the integrity of the building.[289]

§4. Other Cases of Liability

273. Under the title of "other cases of liability," Article 1.379, first paragraph, C.C. provides that "The one who occupies a building even without any right shall be held liable for the damages caused by the falling or throwing of a thing from that building."

274. On the basis of this Article it can be held liable any occupier of a building, no matter if legal or not, or that the building is long term or just temporary occupied. It can be any kind of building, including offices, overground parking, industrial buildings, not just houses or apartment buildings.[290]

275. In order to engage the liability of the occupant, the victim must prove the fact that the damage was caused by the falling or throwing of a thing from the building, the existence of a damage and a causal link between the two. No fault must be proven.[291] The occupant can defend only by proving that the damage is entirely victim's fault or the result of a third-party deed which meets the characteristic of force majeure or a force majeure hypothesis.[292]

276. Though it represents a specific form of liability, if the conditions for engaging tortious liability for the damages caused by things are met, the victim may choose between the two legal grounds, as such possibility is expressly provided by Article 1.379(2) C.C.

---

288. *See* I.I. Neamţ and L.T. Dăuceanu, *supra*, p. 168; L. Pop, *Tratat elementar ...* , *supra*, p. 515; L. Pop, *Curs de drept civil ...* , *supra*, p. 389.
289. *See* I.I. Neamţ and L.T. Dăuceanu, *supra*, p. 168; L. Pop, *Tratat de drept civil. Obligaţiile. Volumul III ...* , *supra*, pp. 457–458; L. Pop, *Tratat elementar ...* , *supra*, p. 515; L. Pop, *Curs de drept civil ...* , *supra*, p. 389. For other hypotheses when the owner could redress, *see* I.F. Mangu, *Răspunderea civilă delictuală ...* , *supra*, p. 291.
290. *See* I.I. Neamţ and L.T. Dăuceanu, *supra*, p. 169; L. Pop, *Tratat de drept civil. Obligaţiile. Volumul III ...* , *supra*, p. 468.
291. *See* I.F. Mangu, *Răspunderea civilă delictuală ...* , *supra*, p. 265.
292. *Ibid.*

Part III. Forms of Strict Liability

Chapter 1. Road and Traffic Accidents

277. Vehicle collisions or other similar cases fall expressly under the regulation concerning the liability for things. According to Article 1376 of the Civil Code the provisions concerning strict liability for things are also applicable in the event of a vehicle collision or in other similar cases. However, in such cases, the burden of repairing all damage will fall only on the person whose culpable act meets the conditions of force majeure toward others. This legal approach raised the question if the damages from all vehicle accidents are from now on to be considered the result of the vehicle's activity or this liability arises only when the vehicle has a causal autonomy.

278. The general doctrine has remained consistent with the view that if the accident is the result of the conduct of the person, the ground for liability is subjective—for one's own act and as a consequence narrowing the field of application of Article 1376 of the Civil Code only to the situations in which the accident was caused by the properties, action or inaction of the vehicle. The matter however presents a reduced importance as the damage resulted from road and traffic accidents is covered either by the insurance company as a result of the conclusion of the compulsory civil liability policy or by the national protection fund established to this end.

279. The compulsory motor third-party liability insurance for damage caused to third parties by vehicle and tram accidents (hereinafter RCA) and its domain of application is regulated by Law No. 132/2017.[293]

280. Natural or legal persons who own vehicles subject to registration in Romania, as well as trams have the obligation to insure themselves for cases of civil liability as a result of damages caused by vehicle accidents within the territorial limits as the EU legislation prescribed. Exceptions from the obligation to conclude the RCA contract regard natural and legal persons who use vehicles exclusively for the purpose of training, racing, competition or rally, legally organized.

293. Law No. 132/2017 on the compulsory motor third-party liability insurance for damages caused to third parties by vehicle and tram accidents published in O.J. No. 431/12.06.2017.

281. The RCA insurance covers damage to third parties caused by vehicle and tram accidents such as: (a) personal injury or death, including nonpecuniary damage; (b) pecuniary damages; (c) costs regarding the restoration of the vehicle to the state before the insured event, proved with documents issued by specialized systems or by documents issued in accordance with the law; (d) damages representing the consequence of the nonuse of the damaged vehicle, including the temporary replacement of the vehicle, based on the option of the injured person; (e) court costs incurred by the injured party or related costs in case of alternative settlement of the dispute if the solution is favorable to the injured party; (f) expenses related to the transport of the damaged vehicle, belonging to the damaged third party, from the place of the accident to the location of the damage detection center, to the repair unit chosen by the injured party to repair the vehicle, the closest to the place of accident or the domicile of the injured person, as the case may be, if the respective vehicle can no longer travel by its own means and the insurer does not provide the transport.

282. Given the large criteria mentioned in regard to pecuniary and nonpecuniary damage, mentioning other damages that would normally be categorized as material damage seems superabundant. Listing all the possible damage by the legislator has however the advantage of proving the causal link of the damage to the accident and thus ensuring a predictable outcome concerning the extent of the damage.

283. Regarding the causes of the accident, RCA covers: the damage caused by the devices or installations with which the vehicle was equipped, including damage caused by accidental detachment of the trailer, semi-trailer or towed attachment of the vehicle; the damage caused by the fault of the driver of the insured vehicle; the damage caused by the act of the vehicle, when the damage has its cause in the properties, action or inaction of the vehicle, through another thing caused by the movement of the vehicle, by leaking, scattering or accidental fall of substances, materials or objects transported; the damage caused to third parties, as a consequence of opening the doors of the vehicle, while driving or when the vehicle is stopped or parked, by its passengers, without ensuring that the safety of the movement of other road users is not endangered; the damages caused to third parties, as a consequence of driving under the influence of alcohol or narcotics. When the accident was caused by the fault of the driver of the insured vehicle, the insurance covers the damage even if in cases where at the date of the accident the driver of the vehicle: drove the vehicle without the express or presumed consent of the insured; is not the holder of a license attesting the right to drive the respective vehicle or he did not comply with the legal obligations regarding the condition and safety of the respective vehicle.

284. The compensations are granted in an amount equal to the extent of the damage up to the maximum liability limit of the RCA insurer which is equal to the highest value between the liability limit provided in the applicable legislation and the one provided in the RCA contract.

285. The insurance covers the damage irrespective of the place where the vehicle accident occurred—on public roads, on roads that are not open to public traffic, on premises and in any other place, both while driving and while the insured vehicle is parked. The insurance also covers the body damage caused to the members of the family of the insured, of the driver or of any other person whose civil liability is involved in a motor vehicle accident and is covered by the compulsory RCA.

286. If the injured party has faultily contributed to the accident or to an increase in the damage, the person called upon to be liable shall be held liable only for the part of the damage attributable to him. In such situations, the extent of each person's liability will be that established by any means of proof. In the event that the extent of the liability of each person cannot be established, it shall be established in equal shares, in relation to the number of parties involved in the accident, each party having the right to compensation insofar as he has not been liable for the accident.

287. The RCA insurer does not grant compensation for: (a) the cases in which the owner, user or driver of the guilty vehicle is not liable, if the accident occurred: (i) in a case of force majeure; (ii) through the sole fault of the injured party; (iii) through the exclusive fault of a third party, except for the situations when the damage caused to third parties as a result of the vehicle's doors being opened while driving or when the vehicle is stopped or parked by its passengers, without ensuring that the safety of other road users is not endangered; (b) the damages caused to the goods belonging to the driver of the vehicle responsible for the accident, as well as those caused as a result of the bodily injury or his death, regardless of who claims these compensations; (c) in the following situations: (i) the damage was caused to property belonging to natural or legal persons, if it was caused by a RCA insured vehicle, owned or used by the same natural or legal person and which is driven by an agent of the same legal person or a another person for whom the natural or legal person is responsible; (ii) the damaged property and the insured vehicle are part of the joint property of the spouses; (iii) the damaged property is used by the owner of the insured vehicle, which caused the damage; (d) damages caused in situations where the validity of the RCA insurance is not proven at the date of the accident or the RCA insurer is not liable; (e) the part of the damage that exceeds the limits of liability established by the RCA contract, produced in one and the same accident, regardless of the number of injured persons and the number of persons responsible for the damage; (f) fines of any kind and criminal expenses incurred by the owner, user or driver of the insured vehicle, liable for the damage; (g) the expenses incurred in the criminal proceedings by the owner, user or driver of the insured vehicle, responsible for the occurrence of the damage, even if during the criminal proceedings the civil side was also resolved; (h) the amounts that the driver of the vehicle responsible for causing the damage is obliged to pay to the owner or user who entrusted the insured vehicle, for the damage or destruction of this vehicle; (i) damages caused to the transported goods, if there was a contractual relationship between the owner or user of the vehicle that caused the accident or the responsible driver and the injured persons at the date of the accident; (j) damages caused to the persons or goods in the vehicle with which the accident occurred, if the RCA insurer can prove that the injured persons knew that the respective vehicle was stolen; (k) damages caused by devices or installations mounted on vehicles, when they are used as machinery or work installations, these constituting risks of the professional activity; (l) damages caused by accidents that occurred during loading and unloading operations, which constitute risks of professional activity; (m) damages caused as a result of the transport of dangerous products: radioactive, ionizing, flammable, explosive, corrosive, combustible, which determined or aggravated the damage; (n) damage caused by the use of a vehicle during a terrorist attack or war, if the event is directly related to that attack or war.

288. For the event in which the owner of the vehicle does not conclude the mandatory insurance policy, the legislator stepped in and constituted a guarantee fund, the Fund of Protection of Street Victims (hereinafter the Fund). This Fund has been constituted in 2006 as an association with legal personality whose members are all insurance companies who have the RCA in their portfolio.

289. The Fund compensates the persons damaged by vehicle accidents, if the vehicle, respectively the tram, which caused the accident remained unidentified or was not insured for civil liability for damages caused by vehicle accidents, although the law provided the obligation to insure. The obligation to compensate the victim of the Fund arises for damages caused by vehicle accidents within the same territorial limits as set for the RCA policy.

290. If the perpetrator of the accident remains unidentified, the Fund will compensate the victim only for bodily injuries or deaths. However, if, as a result of the accident with an unidentified perpetrator, the bodily integrity or health of a person has caused an injury requiring medical care for healing for more than sixty days, the Fund shall also award compensation for material damage caused in that accident. In these cases, a deductible of EUR 500 or the equivalent in lei at the exchange rate of the foreign exchange market, communicated by the National Bank of Romania at the date of the accident, will remain in charge of the injured person, for material damages.

291. If the perpetrator who caused the accident is identified, the Fund shall compensate the injured persons both for material damages and for bodily injuries or deaths. The Fund intervenes as a guarantor for the observance of the obligation of compensation without, however, being able to oppose to the injured persons the benefit of discussion in relation to the persons guilty of the accident.

292. If an entity has compensated the damaged persons or offered them services in connection with the damages suffered, based on concluded contracts or based on the law, they have no right to request from the Fund the recovery of the incurred expenses.

293. The right to benefit of compensation from the Fund belongs to Romanian natural and legal persons as well as residents of Romania or the states of the European Economic Area.

294. For the cases of damage produced on the territory of any state in the European Economic Area of uninsured vehicles that have the usual parking place in Romania only Romanian natural and legal persons, as well as Romanian residents, have the right to benefit from compensation from the Fund. From the date of Romania's accession to the European Union, namely January 1, 2007, for these cases of damage, the residents of the European Economic Area may also benefit from compensations from the Fund, if they have suffered damages during their movement on the territory of another state than the one where they have their residence.

295. The natural and legal persons, as well as the residents from other states than those of the states of the European Economic Area may benefit from compensation from the Fund only under conditions of reciprocity.

296. However, people who voluntarily boarded the vehicle responsible for the accident, if it is proved that they knew that the vehicle in question was uninsured, or those who, at the date of the accident, have the possibility to recover damages suffered on the basis of optional insurance are not entitled to compensation from the Fund.

297. The amount of the damage suffered is established in strict accordance with the provisions of the norms regarding the application of the law in the field of compulsory civil liability insurance for damages caused by vehicle accidents, in force in Romania at the date of the accident.

298. After the Fund pays the compensation, he is subrogated to the rights of the injured persons. The person or persons responsible for repairing the damage have the obligation to reimburse to the Fund the compensation paid to the damaged person, the expenses related to the instrumentation and liquidation of the compensation claims, as well as the legal interest related to the amounts spent by the Fund.

Chapter 2. Product Liability

299. Being a member of the European Union, Romania was bound to transpose Directive 85/374 CEE of 25 July 1985 regarding the liability for defective products which resulted in the adoption of Law No. 240/2004 regarding the liability of producers for damage caused by defective products.[294]

300. According to Article 6 of the law, there are three conditions that need to be proved by the victim in order for the producer to be liable: the damage, the defect and the causation between the defect and the damage, thus placing the producer's liability for defective products among the forms of strict civil liability.

301. The product can be any mobile good, even if it is incorporated in a different mobile or immobile good, including electrical energy. The product has defects if it does not offer the security to which the person is entitled to attend, taking into account all circumstances, including the presentation of the product, all foreseeable uses of the product or the date of release of the product.

302. The damage is defined as: the prejudice caused by the death or injury to the body or health of a person or the damage to or destruction of any property other than the defective product, provided that the property is normally intended for private use or consumption and has been used by the person harmed or personal use or consumption and its value is greater than 200 lei[295] for a product purchased in Romania, namely EUR 500 for a product purchased in the EU.

303. Any contractual clauses limiting or exonerating the producer's liability will be null and void. The producer can exonerate himself only if he proves one of the cases of exemption set by the law such as: (a) he was not the one who put the product into circulation; (b) according to circumstances, the defect that caused the damage did not exist at the moment the product was put into circulation or it appeared after he put the product in circulation for causes that are independent of his fault; (c) the product was not fabricated to be commercialized or for any form of distribution in economic purpose and it was not fabricated or distributed in the course of his business; (d) the defect is due to compliance with mandatory requirements issued by competent authorities; (e) the state of scientific and technical knowledge at the time of putting the product into circulation did not allow him to identify the defect; (f) the defect is due to the noncompliance by the consumer with the instructions for use provided in the technical documents accompanying the product, circumstance proved on the basis of specialized technic expertise.

304. Moreover, the producer's liability can be limited or precluded in court, if the damage is caused both by the defect of the product and the fault of the victim or of a third person for whom he is held liable. However, the producer's liability is

294. Published in O.J. No. 313/22.04.2008.
295. Approximately EUR 40.

not limited in the case in which the damage is caused both by the defect of the product and the action or inaction of a third party. The producer will have a right of recourse against the third party according to the general conditions of the law.

305. The right of action for damages arising from the special legislation has a double time limit. On one hand, it lapses within three years from the date on which the claimant had or should have been aware of the existence of the damage, the defect and the identity of the manufacturer. On the other hand, the action for damages may not be brought after ten years from the date on which the manufacturer put the product into circulation.

306. According to the principles set in the Directive, the application of this form of liability is not mandatory but complementary to other forms of liability that may concur. The law expressly states that the application of its provisions does not exclude the possibility of the victim to claim compensation under contractual or noncontractual liability or another special liability regime, existing at the date of entry into force of this law.

307. The regime of the liability is the same no matter the existence of a contractual relation between the victim and the producer. This led most of the authors of the doctrine to affirm that this is a special legal type of civil responsibility different to tort or contractual liability.

Chapter 3. Liability for Service

308. The liability for service is governed by general contractual liability rules and does not fall under the category of strict liability cases.

309. The contract for service gives rise to the following main obligations: for the entrepreneur to execute the work or provide the service, to procure materials and to inform the beneficiary in exchange of the beneficiary's obligation to pay the price. If the parties fail to comply to these obligations, their contractual liability will incur.

310. Depending on the nature of the service, the obligation to execute the work or provide the service is an obligation of means or an obligation of result. If it is an obligation of result, the nonaccomplishment of the result gives rise to a presumption of noncompliance of the obligation that leads to a presumption of fault. If there is an obligation of means in order to prove the nonaccomplishment of the obligation, the beneficiary will have to prove that the entrepreneur breached the standard of care normally applied to the given situation. Once proven the nonaccomplishment of the obligation, like in the case of the obligation of result, there is a presumption of fault that rises.

311. If by its nature the execution of the work or the service provision implies certain materials or means, the entrepreneur has the obligation to procure them unless the parties stipulated otherwise.

312. The entrepreneur is obliged to inform the beneficiary without delay if the normal execution of the work, its durability or its proper use would be endangered due to the procured materials or other means that, according to the contract, the beneficiary made available, inadequate instructions given by the beneficiary or the existence or emergence of circumstances for which the contractor is not liable.

313. Moreover, the entrepreneur owes a guarantee to the beneficiary against hidden defects and for the agreed qualities that apply according to the rules established in the contract of sale.

314. The beneficiary's obligation to pay the price is a common obligation of result whose failure to perform presents no specificities in the case of this contract.

Chapter 4. Environmental Liability

315. The environmental protection is regulated by Government Emergency Ordinance (O.U.G.) No. 195/2005[296] that was adopted in order to fulfill the commitments assumed by Romania in the process of European integration in view of establishing a framework laying down the principles governing the whole activity of environmental protection and outlining the directions for regulating economic activities in order to achieve the objectives of a sustainable development.

316. Furthermore, in order to complete the Romanian legal framework with a normative act that ensured a unitary and distinct regulation of the environmental damage, the government adopted the O.U.G. No. 68/2007 concerning the environmental liability in regard to the prevention and repair of environmental damage.[297]

317. The environmental damage, including that caused by airborne elements, means: (a) damage to protected natural species and habitats—any damage that has significant negative effects on the achievement or maintenance of a favorable conservation status of such habitats or species;[298] (b) water damage—any damage that has serious negative effects on the ecological, chemical or quantitative status or on the ecological potential of the waters in question[299] or on the ecological status of the marine waters concerned;[300] (c) damage to the soil—any contamination of the soil, which represents a significant risk to human health, which is adversely affected as a result of the direct or indirect introduction of substances, preparations, organisms or microorganisms into the soil or subsoil.

318. Any person who is affected or likely to be affected by an environmental damage or who considers himself harmed in a right or in a legitimate interest has the right to send to the county police station of the National Environmental Guard any observations regarding the occurrence of an environmental damage or an imminent threat of such damage or to request the county agency for environmental protection, in writing or by electronic means of communication, to take the measures provided by the law. This possibility is also applicable to any nongovernmental organization that promotes environmental protection and meets the conditions required by the applicable law, considering that it is harmed in a subjective right or in a legitimate interest.

---

296. Published in the O.J. No. 1196/2005.
297. Published in the O.J. No. 446/2007.
298. The significance of these effects shall be assessed in relation to the initial state, taking into account the criteria set out in the annex 1 of the Ordinance No. 68/2007. Damage to protected species and natural habitats does not include the negative effects previously identified, resulting from the actions of an operator that has been expressly authorized by the competent authorities according to the O.U.G. No. 57/2007 on the regime of protected natural areas, conservation of natural habitats, wild flora and fauna, approved with amendments and completions by Law No. 49/2011.
299. As defined by Law of waters No. 107/1996.
300. As defined by O.U.G. No. 71/2010 on establishing the strategy for the marine environment, approved with amendments by Law No. 6/2011, insofar as the special aspects regarding the ecological status of the marine environment are not already the object of Law No. 107/1996.

319. Environmental protection is an obligation of all natural and legal persons. For this purpose, everybody bears the cost of repairing the damage and removing the consequences of the damage, restoring the conditions prior to the damage, in accordance with the "polluter pays" principle. Thus the environmental liability has as purpose restoration as well as prevention of damage when there is a sufficient probability of causing damage to the environment in the near future. To this end, the ordinances establish both preventive and repair measures.

320. The quality of a polluter can be held by an operator. According to the law, an operator is any natural or legal person governed by public or private law who carries out or controls a professional activity or, where national law so provides, who has been given decisive economic power over the technical operation of such an activity, including the holder of a regulatory act for such an activity or the person who registers or notifies such an activity. Within the meaning of the law, a professional activity signifies any activity carried on in the course of an economic activity, business or enterprise, whether private or public, for-profit or not-for-profit.

321. The liability for environmental damage is objective, independent of fault. Exceptionally, liability may also be subjective for damage caused to protected species and natural habitats, in accordance with specific regulations. However, this type of liability concerns only the environmental damage or imminent threat of such damage, caused by diffuse pollution, only when a causal link can be established between the damage and the activities of the individual operators.

322. In the case of the plurality of authors, the liability is joint and several. The effects of passive solidarity, including the allocation of costs between co-debtors shall be made in accordance with the legal provisions in force, taking into account the provisions regarding the division of responsibility between the producer and the user of a product. When the operator who has caused an imminent damage to the environment or an imminent threat of such damage is part of a consortium or multinational company, he shall be jointly and severally liable with that consortium or company.

323. When a damage to the environment occurs, the operator is obliged to act immediately to control, isolate, dispose of or otherwise manage the respective pollutants and/or any other contaminants, in order to limit or prevent the spread of environmental damage and adverse effects on human health or aggravation of deterioration of services and to take the necessary remedial measures. These reparative measures must be proportionate to the damage caused and lead to the removal of the effects of the damage, by taking into account the precautionary principle in decision-making.

324. In the event of an imminent threat of damage to the environment, the operator is obliged to take the necessary preventive measures immediately. These preventive measures must be proportionate to the imminent threat and lead to the avoidance of injury, taking into account the precautionary principle in decision-making. The operator bears the costs of preventive and remedial actions, including if these costs were incurred by the county agency for environmental protection.

325. If the reparative or preventive measures have been taken by the county agency for environmental protection, the cost will be recovered from the operator who caused the damage or the imminent threat of damage. In order to guarantee the recovery of the costs incurred, the law recognizes a right of the county agency for environmental protection to establish a mortgage on the real estate of the operator and an insurance attachment, according to the legal norms in force.

326. The liability of the operator ceases and thus he cannot be obliged to bear the cost of any preventive or reparative action taken when he can prove that the damage caused to the environment or the imminent threat of such damage was caused by a third party and occurred even if appropriate safety measures were taken or occurred as a result of compliance with a mandatory provision or instruction issued by a public authority, other than an order or instruction issued as a result of an issue or incident caused by the activities of the operator. In these cases the State, through its legal representatives, shall take appropriate measures to enable the operator to recover the costs incurred.

327. Another exemption is provided for the remedial actions taken if the operator can prove that he did not act intentionally or through fault and that the damage to the environment was caused by an issue or event specially authorized and in full accordance with the conditions provided by the regulatory act issued in accordance with the rules implementing the measures provided by the law,[301] in force on the date of issue or event or by an emission, an activity or any way of using a product during an activity, for which the operator demonstrates that it was not possible, according to the state of the art and scientific knowledge existing at the date when the emission was released or when the activity took place, to cause damage to the environment.

328. This special liability ground does not give natural or legal persons under the private law the right to compensation as a consequence of environmental damage or the imminent threat of such damage. For the damage suffered by natural or legal persons, the common law rules apply.

301. Annex No. 3 of the Ordinance No. 68/2007.

Chapter 5. Others

329. The civil liability for nuclear damage that results from the activities of the use of nuclear energy for peaceful purposes is also one of the cases in which the Romanian legislator opted for a strict liability when he adopted Law No. 703/2001.[302]

330. The liability lies mainly with the operator, namely the holder of the authorization issued according to the provisions of Law No. 111/1996 on the safe conduct of nuclear activities.[303]

331. The operator of a nuclear installation is liable objectively and exclusively for any nuclear damage: (1) if it has been shown to be caused by a nuclear accident that occurred in the nuclear installation; (2) that involved nuclear material originating from this nuclear installation (before this liability has been assumed, on the basis of a written contract, by another operator or in the absence of express provisions of such a contract, before another operator has taken over this material or if the nuclear material was sent to a person in the territory of another State before it was unloaded from the means of transport through which it arrived in the territory of that State) or (3) involving nuclear material sent to this nuclear installation after the liability for nuclear damage caused by that nuclear material has been transferred to the operator by the operator of another nuclear installation, under a written contract; in the absence of express provisions of a written contract, after the operator has taken over this nuclear material or if such nuclear material has been sent, with the written consent of that operator, by a person located in the territory of another State, only after the material has been loaded on the means of transport with which it must leave the territory of that State.

332. If the nuclear damage is caused by a nuclear accident that occurred in a nuclear installation and involves nuclear materials stored for transport, the operator will not be held liable if another operator or another person is solely responsible under the cases (2) and (3) stated above.

333. In the event of a nuclear accident occurring during the transport of nuclear material, the civil liability for nuclear damage rests entirely with the carrier, who shall be considered an operator, at his request and with the consent of the operator of the installation.

334. Where a nuclear damage involves the liability of several operators, they shall be liable for the damage jointly and severally, in so far as it is impossible to determine with certainty which part of the damage is attributable to each.

---

302. Law No. 703/2001 concerning civil liability for nuclear damage published in the O.J. No. 818/19.12.2001.
303. Published in the O.J. No. 552/2006.

335. If the operator of a nuclear installation is unable to obtain national and/or international liability insurance cover for nuclear damage or another appropriate financial guarantee, the Romanian state will be liable for the nuclear damage. The State's liability will also be incurred if the nuclear damage is the direct result of an act of terrorism in the nuclear field.

336. Fault of the victim is also a cause of exemption for the operator. Thus, he can be exempted, in whole or in part, if he can prove that the nuclear damage resulted, in whole or in part, from gross negligence on the part of the person who suffered it or that the person acted or failed to act, with the intention of causing damage.

337. The operator is also exonerated from liability if he proves that the nuclear damage is the direct result of acts of armed conflict, civil war, insurrection or hostility. These constitute force majeure cases expressly regulated by the law.

338. The operator shall not be liable for nuclear damage to the nuclear installation itself, to any other nuclear installation, including under construction, located on the site of the actual installation, nor to the goods located on the site of this nuclear installation, which are or must be used in relationship with his.

339. When nuclear damage and nonnuclear damage are caused by a nuclear accident or, in conjunction, by a nuclear accident and one or more different events, the nonnuclear damage, in so far as it cannot be separated with certainty from nuclear, is considered as nuclear damage caused by a nuclear accident.

340. The notion of nuclear damage has been defined by the law and it implies: (1) any death or injury; (2) any loss or damage to property; (3) any economic loss resulting from the damage to a person or property, not included before, if it is suffered by a person entitled to claim compensation in respect of such loss; (4) the cost of measures to restore the environment damaged by a nuclear accident, whether such damage is significant, whether such measures are being taken or are to be taken and whether they are not included in the loss or damage to property; (5) any loss of income arising from an economic interest in any use of the environment due to significant damage to the environment and not included in the loss or damage to property; (6) the cost of preventive measures and any loss or damage caused by such measures; (7) any other economic damage other than that caused by the degradation of the environment, if permitted by the civil liability law of the competent court.

341. The loss or damage referred to the above shall be considered nuclear damage in so far as the loss or damage arises as a result of ionizing radiation emitted by any source of radiation in a nuclear installation or emitted by nuclear fuel, radioactive products or radioactive waste from a nuclear installation or nuclear material from, or sent to a nuclear installation or they are the result of the radioactive properties of such a material or of a combination of radioactive properties with toxic, explosive or other hazardous properties of such material. These conditions do not apply to the cost of preventive measures and any loss or damage caused by such measures.

342. The liability of the operator is limited for each nuclear accident to at least the RON equivalent of 300 million SDR. With the approval of the competent national authority, the liability of the operator may be limited for each nuclear accident to less than the RON equivalent of 300 million SDR, but not less than the RON equivalent of 150 million SDR, provided that the difference is at least the equivalent in lieu of 300 million SDR to be allocated by the state from public funds in order to cover nuclear damage under the conditions of this law.

343. After the payment of the compensation, the operator has the right to take recourse only if such a right has been expressly provided for in a written contract or if the nuclear accident results from an action or omission committed with the intention to cause a nuclear damage against the natural person who acted or failed to act with this intention. This right also extends to the state insofar as it has allocated public funds in order to cover the damage in accordance to the provisions of Law No. 703/2001.

344. The right to compensation against the operator shall lapse if no action is brought within thirty years from the date of the nuclear accident, if the action is related to death or injury or within ten years from the date of the nuclear accident, and if the action is related to the other nuclear damages. Moreover, the right to compensation against the operator will be extinguished if an action is not brought within a period of three years from the date on which the victim of the nuclear damage knew or should have known the damage and the identity of the operator responsible for it, without the deadlines mentioned before to be overcome.

345. In order to guarantee the payment of the damage, the law establishes a legal obligation for the operator and the carrier of nuclear material to conclude an insurance contract or a financial guarantee to cover its civil liability for nuclear damage and to prove to the competent national authority its existence.

Part IV. Defenses and Exception Clauses

346. As a general fact, the Civil Code commonly regulates defenses and exception clauses fort both contractual liability and tortious liability, though some particularities may exist depending on the type of liability. Furthermore, except limitation of action, which is not related to tortious liability itself but to the right of action, most of the other defenses are connected to one of the conditions of tortious liability. For example self-defense, necessity, the order of the legitimate authority, the exercise of a right and the victim's consent are seen as situations which wear off the illicit nature of the deed; force majeure, fortuitous case, victim or third's party deed and contributory fault affect the causation or fault and the lack of discernment averts the fault as previously seen.

Chapter 1. Limitation of Action (Suspension and Interruption)

§1. General Aspects

347. As most of the civil claims, the ones that relate to tortious liability are also the subject of limitation of action. The principle is provided by Article 2.501, first paragraph, C.C. which provides that "The rights of action having a pecuniary object are subject to limitation of action as long as the law does not otherwise provide." The second paragraph of the same Article provides that when the law explicitly provides so, other rights of action, no matter of their object, are subject of limitation of action. Also, Article 2.500 C.C. states that the right of action extinguishes if it was not exercised during the time provide by law and the right of action refers to the right to compel someone, using the public coercive force, to fulfill a certain obligation, to respect a given judicial situation or to abide any other civil sanction. If the time provided by law passed and the victim did not sue the one who could have been held liable, the main effect is that the last can no longer be coerced to repair the damage.[304] Nevertheless, the effect does not operate ex law, as it must be invoked by the defendant within the written answer to the plaintiff's complaint.[305] Plus, the defendant may explicitly or implicitly renounce the benefit of limitation of action[306] and if so, a new term will run from the time of renunciation. Though the norms that regulate limitation of action are mainly dispositive, the parties cannot agree to declare an action that the law provides it to fall within the limitation of action imprescriptible or vice versa. Still, they can prolong or shorten the terms or modify the run of prescription by fixing a new starting point or modifying the cases of suspension and interruption.[307]

348. The general term of prescription provided by law is three years,[308] but multiple exceptions exist. For example, the law provides a ten-year term within which the victim may act in order to obtain redress for the damages caused by torture, acts of barbarism, violence, sexual assault against a minor or a person incapable of defending or expressing the will or for repairing the environmental damage.[309] In the case of tortious liability, Article 1.394 C.C. also provides that whenever the cause of action derives from an illicit deed for which the criminal law provides a longer term of prescription then the civil law, the term provided by the criminal law shall also apply to tortious liability. Thus, if the tort is also a crime and the criminal

304. *See* Art. 2.506(2) C.C. However, the victim may ask the court to be reinstated if the action was not exerted in due time because of solid grounds. Such request must be addressed, together with the action, within thirty days after the solid grounds that detained the victim to act ended. *See* Art. 2.522 C.C.
305. *See* Arts. 2.506, first paragraph, C.C., 2.512 C.C. and 2.513 C.C.
306. *See* Arts. 2.507–2.511 C.C.
307. *See* Art. 2.515 C.C. In any case, the parties cannot agree on terms shorter than one year or longer than ten, except when the term provided by law is ten years or longer, when it can be prolonged to a maximum of twenty years.
308. *See* Art. 2.517 C.C.
309. *See* Art. 2.520 C.C.

law provides a longer term of prescription than the civil law, the term most favorable to the victim shall apply. The right of action for repairing the damage caused by an illicit deed starts to run the moment the victim knew or should have known that a damage was inflicted and the one who is responsible for it.[310] Thus, for the term to start running, the victim must know, or be able to know, two different elements: the existence of a damage and the one who is responsible for that damage. The law provides with two ways for determining *dies a quo*: a subjective one—the moment the victim knew about the damage and who is the tortfeasor or other person that may be held liable, and an objective one—the moment in which though the victim did not knew one or both of this elements, he could have, with sufficient diligence. The existence of an objective moment for determining *dies a quo* is meant to sanction the victim's lack of action in those circumstances in which the victim hold enough data and information to reasonably conclude that a damage existed and who can be held liable, but still remained passive. Both can be proven by any means, including witness testimony. It must be underlined that the victim does not have to be sure about the fact that the conditions for engaging tortious liability of the defendant are met, as this will be determined by the court. For example, if the illicit deed is also a crime, the victim does not have to wait for a criminal decision to be passed. The moment the identity of the tortfeasor is known, the term starts to run. The jurisprudence concluded that any other interpretation would void the objective moment.[311] Furthermore, the objective moment also determines the *dies a quo* when the victim has had enough reasonable clues about the tortfeasor, even though it was not for certain that the one to whom the clues lead to is the wrongdoer.

§2. Suspension Hypothesis

349. The law provides for a series of hypotheses that lead to the suspension and interruption of the prescription term, which are applicable no matter the cause of action. As such, Articles 2.532 and 2.533 provide that the prescription does not run or if it started is suspended: if the parties are husbands and not separated, during the marriage; between parents, tutors and curators and those that lack civil capacity or have a limited civil capacity or among curators and the ones represented, as long as the protection lasts and the accounts were not given and approved; between the one who, under the law, a court decision or a contract administers the assets of another and the one who's assets are administered, as long as the administer lasts and the accounts were not given and approved; when the victim has no civil capacity or has a limited civil capacity, as long as no representative or protector was appointed and the law does not otherwise provides; as long as the debtor deliberately hides from the creditor the existence of debt and its exigibility; for the entire length of negotiation of the parties in order to reach a mutual agreement, but only if the negotiations took place in the last six months of the term; when the one entitled to act must or can, according to the law or contract, use a preliminary procedure, as long as the

310. *See* Art. 2.528, first paragraph, C.C.

311. *See* Judecatoria Baia Mare, civil sentence 1002/2016, available at rolii.ro, last checked on Apr. 19, 2021.

result of that procedure was unknown or needed to be known, but not more than three months since the procedure was initiated, if the law or contract does not provide otherwise; as long as the right holder or the one who breached it are members of the Armed Forces of Romania and as they are in state of emergency or war, even if the victim or the tortfeasor are civilians who became members of the Armed Forces for job considerations related to the necessities of war; against the victim who is impeded to interrupt the prescription term by a force majeure, as long as this impediment lasts. When the force majeure is temporary, it does not constitute a reason for suspending the term, unless it occurs in the last six months prior to *dies ad quem*. Also, the prescription does not run against the creditors of a deceased as long as the succession was not accepted nor was a curator named to represent the successors, or against the successors as long as they did not accept the succession and nor was a curator appointed to represent them, or between the moment the successor accepted the succession and the succession was liquidated. Finally, Article 1.395 C.C. provides a special hypothesis of suspension, stating that the prescription of the right of action for repairing the damage that result from a body injury, a health injury or death is suspended until the pension or other social benefits are established.

350. In all these hypotheses the prescription term does not start to run or if it already started, it is suspended. Once the facts that lead to suspension end, the prescription term starts running again and the period before the suspension will also be considered.[312] However, the prescription term shall not fulfill sooner than six months from the moment the suspension ended, except the situations in which the prescription term is shorter than six months, in which case it shall fulfill in a month.[313] Following the dispositive rationally of the norms that regulate limitation of action, Article 2.535 C.C. provides that the incidence of a suspension hypothesis may be invoked only by the party who was impeded to interrupt the term, if the law does not otherwise provide.

§3. Interruption Hypothesis

351. Article 2.537 C.C. provides that the prescription term interrupts: by an act of voluntary compliance with the obligation or by explicitly or implicitly recognizing the right by the one to whom the prescription benefits;[314] by filling a litigation or arbitration claim, by registering to the mass or creditors in an insolvency procedure, by intervening in a force execution procedure or by invoking the right as an

312. *See* Art. 2.534, first paragraph, C.C.
313. *See* Art. 2.534(2) C.C.
314. Article 2.538 C.C. provides that the recognition can be unilateral or mutual, expressly or tacitly. The tacit recognition must, nevertheless, be undoubtable. The following may be considered as acts of tacit recognition: a partial payment, the payment of interests or penalties, the request of a payment term, etc.

exception;[315] by filling the civil claim in a criminal case or by any act through which the debtor is asked to fulfill the obligation.[316]

352. If prescription is interrupted, the previous prescription time that has run is not counted and prescription commences to run anew from the last day of interruption.[317] If the prescription was interrupted by a litigation or arbitration claim, a new prescription will start only after s final decision was passed.[318] If the interruption rests on the intervention on an insolvency proceeding or force execution proceedings, a new prescription shall run the moment there is a new possibility to obtain the redress.[319]

315. Article 2.539 C.C. provides that the prescription term is interrupted even if the claim was addressed to a court or a criminal prosecution body which was not competent or if the claim was declared void for formal reasons. However, the term shall not be interrupted if the one who filled the litigation or arbitration claim, of intervention in insolvency procedure or execution procedure renounced or if the claim was definitely rejected, voided on other grounds that form or declared obsolete. Still, if the plaintiff, in a six-month term after his claim was rejected or voided fills a new claim, the prescription term is considered interrupted by the first claim, as long as the last claimed is granted.

316. In this latter hypothesis the interruption works only if the request is followed by a call for trial within six months, as Art. 2.540 provides.

317. *See* Art. 2.541, first and second paragraphs, C.C.

318. *See* Art. 2.541(4) C.C.

319. *See* Art. 2.541(5) C.C.

Chapter 2. Grounds of Justification

§1. Consent

353. Usually, victim's consent, as an element which wares off the illicit nature of the deed, or which legitimates it, is analyzed by Romanian legal doctrine together with the exemption clauses,[320] though the last mainly refer to contractual liability. Such an approach is the result of the way in which the law refers to this ground of justification, as Article 1.355 C.C. commonly regulates both the consent and the exemption clauses. The mentioned norm provides that the liability for the material damage caused by a deed committed with intention and gross negligence cannot be averted through conventions and unilateral acts but the ones that exclude liability for the damages caused to victim's assets are valid if the deed was committed with simple imprudence or negligence. Furthermore, the liability for the damages caused to victim's physical or mental integrity may be averted or diminished only when the law so provides. Still, the declaration of the victim that he accepts the risk of certain damage does not signify by itself a renunciation to the right to obtain indemnification. Finally, it can be observed that the norm does not distinguish between tortious liability and contractual liability and it further refers to unilateral acts, which are specific to consent and tortious liability.

354. Though the consent and the exemption clauses are commonly regulated and usually commonly analyzed by Romanian legal doctrine, for the purpose of this monograph we will distinctly analyze the two, addressing in this part only the aspects that are specific to consent.

355. As Article 1.355 C.C. provides, the consent may avert tortious liability only in very specific situations. First, the consent does not produce any effect if the material damage was caused by an intentional or grossly negligence tort. In the meaning of Article 1.355 C.C. intention is similar with bath faith and must be understood as the willingness of the tortfeasor to cause a damage to the victim, and not the willing to have a certain conduct. Thus, what it matters is the way in which the tortfeasor pertained the damage and not the action or inaction that lead to that damage. For this reason, when the victim consented fully aware to the deed, and the consent referred to a right to which the victim could dispose of, as most of pecuniary rights are, the doer cannot be held liable event if it inflicted a material damage as long as such a result was not wished and it cannot have been extremely easy imagined, though the action or inaction that leads to the damage was committed with intention or gross negligence.[321]

---

320. *See* I.I. Neamţ and L.T. Dăuceanu, *supra*, pp. 133–134; L. Pop, *Tratat de drept civil. Obligaţiile. Volumul III ...*, *supra*, p. 249; L. Pop, *Tratat elementar ...*, *supra*, pp. 432–434; L. Pop, *Curs de drept civil ...*, *supra*, pp. 343–344; F.I. Mangu, *Răspunderea civilă. Constantele ...*, *supra*, p. 140.

321. *See* I.I. Neamţ and L.T. Dăuceanu, *supra*, p. 133.

356. Second, the consent can fully avert the liability when a damage was caused to the victim's assets by a tortious deed committed with simple imprudence and negligence. On the other hand, no matter the type of fault with which the illicit deed was committed, damages caused to victim's physical, mental or health integrity may be averted or diminished only in the conditions provided by special law, as it is the case, for example, in the field of medical intervention or contact sports.[322] This is because it is generally accepted that such rights are not disposable, and thus the victim cannot decide to abandon or restrain them.

357. Third, the final paragraph of Article 1.355 C.C. provides that an acceptance of the risk does not imply by itself a renunciation to indemnification if the risk materializes. Therefore, as long as the victim did not explicitly mention or it results so from the circumstance, the mere fact that a risk was assumed, does not avert the right to as for damage reparation. The hypothesis refers to those situations in which the victim takes part or is otherwise involved in an activity that is inherently risky. The victim's decision to nevertheless participate at the activity does not value a consent to being damaged but to take part in that activity.[323] Though this norm is usually analyzed in relation to consent and exemption clauses, the victim's decision to take part in a risky activity may also be relevant in the context of causation, as it can be considered that the victim's conscious and assumed decision to take part in a risky activity contributed to the causation of damage, in which case the liability shall be divided between the victim and the tortfeasor.[324]

358. Finally, in order to produce effect, the consent itself must meet some condition. The consent must be valid (which implies the lack of consent vices such as error or violence) and refer to a right the victim can dispose of.[325] Then, the victim must act with discernment and have full civil capacity, as the consent is considered to be an act of disposition.[326] Furthermore, the consent must be expressed before the illicit deed was committed. If the consent was expressed afterword it may represent a renunciation to the right to ask for damage repairment, but not a ground of justification for the deed.[327] Plus, the law must not provide any explicit or implicit interdictions for the victim to consent to a damageable deed.[328]

322. *Ibid.*
323. *Ibid. See also* L. Pop, *Tratat elementar ... , supra*, p. 434.
324. *See* I.I. Neamţ and L.T. Dăuceanu, *supra*, p. 134.
325. *See* L. Pop, *Tratat de drept civil. Obligaţiile. Volumul III ... , supra*, p. 250.
326. When the law expressly provides so, the consent may be given by a representative of the victim, not only the victim. *See* L. Pop, *Tratat elementar ... , supra*, p. 433.
327. *See* C. Stătescu and C. Bîrsan, *supra*, p. 182; F.I. Mangu, *Răspunderea civilă. Constantele ... , supra*, p. 141.
328. *See* I.I. Neamţ and L.T. Dăuceanu, *supra*, p. 134; L. Pop, *Tratat elementar ... , supra*, p. 433; L. Pop, *Curs de drept civil ... , supra*, p. 389.

§2. NECESSITY

359. Article 1.361 C.C. provides that "The one who, in state of necessity, destroys or deteriorates assets of another in order to protect himself or his assets from damaging or an imminent danger is obliged to repair the damage caused according to the rules applicable to unjust enrichment."

360. The law allows the doer to act in a state of necessity, even if this means damaging another individual. In other words, the damageable deed is considered to be legal when committed in a state of necessity and, as unlawfulness is one of the mandatory conditions for engaging tortious liability, no such liability can be engaged.[329]

361. Though it refers to state of necessity as an element that averts tortious liability, the Civil Code does not define the notion or its conditions. Because of this, the legal doctrine unanimously holds that the notion of "state of necessity" has a similar meaning as the one prescribed by Criminal Code, and therefore the same conditions should be met.[330] As such, considering the provisions of Article 20 Criminal Code, in order to conclude that the doer acted in a state of necessity an imminent danger must exist;[331] that danger has to threaten the doers or another's life, physical integrity, health, an important asset or a general interest; committing the deed must be the only way to avert the danger;[332] the deed must breach a legal or social norm and violate one's subjective rights and interest, the deed must not cause obviously more serious consequences then those that would have occurred if the danger would not have been averted; and the deed must not be committed by a doer who had the legal obligation to face the danger, in order to save himself.[333] If the consequences of the deed are far greater than the ones that may have produced if the doer would not have acted, he can be held fully liable, even though the action was meant to avert a danger. Furthermore, the doer may not invoke necessity in order to escape liability if the saved value or asset has little pecuniary or moral importance. In either case, the necessity can be invoked as a defense by doer even if the action was meant to save another's life, physical integrity, health, important

329. *See* L. Pop, *Tratat de drept civil. Obligaţiile. Volumul III ...* , *supra*, p. 243.

330. *See* I.I. Neamţ and L.T. Dăuceanu, *supra*, p. 132; L. Pop, *Tratat de drept civil. Obligaţiile. Volumul III ...* , *supra*, p. 243; L. Pop, *Tratat elementar ...* , *supra*, p. 429; L. Pop, *Curs de drept civil ...* , *supra*, p. 341; P. Vasilescu, *supra*, p. 655; F.I. Mangu, *Răspunderea civilă. Constantele ...* , *supra*, pp. 133.

331. The danger may be the result of a human action, of natural phenomenon, of a machine, of a technology or of an animal and is must be undergoing or imminent at the time of the deed. Furthermore, the danger must not be a result of a doer's act.

332. This condition shall be analyzed *in concreto*, considering all the circumstances of the act.

333. *See* I.I. Neamţ and L.T. Dăuceanu, *supra*, pp. 132–133; L. Pop, *Tratat de drept civil. Obligaţiile. Volumul III ...* , *supra*, p. 243; L. Pop, *Tratat elementar ...* , *supra*, p. 429; L. Pop, *Curs de drept civil ...* , *supra*, p. 341; P. Vasilescu, *supra*, pp. 656–657. For an extensive analysis of these conditions, *see* F. Streteanu, *Tratat de drept penal. Partea generala. Volumul I (Criminal Law Treaty. General Part. Volume I)*, C.H. Beck, Bucharest, 2008, pp. 505–525; M. Udroiu, *Drept Penal. Partea generală. Noul Cod penal (Criminal Law. General Part. New Criminal Code)*, C.H. Beck, Bucharest, 2014 pp. 67–70.

assets or the general interest. The last hypothesis is meant to conserve and encourage social action and to protect the individuals that do so.

362. Committing the damageable deed in a state of necessity averts tortious liability but does not completely remove liability. The wrongdoer may still be held liable, but not on the grounds of tortious liability, as his deed can no longer be considered illicit, according to the norms applicable to unjust enrichment,[334] which nevertheless may greatly ease the doer's status. First, the prescription rules from unjust enrichment will apply and not those referring to tortious liability. Second, if in the case of tortious liability, as we shall see, the full indemnification principle applies, even if the damage was not foreseeable, unjust enrichment entitles the victim only to the smallest amount between the lost and the enrichment[335] and, furthermore, the enrichment must subsist until the action was filled.[336] Therefore, if the doer obtained, as a result of the deed committed in a state of necessity, a smaller benefit than the value of the damage caused to the victim, the latter may request only the equivalent of that benefit. Also, if after committing the deed, the doer lost unimputably the benefit (e.g., the initially saved asset was afterwards stroke by a lightning and destroyed), the victim can no longer ask for any damage repairment. Furthermore, if an enrichment and a lost may exist when the deed was committed in order to save an asset belonging to the doer, an enrichment will be impossible to find when the action was meant to save the doer himself or to conserve, for that matter, any other nonpecuniary subjective right.

363. When the damageable deed was committed in order to save another's life, physical integrity, health or important assets, Article 1.362 C.C. provides that the victim may head against the beneficiary based of unjust enrichment. Thus, in this situation not the doer, but the beneficiary of his deed, shall be held liable.

§3. Self-Help and Self-Defense

364. First, we underline that the Romanian law does not regulate the institution of self-help, in the meaning given to this notion in other legal systems, respectively the personal implementation of own's rights without resorting to public authorities. For this reason, we will further address only the issue of self-defense.

365. Article 1.360, first paragraph, C.C. provides that no indemnification is due by the one who, in self-defense, caused a damage. As in the case of necessity, the Civil Code does not provide a definition or the conditions for self-defense. Therefore, the legal doctrine has turned once again to the provisions of Criminal Code,

334. *See* L. Pop, *Tratat de drept civil. Obligaţiile. Volumul III* ..., *supra*, p. 244.
335. *See* Art. 1.345 C.C. For further details, *see* F.I. Mangu, *Răspunderea civilă. Constantele* ..., *supra*, pp. 134–135.
336. *See* Art. 1.347, first paragraph, C.C.

which regulates self-defense in Article 19.[337] The mentioned Criminal Code Article provides a series conditions for both the attack and the defense.

366. Referring to the *attack*,[338] first, the attack must be material, which means that it consists in a physical violence or other manifestation that endangers the physical existence of the protected value or the item that incorporates it.[339] The verbal or written violence does not meet the conditions of a material attack and cannot justify a self-defense.[340]

367. Second, the attack must be direct, which means that it directly threatens the doer or another, their rights or a general interest.[341] No direct physical contact between the aggressor and the protected social value is needed in order to satisfy the condition; but, no insurmountable obstacle must exist either.[342]

368. Third, the attack must be immediate, which means that it must be undergoing or imminent and not a mere eventuality.[343] Generally, if the attack already occurred, a reaction will no longer satisfy the conditions of self-defense, except in those cases when the attack had a reversible consequence, such as when the victim of a robbery experts' violence over the robber in order to recover the stolen goods.

369. Fourth, the attack must be unjust, meaning it must come from a responsible person and not be allowed by law.[344] Thus, if the attacker had no discernment at the time of the attack and the doer knew this aspect or the attack was allowed by law, the condition is not met. An attack coming from an animal shall not be considered unjust unless the animal was determined by a person to attack. If the attack is allowed by law, such as the intervention of a firefighter at a fire, or of a policeman at a crime, it remains just only as long as is within the limits prescribed by law. If those limits are overpassed, a reaction may fall within the self-defense.

370. Finally, the attack must be directed against the defender, against another, their rights or a general interest, which means that it can target either the doer or his rights or other persons or their rights.[345]

---

337. *See* L. Pop, *Tratat de drept civil. Obligaţiile. Volumul III ... , supra*, p. 241.
338. For an extensive presentation of this conditions, *see* F. Streteanu, *supra*, pp. 476–505; M. Udroiu, *supra*, pp. 61–63.
339. *See* L. Pop, *Tratat de drept civil. Obligaţiile. Volumul III ... , supra*, p. 241; P. Vasilescu, *supra*, p. 652. The attack can take the shape of an action or inaction, as long as the inaction threatens the physical existence of the social value.
340. *See* P. Vasilescu, *supra*, p. 652; C. Stătescu and C. Bîrsan, *supra*, p. 179; F.I. Mangu, *Răspunderea civilă. Constantele ... , supra*, p. 131.
341. *See* L. Pop, *Tratat de drept civil. Obligaţiile. Volumul III ... , supra*, p. 241; C. Stătescu and C. Bîrsan, *supra*, p. 179; F.I. Mangu, *Răspunderea civilă. Constantele ... , supra*, p. 131.
342. *See* P. Vasilescu, *supra*, p. 652.
343. *See* L. Pop, *Tratat de drept civil. Obligaţiile. Volumul III ... , supra*, p. 241; P. Vasilescu, *supra*, p. 652; F.I. Mangu, *Răspunderea civilă. Constantele ... , supra*, p. 131.
344. *See* L. Pop, *Tratat de drept civil. Obligaţiile. Volumul III ... , supra*, p. 241; P. Vasilescu, *supra*, p. 652; C. Stătescu and C. Bîrsan, *supra*, p. 179.
345. *See* C. Stătescu and C. Bîrsan, *supra*, p. 179.

371. In which the *defense* is concerned,[346] it must consist in an action or inaction which causes a damage to the attacker. In any case, the doer must act aware of the existence of the attack. Then, the deed must be necessary to repeal the attack, which means that it has to be committed while the attack is undergoing or imminent and be able to repeal the attack. The condition is not satisfied if the deed is committed before the attack became imminent or after the attack ended or is not reasonably capable of repealing the attack.[347] Nevertheless, it is not necessary for the deed to be the only way to reject the attack. Furthermore, the deed must be directed against the aggressor or object used by the aggressor, it must be preceded by the attack and be proportional with the attack. The proportionality is analyzed considering the circumstances in which the attack took place and the social values there affected by the attack and the defense.[348]

372. Though the Criminal Code regulates the presumed self-defense, the legal doctrine alleged that because Civil Code makes no reference to such presumption, the doer must prove in all circumstances that the conditions of self-defense are met.[349]

373. Article 1.360(2) C.C. provides that the doer may be obliged to pay an adequate and equitable compensation if he acted in the conditions of justified excess of defense. A justified excess of defense exists, according to the Article 19(2) Criminal Code, when all the conditions of self-defense are met, except the proportionality, which was voluntarily or involuntarily breached because of the emotions or fear caused by the attack. In such case, the illegal nature of the deed is still averted, and the tortious liability cannot be engaged, but the victim is entitled to an adequate and equitable compensation based on 1.360(2) C.C., which represents an independent and autonomous case of liability which has as fundament the principle of equity.[350]

374. Finally, as in the case of necessity, if the damageable deed was committed in the interest of another, Article 1.362 C.C. provides that the victim may head against the beneficiary based of unjust enrichment, but only when the deed was committed in the conditions of justified excess of defense. Thus, unlike necessity, self-defense completely averts the doer liability. The doer can be held liable only if he acted in justified excess of defense or, when the doer acted in the interest of another with justified excess of defense, the latter can be held liable based on unjustified enrichment.[351]

346. For an extensive presentation of this conditions for defense, *see* M. Udroiu, *supra*, pp. 63–65.
347. *See* P. Vasilescu, *supra*, pp. 653–654.
348. *See* F.I. Mangu, *Răspunderea civilă. Constantele ...* , *supra*, p. 132.
349. *See* I.I. Neamţ and L.T. Dăuceanu, *supra*, p. 132. For the opposite opinion, *see* L. Pop, *Tratat de drept civil. Obligaţiile. Volumul III ...* , *supra*, p. 242.
350. *See* P. Vasilescu, *supra*, p. 654.
351. *See* L. Pop, *Tratat de drept civil. Obligaţiile. Volumul III ...* , *supra*, p. 243.

§4. Others

375. Besides consent, necessity and self-help, the Civil Code regulates two other hypotheses in which the deed, though damageable, does not entitle the victim to indemnification. First of this, known as *the authorization of law or the order of the superior*, is provided by Article 1.364 C.C., which states that fulfilling an activity permitted or required by law or the order of the superior does not avert liability of the one who could have realized the illicit nature of the deed committed in such circumstances. For good reason, the norm was highly criticized because of its ambiguous wording.[352] Thus, the legal doctrine underlined that a clear distinction should be drawn between the situation in which the damageable deed is committed in order to fulfill a legal duty (such as extinguishing a fire by the firefighters) or it is expressly allowed by the law (such as the veterinarians who sacrifice animals in order to stop the spreading of a epidemy) and the situation in which the deed is the result of executing an order of the superior.[353] This distinction results from the provisions of Article 21 Criminal Code, which in first paragraph provides that "It is justified the deed prescribed by criminal law consisting in the exercise of a right provided by law or the fulfillment of a legal duty, in compliance with the conditions and limits prescribed" while the second paragraph of the same Article provides that "It is also justified the deed prescribed by criminal law consisting in the fulfillment of an obligation imposed by the competent authority, in the form provided by law, as long as it is not manifestly illegal."

376. In the first hypothesis, when the damageable deed consists in the exercise of a right provided by law or the fulfillment of a legal duty, the doer can be held liable only if he acted outside the limits or conditions prescribed by law, otherwise his action or inaction remains legal no matter the damage caused.[354] For example, if the law states that the veterinarian can proceed to animal sacrifice only after the blood samples confirm the disease, when the sacrifice is done before the disease confirmation, the veterinarian's deed does not respect the conditions prescribed by law and, thus, he cannot be absorbed of liability. Furthermore, the notion of law must be widely interpreted, both when it comes to fulfilling a legal duty and performing an activity prescribed by law. Therefore, not only the laws adopted by the Parliament but also any legal norm, no matter of its position the hierarchy of norms, shall be considered.

377. Regarding the order of the superior or the order of the authority, they may stand as a justification if three conditions are met. First, the order must come from a competent authority or from a superior that is entitled to pass an order to the doer and in that domain.[355] Second, the order must respect the forms prescribed by

352. *See* L. Pop, *Tratat de drept civil. Obligaţiile. Volumul III … , supra*, p. 245; L. Pop, *Tratat elementar … , supra*, p. 430.
353. *See* L. Pop, *Tratat de drept civil. Obligaţiile. Volumul III … , supra*, p. 245; L. Pop, *Tratat elementar … , supra*, p. 430; F.I. Mangu, *Răspunderea civilă. Constantele … , supra*, p. 136.
354. *See* F.I. Mangu, *Răspunderea civilă. Constantele … , supra*, p. 136.
355. *See* L. Pop, *Tratat de drept civil. Obligaţiile. Volumul III … , supra*, p. 246; F.I. Mangu, *Răspunderea civilă. Constantele … , supra*, p. 138.

law.[356] If, for example, the law imperatively provides that the order must be written, a verbal order cannot be considered even if it comes from a competent authority. Finally, the order must not be manifestly illegal.[357] An order is considered to be manifestly illegal when its illegality could have been ascertained even by the least diligent person. An order which is not manifestly illegal, but still illegal, will avert liability as long as it comes from the competent authority or superior and in the form prescribed by law. In all circumstances, for the liability to be averted, the doer must act precisely according to the order. If the conditions prescribed in the order are breached, the liability may be engaged.

378. If these conditions are fulfilled, the deed is no longer considered as being unlawful and the victim cannot request any indemnification from the doer, even though a damage was caused. Nevertheless, in the hypothesis of superior's order, if the order was illegal, but not manifestly illegal, the victim may engage the liability of the superior based on the liability for own's fault.

379. The second justification, known as the *normal and legal exercise of the rights*, results from Article 1.353 C.C. which provides that "the one who causes a damage by exercising his rights cannot be obliged to repair it, except the case when the right was abusively exercised." As the abuse of right is analyzed in another section, we are going to further address only the specific elements of this ground of justification.

380. Essentially, the norm is a materialization of the principle *neminem laedit qui suo jure utitur*,[358] according to which when a damage results from a regular exercise of a subjective right, the deed cannot be considered illegal. As the subjective rights of the individuals that form communities are not isolated one from each other, there are a lot of situations in which the exercise of an individual's right damages another's subjective rights or, more often, legal interest. A different solution would empty of meaning the idea of subject right itself, considering that it is within the essence of any subjective right to provide, under the protection of law, a series of powers and liberties whose exercise may not lead to liability.[359]

381. In order to avert any liability, the subjective right must be exercised in its internal and external limits, as an exercise outside these limits transforms the action or inaction in an abuse of right. Though most of civil rights may be exercised abusively, there is a category of rights that cannot, by default, be exercised abusively as they confer the owner a complete power of discretion, such as the right to conclude

---

356. *See* L. Pop, *Tratat de drept civil. Obligaţiile. Volumul III ...*, *supra*, p. 246; P. Vasilescu, *supra*, p. 661; C. Stătescu and C. Bîrsan, *supra*, p. 181; F.I. Mangu, *Răspunderea civilă. Constantele ...*, *supra*, p. 138.
357. *See* L. Pop, *Tratat de drept civil. Obligaţiile. Volumul III ...*, *supra*, p. 246; P. Vasilescu, *supra*, p. 661.
358. *See* L. Pop, *Tratat elementar ...*, *supra*, p. 431; L. Pop, *Tratat de drept civil. Obligaţiile. Volumul III ...*, *supra*, p. 252.
359. *See* L. Pop, *Tratat elementar ...*, *supra*, p. 431; L. Pop, *Tratat de drept civil. Obligaţiile. Volumul III ...*, *supra*, p. 253.

a contract, to disinherit, to accept an offer, etc. In such cases, no matter the way in which the right is exercised, a tortious liability cannot be engaged.[360]

382. Besides the situations when the unlawfulness of the deed is averted, there also situations in which one cannot be held liable because of an element that interfered with the casual link between the deed and the damaged inflected to the victim. So is the case when the damage is the result of a thirds' party action or inaction, of a force majeure or of a fortuitous case.

383. Regarding the first hypothesis, *the act of a third party*, Article 1.352 C.C. provides that the third's party act averts liability even if it does not have the characteristics of a force majeure, but of a fortuitous case, but only in those cases when fortuitous case may, according to the law or the provisions of a contract, avert liability. The norms must be corroborated with Article 1.371(2) C.C., which provides that when the damage is the result of both the doer's act and the act of a third party for whom the doer cannot be held liable, the doer shall be held liable only for the part of damage he caused.

384. Considering the two norms, it must be first underlined that in all hypotheses, there must be an act committed by the defendant (or by the one for whom the defendant can be held liable) which is invoked by the victim as a factual justification for the claim. Third's party action or inaction adds to the defendant's act (or to the act of the one for whom the defendant can be held liable) and contributes to the damage. If the doer has not committed any unlawful act, then the first condition of tortious liability is not fulfilled and there is no reasoning to going further with the analysis.[361] Thus, the existence of a deed for which the defendant can be held liable is essential and, without it, tortious liability cannot be engaged. The fact that third's party act interferes between the deed for which the defendant can be, *in abstracto*, held liable and the damage inflicted to the victim affects the causal relation and may lead to total or partial exemption from tortious liability.[362] Furthermore, between the third party and the defendant there must not exist a collaboration in committing the deed. If the third party is actually a joint author, accomplice, instigator or a fence, then the deed of the third party will not avert liability, but both shall be considered jointly and several liable.[363] In other words, the third party needs to act independently, and his deed must appear for the defendant at least as a fortuitous case, if not a force majeure.

---

360. *See* V. Stoica, *Pot fi drepturile potestative exercitate abuziv? (May Potestative Rights Be Exerted Abusively?)*, available at https://www.juridice.ro/essentials/517/pot-fi-drepturile-potestative-exercitate-abuziv, last checked on Apr. 17, 2021; L. Pop, *Tratat de drept civil. Obligațiile. Volumul III ... , supra*, p. 260.
361. In the sense that in such a case the condition which is not met is casuality, *see* P. Vasilescu, *supra*, p. 616.
362. *See* F.I. Mangu, *Răspunderea civilă. Constantele ... , supra*, pp. 217–218.
363. *See* Supreme Court of Justice, civil section, Decision No. 1834/1991, in Dreptul, No. 6/1992, p. 88.

385. For this ground of justification to be applicable, the defendant must prove that the act of another, who may or may have not already been called to trial by the victim, contributed in whole, or in part, to the damage. Any proof is allowed, including expert testimony or witness testimony. If the damage is partially the result of the deed for which the defendant can be held liable and partially the result of the third's party deed, then each shall be held liable proportionally with the damage inflicted.[364]

386. A further distinction must also be drawn. As shown, the third party's act must appear for the defendant as a fortuitous case or a forces majeure. When the act has the characteristics of force majeure it will partially or completely exonerate the defendant of liability, no matter the type of tortious liability which is incident (for own's act, for things, for animals, for minors, for agents, etc.).[365] On the other hand, when the act has the characteristic of fortuitous case, the defendant shall be exonerated only in those cases of liability in which fortuitous case acts as a ground of justification (such as liability for own's act) and shall still be held liable in those cases in which only force majeure is a cause of exoneration (such as liability for things or animals).

387. Force majeure (*vis maxima*) is regulated as a cause of exoneration by Article 1.351, first paragraph, C.C., which provides that if the law or parties do not otherwise stipulate, the liability is averted when the damage is the result of a force majeure. The notion of force majeure is defined by the second paragraph of the same Article as any external, unforeseeable, absolutely invincible and inevitable event. Thus, in order to be considered a force majeure, an event must be exterior, unforeseeable, absolutely invincible and inevitable.

388. An event is exterior, and therefore may be considered a force majeure, when its etiology is placed outside the defendant and his activities or assets.[366] In other words, the event must not have any connection with the defendant. Enter within this category natural phenomena which are outside human activity, such as majeure earthquakes, flooding, tornados, lightnings,[367] or, in particular cases, social events such as wars, riots or strikes, as long as the defendant was not a participant,[368] and it cannot be considered a force majeure, as they originate within the defendants field of activity or assets, but, eventually a fortuitous case, events such as a tire explosion, a mechanism malfunction or a manufacturing error.[369]

---

364. *See* I.I. Neamţ and L.T. Dăuceanu, *supra*, p. 140.
365. *See* I.I. Neamţ and L.T. Dăuceanu, *supra*, p. 140; L. Pop, *Tratat elementar ...* , *supra*, p. 446; L. Pop, *Curs de drept civil ...* , *supra*, p. 351.
366. *See* I.I. Neamţ and L.T. Dăuceanu, *supra*, p. 139; L. Pop, *Tratat elementar ...* , *supra*, p. 441; L. Pop, *Curs de drept civil ...* , *supra*, p. 348; P. Vasilescu, *supra*, p. 608; F.I. Mangu, *Răspunderea civilă. Constantele ...* , *supra*, p. 206; L.R. Boilă, *supra*, p. 1491.
367. *See* I.I. Neamţ and L.T. Dăuceanu, *supra*, p. 139; L. Pop, *Tratat elementar ...* , *supra*, p. 441; L. Pop, *Curs de drept civil ...* , *supra*, p. 348; P. Vasilescu, *supra*, p. 608; F.I. Mangu, *Răspunderea civilă. Constantele ...* , *supra*, p. 206.
368. *See* I.I. Neamţ and L.T. Dăuceanu, *supra*, p. 139; P. Vasilescu, *supra*, p. 608.
369. *See* L. Pop, *Tratat elementar ...* , *supra*, p. 441.

389. The unpredictability refers to both the happening of the event and its consequences.[370] If the event and its consequences were foreseeable, then the defendant may be held liable because he did not foresee them and did not took the necessary safety measures to prevent the event from happening or for avoiding the negative consequences.[371] Nevertheless, *in abstracto*, almost any event is foreseeable, at least when it already happened in the past. One cannot reasonably declare that a storm, a war or a riot was absolutely unpredictable, as long as such events happen quite often. Not even extremely rare events, such as an asteroid explosion, are absolutely unpredictable and, with enough imagination, events that never occurred before, such as a gamma ray burst, may be foreseen. The problem is that such a standard of foreseeability would completely void the force majeure of any practical relevance because as long as any event can be, *in abstracto*, foreseen, then the incidence of a force majeure could never be retained. This led to a doctrinal debate on which should be the standard of foreseeability applicable.[372] The answer is provided by Article 1.351(2) C.C. which associates the term "absolutely" only with the conditions of invincibility and inevitability. Thus, the event does not have to be absolutely unpredictable, but only reasonable unpredictable.[373] Legal doctrine has stated that an event is predictable or unpredictable, depending on a "normality" criterion, meaning an event is unpredictable if it never happened before or it rarely happens and is predictable when it happens quite often or regularly.[374] For example, if a region is regularly hit by strong earthquakes, an earthquake cannot be considered a force majeure event.[375] The standard considered when the reasonability is assessed is a medium individual, who pays a normal care and diligence in his businesses—a *bonus pater familias*, acting in the same circumstances and benefiting by the same information and education as the doer.[376]

390. The final two conditions, which must be analyzed together, are invincibility and inevitability. As Article 1.351(2) C.C. provides, the event must be absolutely invincible and inevitable, which means that is must be so not only for the defendant but for any other individual.[377] Therefore, unlike unpredictability, this time the analysis is *in abstracto*, taking as a landmark the most capable, well-informed and diligent individual.[378] If the event was invincible and inevitable only for the defendant, then the fortuitous case and not force majeure is incident, and he

370. *See* I.I. Neamţ and L.T. Dăuceanu, *supra*, p. 139; L. Pop, *Tratat elementar ...*, *supra*, p. 441; L. Pop, *Curs de drept civil ...*, *supra*, p. 348; L.R. Boilă, *supra*, p. 491.
371. *See* L. Pop, *Tratat elementar ...*, *supra*, p. 441; L. Pop, *Curs de drept civil ...*, *supra*, p. 348.
372. *See* L. Pop, *Tratat elementar ...*, *supra*, p. 441.
373. *See* I.I. Neamţ and L.T. Dăuceanu, *supra*, p. 139.
374. *See* L. Pop, *Tratat elementar ...*, *supra*, p. 442; F.I. Mangu, *Răspunderea civilă. Constantele ...*, *supra*, p. 210.
375. *See* Supreme Tribunal, civil section, Decision No. 1096/1978, in RRD, No. 1/7979, p. 55.
376. *See* I.I. Neamţ and L.T. Dăuceanu, *supra*, p. 139; L. Pop, *Tratat elementar ...*, *supra*, p. 442; L. Pop, *Curs de drept civil ...*, *supra*, p. 349; P. Vasilescu, *supra*, p. 609.
377. *See* I.I. Neamţ and L.T. Dăuceanu, *supra*, p. 139; L. Pop, *Tratat elementar ...*, *supra*, p. 443; L. Pop, *Curs de drept civil ...*, *supra*, p. 349; P. Vasilescu, *supra*, p. 609.
378. *See* I.I. Neamţ and L.T. Dăuceanu, *supra*, p. 139; L. Pop, *Tratat elementar ...*, *supra*, p. 443; L. Pop, *Curs de drept civil ...*, *supra*, p. 349; F.I. Mangu, *Răspunderea civilă. Constantele ...*, *supra*, p. 212.

shall be exonerated solely in those situations when fortuitous case has such an effect. The two conditions are variable and dynamic, as they must be analyzed considering the human knowledge and technology from the time of the damageable deed and these are under a continuous evolution.[379]

391. Like the third's party deed, force majeure implies a deed for which the defendant may be held liable *in abstracto*, on which the event that meets the characteristics of force majeure overlaps, and the latter affects the causal link between the deed and the damage.[380] If the damage is entirely the consequence of the force majeure event, meaning that no damage would have occurred without the interference of the event, tortious liability is completely averted, no matter the type of liability which is incident.[381] When the damage is the result of both a force majeure event and the deed for which the defendant may be held liable, then the defendant's liability may still be engaged proportionally with the damage inflicted, as Article 1.371(2) C.C., provides.[382]

392. Finally, Article 1.351, first paragraph, C.C. provides that if the law or parties do not otherwise stipulate, the liability is averted when the damaged is the result of a *fortuitous case* (*casus*). The third paragraph of the same Article defines the fortuitous case as an event unpredictable and unavoidable by the one that would have been liable if the event would have not occurred. The legal doctrine has underlined that there are two types of event that fall within the legal definition of fortuitous case: internal and external events.[383]

393. Internal events originate within the field of activity of the defendant, being intrinsic to his animals and things, such as hidden vices, manufacturing error, and a sick animal, whereas external events originate outside defendant's filed of activity. The latter have no extraordinary nature, but could not have been foreseen and avoided by an individual with a medium diligence and care, but only by the most capable and diligent individual. Those that fall within this category are torrential rains, regular flooding or earthquakes.[384] Thus, unlike force majeure, fortuitous case may have an internal or external origin and its unpredictability and inevitability are no longer analyzed considering an abstract individual, but the defendant and his characteristics.[385]

---

379. *See* L. Pop, *Tratat de drept civil. Obligaţiile. Volumul III* … , *supra*, p. 283.
380. Indirectly, in the case of subjective liability, force majeure also excludes fault, considering that event and its consequences could not have been foreseen or avoided. *See* I.I. Neamţ and L.T. Dăuceanu, *supra*, p. 139; L. Pop, *Tratat elementar* … , *supra*, p. 443.
381. If the conditions are met, force majeure averts liability no matter the type of tortious liability as no type of liability may be engaged when the damage was caused by a force majeure event. *See* I.I. Neamţ and L.T. Dăuceanu, *supra*, p. 139; L. Pop, *Tratat elementar* … , *supra*, p. 443.
382. *See* I.I. Neamţ and L.T. Dăuceanu, *supra*, p. 139; L. Pop, *Tratat elementar* … , *supra*, p. 443; L. Pop, *Curs de drept civil* … , *supra*, p. 349.
383. *See* L. Pop, *Tratat elementar* … , *supra*, p. 444; L. Pop, *Curs de drept civil* … , *supra*, p. 350; P. Vasilescu, *supra*, p. 611; F.I. Mangu, *Răspunderea civilă. Constantele* … , *supra*, p. 213.
384. *See* L. Pop, *Tratat elementar* … , *supra*, pp. 444–445; L. Pop, *Curs de drept civil* … , *supra*, p. 350.
385. *See* I.I. Neamţ and L.T. Dăuceanu, *supra*, p. 139; P. Vasilescu, *supra*, p. 611.

394. Furthermore, for a fortuitous case to exist it is enough for the event to be unpredictable and inevitable considering the person liable. Thus, both unpredictability and inevitability shell be subjectively analyzed, considering the doer and his particularities.[386]

395. Just as force majeure, if the conditions are met, fortuitous case averts tortious liability. Nevertheless, the distinction between the two remains important, as there are situations in which only the force majeure has such an effect, and not the fortuitous case. Fortuitous case excludes the idea of fault and so it becomes relevant only in case of subjective liability, based on fault and it has no impact on strict liability. As such, in case of tortious liability for things, animals, the ruin of edifice or environmental damages only force majeure may avert liability and not the fortuitous case.[387]

386. *See* F.I. Mangu, *Răspunderea civilă. Constantele ...*, *supra*, p. 214.
387. *See* I.I. Neamţ and L.T. Dăuceanu, *supra*, p. 139; L. Pop, *Tratat elementar ...*, *supra*, p. 445; L. Pop, *Curs de drept civil ...*, *supra*, p. 350.

Chapter 3. Contributory Fault

396. There are multiple situations in which the damage is the result of a multitude of factors and circumstances that together or independently contribute to the result. In some cases, even the victim, willingly or not, contributes to causation or augmentation of damage. For example, wanting to get a higher indemnification, the victim to whom the tortfeasor inflicted an injury refuses to go to the hospital and this leads to a series of medical complications and highly expensive treatments. In such hypothesis the tortfeasor cannot be made to pay for the entire damage as not the entire damage is the result of his deed.

397. For this reason, Article 1.352 C.C. provides that the victim's act averts liability even if it does not have the characteristics of a force majeure, but of a fortuitous case, but only in those cases when fortuitous case may, according to the law or the provisions of a contract, avert liability.[388] The norms must also be corroborated with Article 1.371, first paragraph, C.C., which provides that when the victim contributed, intentionally or by negligence, to the causation of damage or its augmentation, or did not avoid it, in whole or in part, though he could have, the tortfeasor can be held liable only for the rest of the damage.

398. The above-mentioned norms require further attention. First, in order to avert liability, the victim's act must at least meet the conditions of fortuitous case, which means that the act itself could not have been foreseen or avoided by the doer. If, by contrary, the act could have been foreseen or avoided by the doer, he shall still be held liable. Nevertheless, in those cases in which only force majeure avert tortious liability, such as liability for thing, animals or the ruin of edifice, the act of the victim must also meet the conditions of force majeure, which means that it must be exterior (e.g., the victim cannot be an employee which was damaged during the professional activity), unforeseeable and absolutely invincible and inevitable. Otherwise, the defendant shall still be held liable, even if the victim's deed meets the conditions of fortuitous act.[389] Moreover, the victim's deed does not have to be of the same nature as the tortfeasor's deed or committed with the same type of fault. One can be an action and the other an abstention, one can be committed with intention while the other one by negligence or any combination between those.

399. Second, if the victim's act does not meet the conditions of force majeure or fortuitous case (when the last averts liability) the liability of the doer may still be partially or fully averted but only when a fault can be attributed to the victim.[390] It does not matter the victim's type of fault. It can be either intentional or by negligence. The type of fault will not influence the extent of the liability as the defendant

388. Contributory fault and third's party act are regulated by the same norm and the same conditions are applicable to both. Therefore, all the above mentioned, when we have analyzed third's party act as a ground of justification, are, *mutatis mutandis*, applicable to contributory fault.

389. *See* I.I. Neamţ and L.T. Dăuceanu, *supra*, p. 140; L. Pop, *Tratat elementar ...* , *supra*, p. 446; L. Pop, *Curs de drept civil ...* , *supra*, p. 351.

390. *See* F.I. Mangu, *Răspunderea civilă. Constantele ...* , *supra*, p. 218.

shall be held liable only for the part of the damage he has caused and the victim will have to endure the personally caused damage, no matter if the victim acted intentionally or by negligence.

400. Third, the victims must not only abstain from causing or increasing the damage, but he must also put all the reasonable diligences to avoid or reduce the damages. If the damages could have been, in all or in part, avoided with reasonable efforts, then the doer shall only be liable for the part of damage that could not be avoided. In order to analyze this aspect, the personal circumstances of the victim shall be considered, including the level of education, the social status, the emotions caused by the illicit deed. In other words, the analysis is *in concreto* and not *in abstracto*. Furthermore, the victim is not required to take measures that are economically infeasible, such as those that would cost more that the damage.

Chapter 4. Exemption Clauses

401. As we have previously seen, when we have analyzed the consent as a ground of justification, the law regulates within the same norm both consent and exemption clauses. The reason for this approach is that, despite the differences, in the end, what leads to exoneration is the same element: the victim's acceptance to be exposed to certain risks or to be inflicted certain damages.

402. Because the conditions are identical, most of the arguments presented when consent was analyzed shall apply *tale quale* to exemption clauses. What mainly differentiates the two is the mechanism behind the ground of justification, or the judicial instrument through which the will of the victim not to engage the liability becomes effective. Consent, as a ground of justification, implies a unilateral manifestation of will coming from the victim. Though the consent may originate in a proposal coming from the doer, no mutual agreement is needed. The victim's consent itself is enough to avert liability. On the contrary, exemption clauses imply a contract, a mutual agreement between the doer and the victim. In order to avert liability, the contract must be concluded before the damageable deed is committed. As the deed cannot be considered *ex tunc* legal, if the contract is concluded afterwards, it does no longer work as an exemption clause, but a renunciation of the victim to the right to be compensated for the damage inflicted or other arrangement of the remedies. For this reason, usually, exemption clauses are only applicable in contractual liability[391] and are, in most of the cases, accessory to another contract.

403. Considering the fact that exemption clauses are contractual by nature, they must fulfill all the conditions provided by law for any contract, the capacity to conclude a contract, a valid consent of the parties, a specific and legal object and a legal and moral cause.[392] To those, the special conditions provided by Article 1.355 C.C. shall be added.

404. It must be underlined the clauses based on which the liability is aggravated are valid, no matter the type of damage or the type of fault with which the deed is committed.[393] Thus, the imperative conditions, meant to protect the victim, are applicable only when the clause diminishes or averts the tortious liability.

405. Referring to the last hypothesis, when the clause diminishes or averts liability, several distinctions must be drawn based on the provisions of Article 1.355 C.C.

406. First, it must be distinguished between material damages, or damages caused to the victim's assets, and damages caused to the victim's physical, mental

391. *See* L. Pop, *Tratat elementar …* , *supra*, p. 432; P. Vasilescu, *supra*, p. 624.
392. *See* Art. 1.179, first paragraph C.C.
393. The conclusion result interprets *per a contrario* the provisions of Art. 1.355, first paragraph, C.C., which states that it cannot be excluded or limited the tortious liability for the material damaged caused by a deed committed with intention or gross negligence. Thus, *per a contrario*, no matter the fault, the liability can be aggravated.

or health integrity. While in the case of material damages exemption clauses are allowed, in certain conditions, when the deed interfered with the victims physical, mental or health integrity, tortious liability cannot be averted or diminish except in those situations in which the law expressly provides so.[394] If the same deed inflicted both a material and a bodily damage, the exception clause shall be applicable only partially, respective to the material damages, and only as long as the intention of the parties was for the clause to be applicable even in this manner.

407. Second, when it comes to material damages, the validity of the exemption clause further depends on the type of fault with which the deed was committed. If the damageable deed was intentional or grossly negligent, the liability cannot be averted or diminished, no matter the provisions of the exemption clauses.[395] On the contrary, if the damaged to the victim's assets was caused with simple negligence or imprudence, the exemption clause is perfectly valid, and the doer's liability may be averted or diminished.[396]

408. The norms that prohibit the exemption clauses for the damages caused to the victim's physical, mental or health integrity or those referring to the materials damages inflected intentionally or by gross negligence are imperative. Therefore, the parties may not choose to stipulate the contrary.

409. Finally, the exemption clauses may refer to liability itself, stating the one shall not be held liable for any acts, or to the extent of liability. The last can be contractually regulated from two perspectives. The parties may decide to avert liability in reference to certain acts and keep the liability active in relation to others, or they may decide to cap the damages, by establishing a maximum amount to which the doer can be held liable.

410. Another hypothesis that may be assimilated to that of exemption clauses are the announcements referring to liability. In this regard, Article 1.356, first paragraph, C.C., provides that an announcement that limits or averts contractual liability, made or not available to the public, shall have no effect unless the one who invokes it proves that the victims knew about the existence of the announcement when the contract was concluded.[397] Thus, a simple announcement made by one of the contractual parties in order to reduce or avoid contractual liability has no effect as long as that party is unable to prove that the other party was fully aware of that announcement when the contract was concluded. For example, an announcement posted on the door of a hotel stating that the hotel assumes no liability for the assets left unattended by the customers in their rooms, shall have no effect unless the hotel is able to prove that the client knew about this announcement when the contract was concluded. Furthermore, the second paragraph of the same Article provides that an announcement cannot exclude or limit tortious liability, but it may be seen a danger

394. *See* Art. 1.355(3) C.C.
395. *See* Art. 1.355, first paragraph C.C.
396. *See* Art. 1.355(2) C.C.
397. For an analysis of this provision, *see* P. Vasilescu, *supra*, p. 624.

warning and may lead to contributory fault. As such, an announcement may impact only contractual liability, while tortious liability may be affected only when the victim's will is beyond any doubt, otherwise the announcement can be consider as an element of reference to conclude that the victim has also contributed to the damage by not considering the announcement.

Part V. Causation *(Concept; Joint and Several Liability, Etc.)*

411. Causation represents a general and an essential condition of any form of civil liability. The causal relationship presupposes the existence of a link between the wrongful act and the damage.

412. In other words, compensation can be awarded only for the direct damage, namely the damage that represents a consequence of the wrongful act or damage. In the case of indirect damage there is no right of the aggrieved person to compensation unless the law provides otherwise. However, the direct damage can be the result of a direct or indirect causation link between the damage and the wrongful act.

413. Together with the condition of damage and wrongful act, causation is an objective element of the civil liability differentiating itself from the subjective element of fault. As a consequence, causation theories relying on subjective elements are repudiated in the Romanian legal system.

414. Frequently, establishing the existence of the causal relationship does not raise any difficulties as it is obvious from the dynamics of the facts. However, there are also situations in which the existence of certain conditions, events or actions, previous or concomitant, that work together in order to produce the damageable result. In these cases, it is the judge's role to determine the causal events and decide their contribution to the damage.

415. As the legislator chose not to set any criteria in order to establish a general mechanism applicable in these situations, it was the jurisprudence and the doctrine that developed some theories in order to determine existence of the causal relationship.[398] In this sense, it can be mentioned the theory of the *sine qua non* condition—according to this theory, all those facts or circumstances without which the result would not have occurred have cause value; theory of adequate—according to this theory all those facts or circumstances *sine qua non* that are usually capable of leading to the result produced have causal value; the theory of the proximate cause—according to which only the deed or circumstance immediately prior to the production of the result has causal value; and the theory of the indivisible unity between cause and conditions—according to which the causal field includes not

398. L. Pop, I.Fl. Popa, and S.I. Vidu, *Curs de drept civil …* , *supra*, pp. 344–347.

only those facts and circumstances with necessary and direct causal value but also those that facilitate the production of the result, having the value of causal conditions. The first three theories have been criticized and abandoned because causal spectrum was considered to be either too large—in the case of the *sine qua non* condition—or too narrow—in the case of the proximate cause or because they included a subjective approach like in the case of the adequate cause. Thus, the embraced theory that is applied by judges is the theory of the indivisible unity between cause and conditions.

416. For certain hypothesis, the legislator decided to intervene and establish the causal relevance of certain facts and the existence of a causal link between them and the damage.

417. For instance, the acts of complicity, instigation or concealment are considered to be in direct causal relationship to the damage.[399] As a result, if the perpetrator was determined by a third party to commit the wrongful act or was helped in any way, including morally, or if the third party benefited from the act or concealed property from the wrongful act, the victim will be able, at its choice, to direct for the reparation of the damage suffered against the author or the third party or both. The same liability also lies on the person who, in any way, prevented or delayed the prosecution of the perpetrator.

418. A similar regulation exists for the situations in which the damage was caused by the simultaneous or successive action of several persons, without it being possible to establish that it was caused or, as the case may be, could not have been caused by the deed of any of them. As it results from the premise of this norm, it becomes incident whenever, due to the indissoluble link between the actions and their result, it is impossible to individualize which is the illicit deed or deeds that led to the damage. In such a situation, each deed will be able to incur the tortious liability of the respective person.

419. In both of the abovementioned cases, all such persons shall be jointly and severally liable toward the victim. This consequence is also an application of the general rule according to which those who are liable for a prejudicial act are jointly and severally liable for reparation to the injured party.

399. Article 1369 of the civil code.

Part VI. Remedies

420. If all the conditions for engaging tortious liability are met, a legal relationship is created between the victim and the one who can be held liable for the damage (the tortfeasor, the principal, the parents, the legal guardian, etc.) based on which the victim is entitled to ask for damage repairment and the one liable is bound to repair the damage.[400] Though the law extensively regulates the mechanism of damage reparation, in Articles 1.381–1.395 C.C., there are still multiple aspects left unregulated. Some found a jurisprudential or doctrinal solution, while others remain to be addressed.

400. *See* I.I. Neamţ and L.T. Dăuceanu, *supra*, p. 169; L. Pop, *Tratat elementar ...* , *supra*, p. 557; L. Pop, *Curs de drept civil ...* , *supra*, p. 412.

Chapter 1. General Principles

421. Legal doctrine unanimously holds that at least two principles govern the field of remedies when it comes to tortious liability: the principle of full restoration or complete damage repairment and the principle of reparation in kind of the damage. The two principles were not expressly regulated by the former Civil Code, but they were a creation of legal doctrine and jurisprudence, which emerged from the general regime of remedies and the scope of tortious liability.[401] On the contrary, the new Civil Code, though it does not name them as principles, expressly regulates the problem of full restoration and the reparation in kind.

§1. The Full Compensation Principle

422. By violating the subjective rights or legitimate interest of the victim, the tortious deed affects the social balance and the equilibrium that must exist among community members. The main purpose of tortious liability is to reinstate this equilibrium by removing all the negative effects of the tortious deed, and to deter similar acts from happening further by placing the task of repairing the damage on the doer or the guardian of the risky activity or thing. In other words, a *restitutio in integrum* must be achieved.[402] The victims must be placed in the same situation as he would have been in lack of damageable deed, no matter the type of damages that was inflicted, pecuniary or nonpecuniary, or the type of fault with which the deed was committed.[403]

423. The full compensation principle refers exactly to this aspect, the victim's entitlement to a true *restitutio in integrum*, and it dictates both the limits of liability and the limits of victim's right to indemnification. In this respect, Article 1.385, first paragraph, C.C., provides that "the damage shall be fully compensated, unless the law does otherwise provide." Thus, the general rule is that the victim is entitled to *restitutio in integrum,* as long as a legal provision does not otherwise provide. With regard to the last aspect, it can be noticed that the reference is made only to a legal exemption. Nevertheless, it must be remembered that an exception clause may also cap the damages to which the victim is entitled. In such case, if the total damages inflicted is higher than the maximum limit set by the parties, than the victim shall be entitled only to the maximum amount agreed and the principle of full compensation or restoration will not be applicable, though not because of a special legal provision, but of a contractual engagement. Furthermore, the victim is the only one entitled to decide whether or not to sue the doer and to establish the extent of the remedy requested, even if, of course, in the end the court shall decide the amount allowed to the victim as damage, which may imply a partial granting of the claim.

401. *See* L. Pop, *Tratat elementar ... , supra*, p. 562; C. Stătescu and C. Bîrsan, *supra*, p. 159.
402. *See* I.I. Neamţ, *Acţiunea colectivă ... , supra*, p. 118; L. Pop, *Tratat de drept civil. Obligaţiile. Volumul III ... , supra*, p. 492; F.I. Mangu, *Răspunderea civilă. Constantele ... , supra*, p. 34. *See also* C.A. Constanta, s. civ., dec. No. 354/2008, in V. Terzea, *supra*, p. 405.
403. *See* I.I. Neamţ and L.T. Dăuceanu, *supra*, p. 171.

Still, the victim could decide to ask for less than he would be entitled. In this case, as the victim's will manifests after the damage occurred, the full restoration principle is still applicable and the victim's decision is nothing more than a partially renunciation to the right.

424. In order to fully restore the situation, the extent of negative consequences of the illicit deed must be known, which means the damage needs to be *certain*. The damage is certain whenever its existence is undoubted, and its extent can be fully assessed.[404] Thus, the certainty of the damage refers to both its existence and extent.[405] All the damages that have already occurred at the time of the victim's claim are certain as they have already produced, and a present damage can always be evaluated.[406] In this regard, though it refers to contractual liability, the provisions of Article 1.532(3) C.C. are *mutatis mutandis* applicable. The norm provides that when the extent of the damage cannot be assessed for sure, it shall be determined by the court. Therefore, as long as the damage already manifested, the fact that the victim cannot fully prove its extent will not lead to a claim dismiss, but the court is bound to establish the damage considering the elements available. The problem is that sometimes the damage occurs after a long period of time or it manifests gradually. In such case, if the victims were to expect damage manifestation before submitting a court application, the chance of obtaining compensation may drastically decrease because the doer may become insolvent, die or the maximum coverage of an eventual civil liability assurance limit may be reached. For this reason, a future damage can also be compensated as long as it is undoubted that it will occur and there are sufficient elements to assess its dimension.[407] The conclusion is supported by Article 1.385(2) C.C. which provides that compensations shall be granted for future damage as longs as its emergence is unquestionable. A perfect determination of damage is not required, but a preliminary determination shall suffice, especially in the case of those damages that occur *pro rata temporis*, such as work incapacity. If after the judgment was passed new elements allow the conclusion that the amount is either too high or too low, or even that the compensation should not have been granted, Article 1.386(4) C.C. provides that the compensation can be reduced, diminished or even averted. Still, the decision to request for compensation before the damage occurs belongs to the victim, who can decide to assume the risk of having to return the compensation or to fill a new court action in order to obtain the difference.

---

404. *See* I.I. Neamţ and L.T. Dăuceanu, *supra*, p. 135; L. Pop, *Tratat de drept civil. Obligaţiile. Volumul III ...* , *supra*, pp. 492–493; L. Pop, *Tratat elementar ...* , *supra*, pp. 562–563; L. Pop, *Curs de drept civil ...* , *supra*, p. 414; C. Stătescu and C. Bîrsan, *supra*, p. 154; F.I. Mangu, *Răspunderea civilă. Constantele ...* , *supra*, p. 148. *See also* C.A. Craiova, S. civ., dec. No. 5086/1997, in V. Terzea, *supra*, p. 404.
405. *See* L. Pop, *Tratat de drept civil. Obligaţiile. Volumul III ...* , *supra*, p. 492; L. Pop, *Tratat elementar ...* , *supra*, p. 563.
406. *See* C. Stătescu and C. Bîrsan, *supra*, p. 154; F.I. Mangu, *Răspunderea civilă. Constantele ...* , *supra*, p. 148. *See also* C.A. Craiova, S. civ., dec. No. 5086/1997, in *supra*, p., 404.
407. *See* I.I. Neamţ and L.T. Dăuceanu, *supra*, p. 135; L. Pop, *Tratat de drept civil. Obligaţiile. Volumul III ...* , *supra*, p. 493; L. Pop, *Tratat elementar ...* , *supra*, pp. 562–563; L. Pop, *Curs de drept civil ...* , *supra*, p. 414; C. Stătescu and C. Bîrsan, *supra*, p. 155; F.I. Mangu, *Răspunderea civilă. Constantele ...* , *supra*, pp. 42, 149.

425. Another problem related to certainty is that sometimes the unlawful act interferes with the victim's possibility to obtain a gain or avoid a loss. In such case, it cannot be stated that a clear damage was caused as with or without the unlawful deed, it is not sure if the victim would have actually obtained the gain or avoid the loss.[408] It is what the legal doctrine calls the damage in the form of losing a chance, because what the victim has lost is not a clear benefit, but a chance to obtain that benefit. According to legal scholars, the damages resulted from the loss of a chance are halfway between certainty and uncertainty.[409] The damage is not certain because the benefit the victim expected, and which the victim may have been deprived of, is not certain. Nevertheless, it is undoubtable that a damage was caused, as the victim's chance completely vanished because of the deed. Under the previous legislation no norms existed for such situations; but, the legal doctrine has advanced the idea that the loss of a chance may stand as ground for tortious liability. The opinion remained mainly at doctrinal level, as it was not gladly embraced by jurisprudence. The new Civil Code addressed the issue and Article 1.385(4) C.C. provides that if the illicit deed determined the loss of a chance for obtaining an advantage or avoiding a damage, the compensation shall be proportional with the probability of obtaining the advantage or avoiding the loss, taking into account the circumstances and the victim's concrete situation.[410] In order to give rise to tortious liability, the lost chance must be real (which means that the victim is in the exercise of the chance or the chance fulfillment is imminent) and serious (meaning that there was a reasonably high probably for the chance to materialize if the illicit deed would not have been committed).[411] In all cases, because in the end no certainty exists, the victim is not entitled to full compensation, but only to a compensation which is proportional with the probability for obtaining an advantage or avoiding a loss.

426. The full restoration principle requires not only a compensation for the direct damage inflicted (*damnum emergens*) but also for the gain or the profit the victim lost because of the tortious act (*lucrum cessans*).[412] In this regard, Article 1.385(2) C.C. provides that compensation shall include the damaged actually suffered and the profit that, in regular circumstances, could have been obtained by the

408. *See* P. Vasilescu, *supra*, p. 599.

409. *See* I.I. Neamţ and L.T. Dăuceanu, *supra*, p. 136. In this case, the certainty does not refer to the damage itself, as in relation with the damage there is always an alea, but to the chance that was lost. In other words, though the damage is not certain, a chance was certainly lost.

410. An almost identical norm is provided in the matter of contractual liability by Art. 1.532, second paragraph, C.C.

411. *See* I.I. Neamţ and L.T. Dăuceanu, *supra*, p. 136; L. Pop, *Tratat elementar ... , supra*, p. 564; L. Pop, *Curs de drept civil ... , supra*, pp. 415–416; P. Vasilescu, *supra*, pp. 599–600; F.I. Mangu, *Răspunderea civilă. Constantele ... , supra*, p. 43; F.I. Mangu, *Răspunderea civilă. Constantele ... , supra*, pp. 163–164; O. Podaru and A. Buciuman, *Despre pierderea sansei în contenciosul administrativ (About Loss of Opportunity in Administrative Litigation)*, in Revista Română de Drept Privat No. 3/2020, pp. 303–308.

412. *See* L. Pop, *Tratat de drept civil. Obligaţiile. Volumul III ... , supra*, p. 432; P. Vasilescu, *supra*, p. 601; C. Stătescu and C. Bîrsan, *supra*, p. 159; F.I. Mangu, *Răspunderea civilă. Constantele ... , supra*, pp. 36–37.

victim, but was lost because of the tortious act. The victim is entitled to *lucrum cessans* starting the moment the damage was inflicted[413] and until *damnum emergens* was fully compensated or negative effects cease.[414] When the victim lost an amount of money as a result of the legal deed, the law presumes that *lucrum cessans* is equivalent with legal interest and the victim is not required to prove any damage. Still, if the damage inflicted is higher, the victim is entitled to ask for more than the legal interest, but the exact damage must be proven.[415] Furthermore, according to the final thesis of Article 1.385(2) C.C., the victim may ask for the mitigation damages, an aspect that will later addressed.

427. Unlike contractual liability, in the case of tortious liability, of any kind, the damage shall be fully repaired even if at the time of the tortious act the doer could have not foreseen the entire amplitude of the negative consequences or some form of damages were unpredictable.[416]

428. Though Article 1.385 C.C. makes no distinction, the principle of full restoration will apply mainly when a material damage was caused,[417] considering that in the case of body injuries full damage repairment is more of an illusion then a reality. The remedies that are available in such case, pecuniary or nonpecuniary, are unable to provide a true *restitutio in integrum* as they lead only to a diminish of the negative consequences or to a substitutive reparation.[418]

429. Finally, there are multiple situations in which full compensation will not be achieved either because the law provides an exemption[419] or because the factual circumstances lead to such a result.[420] In any case, the fact that the victim is entitled to full restoration does not mean that in the end the doer will have to bear the entire amount. For example, if, as a result of the tortious deed, the victim is entitled to a form of pension or other social benefits, the doer shall be obliged to pay only the difference.[421]

---

413. This is because Art. 1.381, second paragraph, provides that the right to compensation arises the day the damage was caused even if it cannot be valued immediately.
414. *See* I.I. Neamţ and L.T. Dăuceanu, *supra*, p. 171.
415. *See* Art. 1.535, first paragraph, C.C., applicable *mutatis mutandis*.
416. *See* I.I. Neamţ and L.T. Dăuceanu, *supra*, p. 172.
417. *See* L. Pop, *Tratat elementar ...*, *supra*, p. 562; L. Pop, *Curs de drept civil ...*, *supra*, p. 414.
418. *See* I.I. Neamţ, *Acţiunea colectivă ...*, *supra*, p. 119. *See also* First Instance Court of Iasi, civil sentence No. 2465/2011, in V. Terzea, *supra*, pp. 425–426.
419. One such example is Art. 1.368 C.C., already mentioned, which provides that when the doer lacks discernment and no one else can be held liable, the victim is entitled to an equitable indemnity, determined by considering the patrimony of the parties. In most of the cases, the norm will lead to an under-compensation, though a full compensation is not impossible.
420. One example would be the case when the doer's assets and incomes are insufficient to cover the entire damage. For more details, *see* I.I. Neamţ, *Acţiunea colectivă ...*, *supra*, p. 120.
421. *See* Art. 1.393 C.C.

§2. The Principle of in Kind Reparation of Damage

430. As the principle of full restoration, the one of in-kind repairment of damage had no explicit reflection in the old civil law, but the legal doctrine and jurisprudence held that as long as it is possible, the damage should be repaired in kind, and the victim is entitled to compensation only if in-kind repair is not possible.[422]

431. The enactment of the new Civil Code brought some major changes in this respect as well, with Article 1.386, first paragraph, C.C. providing that the damage shall be repaired in kind, by restoring the facts to the previous situation, and, if this is not possible or the victim does not wish so, by paying a compensation, agreed by the parties or determined by the court. Thus, though the law keeps as a principle the in-kind reparation of damage, it also provides an extra exemption: the will of the victim. As such, compensation may be allowed not only in those cases when in-kind reparation of damage is no longer possible but also when the victim prefers this remedy. Therefore, it can be asserted that in-kind reparation of damage is dispositive and it depends on two elements: the objective possibility and the will of the victim.[423]

432. The victim can freely decide whether to ask for in-kind reparation or for pecuniary compensation. The question is if the decision made can be censored by the court or it is completely discretionary, being a purely potestative right. From our standing point, the answer is yes, but only in limitative circumstance. If the victim has the possibility to mitigate the damage, then a decision, for example, to opt for an in-kind reparation of damage which is obviously more expensive than the value of compensation or extremely difficult to obtain with almost no benefit for his, could be considered an abuse of right by the court, if the other conditions are met.[424] In such circumstances, if the defendant makes a request, the court should be able to afford compensation instead of in-kind compensation.

433. The in-kind reparation must first consider the nature and the specificity of the damage and may consist in the restitution of stolen goods, the replacement or the destroyed goods with similar ones, the repairment of the good or other similar mechanisms.[425] Considering that in most of the cases the tortious act impacts on the reality, the legal doctrine underlined that in-kind repairment of damage is the best

422. *See* C. Stătescu and C. Bîrsan, *supra*, p. 160; F.I. Mangu, *Răspunderea civilă. Constantele …* , *supra*, pp. 45–46. For a history and evolution of the principle, *see* F.I. Mangu, *Despre formele reparaţie (art. 1.386 din Codul civil)(About the Forms of Remedy (Art. 1386 of the Civil Code))*, in Revista Română de Drept Privat, No. 2/2020, pp. 123–129.

423. *See* I.I. Neamţ and L.T. Dăuceanu, *supra*, p. 172.

424. For an opposite view, *see* F.I. Mangu, *Răspunderea civilă. Constantele …* , *supra*, p. 46. Nevertheless, the same author in a later study underlined that an abusive exercise of the right to choose the remedy may be censored by the court. *See* F.I. Mangu, *Despre formele …* , *supra*, pp. 170–171.

425. *See* I.I. Neamţ and L.T. Dăuceanu, *supra*, p. 172; L. Pop, *Tratat elementar …* , *supra*, p. 565; L. Pop, *Curs de drept civil …* , *supra*, pp. 416–417; F.I. Mangu, *Răspunderea civilă. Constantele …* , *supra*, p. 45.

way to ensure a true *restitutio in integrum*.[426] Nevertheless, the specificity of in-kind repairment makes it applicable mainly to material damages.[427] For the damage to be repairable in kind the negative effects of tortious act must be reversible or the affected asset must be fungible. Or, in most of the cases, the negative effects of violating a subjective nonpecuniary right are not reversible as the rights are not flexible.[428] For example, once an injury was inflicted, the pain and sufferance cannot be reversed nor a work incapacity that resulted from the injury.[429] Furthermore, most of the "in-kind remedies" that are provided by law for the situation in which a nonpecuniary subjective right was breached, such as obliging the doer to publish the court decision[430] are not truly in-kind remedies.[431] A true in-kind remedy leads to a veritable *restitutio in integrum*, a restoration of fact to the form previous to the illegal deed. Or, the publishing of a court decision which concludes that an illegal deed was committed that can at most offer a substitutive remedy, but not one in-kind.

426. *See* I.I. Neamţ and L.T. Dăuceanu, *supra*, p. 172; F.I. Mangu, *Răspunderea civilă. Constantele* ..., *supra*, p. 47.
427. *See* I.I. Neamţ, *Poate frica* ..., *supra*, p. 230; L. Pop, *Tratat elementar* ..., *supra*, p. 565; L. Pop, *Curs de drept civil* ..., *supra*, pp. 416–417.
428. *See* I.I. Neamţ, *Poate frica* ..., *supra*, p. 230.
429. There are a lot of situation in which in-kind damage reparation is not possible. For example, whenever a good was destroyed and that good is not fungible, in-kind reparation is not possible. Furthermore, if the tortious deed has led, for example, to a species extinction, in-kind reparation is obviously, once again, impossible.
430. *See* Art. 253, third paragraph, let. (a), C.C.
431. For the opinion that they are in-kind remedies, *see* L. Pop, *Tratat elementar* ..., *supra*, pp. 565–566; F.I. Mangu, *Răspunderea civilă. Constantele* ..., *supra*, pp. 49–50.

Chapter 2. Kinds of Damage

434. When it comes to the kinds of damage for which the victim is entitled to seek relief, the Romanian legislation is quite flexible, especially because the norms are highly permissive, allowing the judge to take into account most of the negative aspects that may result from a tortious deed. Nevertheless, some type of damages would have required a closer attention, but though the Civil Code just recently entered into force, on October 1, 2011, it failed to address aspects that are on the center of academic debate across Europe, such as collective damages. Still, the legal doctrine tried to overpass these inconveniences by coming up with solutions that are compatible with the legal framework.

§1. Individual and Collective Damages

435. The Romanian legal norms on tortious liability were, beyond doubt, constructed around the idea of individual damage, as all the conditions of civil liability are highly impregnated with the idea of individuality.[432] In this regard, almost obsessively, and without such an approach being required by legislative technique, all the norms that regulate the conditions of tortious liability use the singular and refer to individual.[433] It is, thus, practically superfluous to state that in order to be unlawful the deed must violate the subjective right or legal interest of a given individual, or that the damage assessment requires the analysis of the negative consequences endured by a specific individual as a result of the tortious deed. As it has been underlined, in the current normative framework a specific individual is both the raison d'etre for tortious liability and its final recipient, because tortious liability cannot exist without a clearly identifiable victim.[434]

436. For these reasons, the legal doctrine does not even directly analyze the individual nature of damage, nor does it state that the damage must be individual. Instead, another condition is underlined, which is in direct relation with the individual nature of the damage: the fact that the damage must be personal. In this regard, the scholars have stated that only those individuals that actually suffered the negative consequences of tortious deed may ask for compensation.[435] The personal nature of damage emerges from both the condition of causation, which implies the existence of a causal link between every damage and tortious act that the victim is bound to prove,[436] and, in the case of subjective liability, from the condition of fault,

432. *See* I.I. Neamţ, *Acţiunea colectivă ... , supra*, p. 24.
433. *Ibid.*, p. 25.
434. *Ibid.* Nevertheless, the legal scholars have noticed in recent years a clear deviation from the individual perspective over the civil liability toward a more collective one—*see* L. Pop, *Tratat de drept civil. Obligaţiile. Volumul III ... , supra*, pp. 109–111.
435. *See* I.I. Neamţ, *Acţiunea colectivă ... , supra*, p., p. 114; I.I. Neamţ and L.T. Dăuceanu, *supra*, p. 136; L. Pop, *Tratat elementar ... , supra*, p. 420; L. Pop, *Curs de drept civil ... , supra*, p. 335.
436. *See* I.I. Neamţ, *Acţiunea colectivă ... , supra*, p. 114; V. Stoica, *Relaţia cauzală complex ca element al răspunderii civile delictuale în procesul penal (Complex Causal Link as Element of Civil Liability in Criminal Trial)*, in RRD, No. 2/1994, pp. 35 et seq.

considering that it may be repaired only the damage for which a fault of the doer may be proven.[437] Nevertheless, the legal doctrine admits that the personal nature of the damage does not oppose damage reparation when the damage resulted not from violating individual subjective rights or legitimate interests, but subjective rights and legitimate interest that belong to groups.[438] This brings into attention the problem of collective damages.[439]

437. As we have already mentioned, the problem of collective damages was not addressed by the Civil Code and, furthermore, with a few exceptions, it was almost ignored by the legal doctrine, even though they have become a incontestable reality as a result of mass production, globalization and the development of technologies[440] and it is one of the most debated legal topics at European level. Still, things started to change, at least at doctrinal level, and scarce decisions that mostly indirectly refer to collective damages have started to be passed by domestic courts.

438. In which the doctrine is concerned, in the only monograph that addressee the issue of collective damages and their procedural counterpart, the class action has been underlined that there are four characteristics that apart collective damages to individual ones.[441]

439. The most obvious is the *quantitative component*: a collective damage implies a plurality of victims.[442] How many victims exactly and how this plurality should be determined is still highly controversial even in comparative law. In one approach a fixed threshold is established which, once exceeded, the damage is considered by default as collective. The numbers go from two victims[443] to 10,000 victims.[444] This approach was criticized on the grounds that collective damages are so diverse and heterogeneous that establishing a fix threshold may lead to undesirable results, and it is, in all cases, arbitrary and sometimes impossible to assess, because

---

437. *See* I.I. Neamţ, *Acţiunea colectivă ...* , *supra*, p. 114.
438. *Ibid. See also* L. Pop, *Tratat elementar ...* , *supra*, p. 420; L. Pop, *Curs de drept civil ...* , *supra*, p. 335.
439. On the fact that collective damages may nevertheless rise doubts from the perspective of the condition that the damage must be personal, *see* L. Pop, *Tratat elementar ...* , *supra*, p. 421.
440. For a deep analysis of causes that led to the wide spread of collective damages, *see* I.I. Neamţ, *Acţiunea colectivă ...* , *supra*, pp. 25–37.
441. *See* I.I. Neamţ, *Acţiunea colectivă ...* , *supra*, pp. 72–88.
442. *See* I.I. Neamţ, *Instrumente ...* , *supra*, p. 189.
443. *See*, *e.g.*, para. 3, let. (b) from European's Commission Recommendation of 11 June 2013 on common principles for injunctive and compensatory collective redress mechanisms in the Member States concerning violations of rights granted under Union Law, available at https://eur-lex.europa.eu/legal-content/EN/TXT/HTML/?uri=CELEX:32013H0396&from=EN, last checked on Nov. 20, 2019, which defines mass harm as "a situation where two or more natural or legal persons claim to have suffered harm causing damage resulting from the same illegal activity of one or more natural or legal persons."
444. *See*, *e.g.*, the proposal of T.E. Willging, *Mass Torts, Problems & Proposals. A Report to the Mass Torts Working Group. Appendix C*, p. 9, available at http://www.uscourts.gov, last checked on Nov. 20, 2019. For comparative law examples of threshold, *see* I.I. Neamţ, *Elemente de particularitate ale acţiunii colective (The Particularities of Class Action)*, in RRDP No. 4/2018, pp. 373–374.

the exact number of victims cannot be determined.[445] Another approach would require determining the plurality not by referring to a threshold but the particularities of the damage. In this regard, we have proposed that two criteria may be considered, one substantial and one material. From the substantial standing point, the number of victims must be high enough to reflect an abnormal exposure of a community to a risk, a systemic malfunction, an highly illicit behavior or the deed violates the subjective right or legitimate interest belonging not to individuals, but to communities or a group of individuals.[446] Regarding the last element, we have underlined that some damages are inherently collective while others are accidently collective. The damages are in all cases collective when the deed violated a diffuse or collective right or legitimate interest. A diffuse right is a transindividual and indivisible subjective right, that belongs to a group of indeterminate and indeterminable individuals, who usually had no previous connection and became connected as a result of the tortious deed.[447] These are not a simple sum of individual rights, as they are distinct from the subjective rights belonging to individuals, and belong to an amorphous entity, such as a group of persons with similar characteristics.[448] Diffuse rights are the rights that belong to everybody and nobody in particular.[449] A collective right is also a transindividual and indivisible subjective right but unlike diffuse right, it implies a more characteristic relationship between the members of the group, based on previous legal relation between them or between them and the tortfeasor.[450] When a plurality of classical subjective right or legitimate interest is infringed, the damages are accidently collective. In such case, because a collective damage was caused, the classical subjective right transforms into an individual homogenous right. Individual homogenous rights are classical individual and divisible subjective rights which are particularized by the fact that they were all damaged by the same illicit deed or a series of illicit deed having a common origin.[451] From the material criteria perspective, a damage can be considered collective when using the mechanism of individual civil action to repair it may create dysfunctionalities in the judiciary, or the remedy searched for is indivisible.[452]

445. For example, when a diffuse right was violated, it is impossible to determine the exact number of victims, as the right does not belong to individual, but a community whose members cannot be exactly determined. For all the above-mentioned critics and more, *see* I.I. Neamţ, *Acţiunea colectivă … , supra*, pp. 73–74.

446. For a more detailed presentation of this criteria, *ibid.*, pp. 75–76.

447. *See Acţiunea colectivă … , supra*, p. 91; I.I. Neamţ, *Elemente de particularitate … , supra*, p. 381; I.I. Neamţ, *Instrumente vechi … , supra*, p. 222.

448. *See* I.I. Neamţ, *Elemente de particularitate … , supra*, pp. 381–382.

449. *See* I.I. Neamţ, *Class action la porţile cetăţii! (?) (Class Action at City Gates)*, in Liber Amicorum Liviu Pop, Universul Juridic, Bucharest, 2015, p. 571.

450. *See* I.I. Neamţ, *Acţiunea colectivă … , supra*, pp. 92–93; I.I. Neamţ, *Elemente de particularitate … , supra*, p. 382; I.I. Neamţ, *Class action … , supra*, p. 571; I.I. Neamţ, *Instrumente vechi … , supra*, p. 222.

451. *See* I.I. Neamţ, *Acţiunea colectivă … , supra*, pp. 94–95; I.I. Neamţ, *Elemente de particularitate … , supra*, p. 383; I.I. Neamţ, *Class action … , supra*, pp. 571–572; I.I. Neamţ, *Instrumente vechi … , supra*, p. 223.

452. For a more detailed presentation of the criteria, *see* I.I. Neamţ, *Acţiunea colectivă … , supra*, pp. 76–77.

440. The second element of particularity is the qualitative one, which consists in the existence of a *common core of element and features shared by the victims*. The commonality most often results from the fact that all the victims were damaged by the same tortious conducts or a series of tortious conducts that have a common origin.[453] In such cases, element such as the unlawfulness of the deed and the type of liability applicable will be common among the victims. Often, other aspects such as the causation or even the type and the extent of the damage shall be similar. The fact that the victims share a substantial number of common features is what allows a unitary approach of the negative consequences of tortious conduct. Moreover, in the case of diffuse or collective rights, with rare exceptions, the situation of the victims is, under all aspects, identical.[454]

441. The third element of particularity, or the public one, refers to *the existence of a public interest*, distinct and competing with the interest of the victims which consists of the need to repair the damage caused to community and to take all the reasonable measure in order to deter similar tortious conducts for future or at least to reduce the risk.[455]

442. Finally, the fourth characteristic, the substantial one, refers to the fact that the collective damages are *transubstantial*, meaning they can take any shape or form and can result from any human conduct or activity, no matter their nature.[456]

443. Considering all the above-mentioned particularities, the collective damages were defined as the situation in which a unique tortious act or a series of tortious acts having a common origin infringes the subjective rights or legitimate interest belonging to a high number of individuals, a group or a community giving rise to legal relations that are highly cohesive, and the public interest demands special measures to be taken in order to repair the damages inflicted or to prevent or reduce the risk of future similar damageable conducts.[457]

444. Though unregulated and often treated in the same way as individual damages, collective damages have nevertheless impacted the Romanian judicial system, from the most obvious impact, referring to the increased pressure on court dockets, to the adoption of special norms in some domains, or even a reconfiguration of classical legal institution such as causation and damage.[458] Regarding the last aspect, in one of the very few judicial decisions which directly addressed the collective component, the court seemed to agree with the theory according to which, in the case of collective damages, the total is more than the sum of its parts or that the collective

---

453. *See* I.I. Neamţ, *Instrumente vechi* ... , *supra*, p. 195.
454. For further details, *see* I.I. Neamţ, *Acţiunea colectivă* ... , *supra*, pp. 78–82.
455. *Ibid.*, pp. 82–86. *See also* I.I. Neamţ, *Instrumente vechi* ... , *supra*, pp. 197–200.
456. *See* I.I. Neamţ, *Acţiunea colectivă* ... , *supra*, pp. 86–87; I.I. Neamţ, *Instrumente vechi* ... , *supra*, pp. 200–201.
457. *See* I.I. Neamţ, *Acţiunea colectivă* ... , *supra*, p. 88; I.I. Neamţ, *Elemente de particularitate* ... , *supra*, p. 363.
458. For a detailed presentation on the substantial and procedural effects of collective damages, *see* I.I. Neamţ, *Acţiunea colectivă* ... , *supra*, pp. 112–177.

component impregnates by itself to a higher gravity than each individual damages, at least when it comes to moral damage. Thus, in 2010 a fire in a maternity hospital, in which six newborns were killed and five badly injured, covered the headlines and news reports for weeks and even months, being considered one of the worst tragedies in current history.[459] In the criminal proceedings that followed the parents asked for the compensation of the moral damages endured. When analyzing the claims, the first instance court held, among others, that by its magnitude and consequences the fire determined a strong emotion among the patients, visitors, relatives and the public in general, while the intense mediatization made it impossible for the victims to forget it as time passed. The court also held that the event was at that time unique in Romania and that it determined special psychological pains to the victims which must lead to a higher compensation than the ones afforded in similar individual tortious conducts.[460]

445. Furthermore, as already stated, special legislation was passed for situations that imply, by default, collective damages, such as the damages caused by nuclear accidents,[461] environmental damages,[462] damages caused by defective products[463] or the damages caused as a consequence of breaching competition norms.[464] In most of these cases, there are only slight deviations from general rules regulating tortious liability, usually in the sense that the norms provide strict forms of liability or presumptions that are meant to ease the victim's task.[465]

§2. Direct and Indirect

446. The legal doctrine unanimously underlines that only a direct damage may entitle the victim to compensation.[466] Nevertheless, the notion of "direct damage" has a different meaning than in most of the other legal systems. The damage is considered to be direct as long as a causal link exist between it and the tortious deed, no matter if the causal link is direct or indirect.[467] Thus, the damage is direct both

459. Unfortunately, not the worst, as five years later, another fire in a nigh pub killed sixty-five persons, becoming the worst tragedy that happened after 1990s.
460. *See* I.I. Neamţ, *Acţiunea colectivă ...* , *supra*, p. 121.
461. *See* Law No. 703/2001 on the civil liability for nuclear damages, published in Official Monitor (M. Of.) No. 818/19 December 2001.
462. *See* O.U.G. No. 195/2005 referring to the protection of public environment, published in Official Monitor (M. Of.) No. 1196/30 December 2005 and O.U.G. No. 68/2007 referring to environmental liability, published in Official Monitor (M. Of.) No. 446/29 June 2007.
463. *See* Law No. 240/2004 referring to the liability of the producers for the damages caused by defective products, republished in Official Monitor (M. Of.) No. 313/22 April 2008.
464. *See* O.U.G. No. 39/2017 on the action in which compensation is requested for the breach of competition norms, published in Official Monitor (M. Of.) No. 422/8 June 2017.
465. For a detailed analysis of all these hypotheses, *see* I.I. Neamţ, *Acţiunea colectivă ...* , *supra*, pp. 134–154.
466. *See* I.I. Neamţ and L.T. Dăuceanu, *supra*, p. 136; L. Pop, *Tratat de drept civil. Obligaţiile. Volumul III ...* , *supra*, p. 222; L. Pop, *Tratat elementar ...* , *supra*, p. 418; L. Pop, *Curs de drept civil ...* , *supra*, p. 335; F.I. Mangu, *Răspunderea civilă. Constantele ...* , *supra*, p. 167.
467. *See* I.I. Neamţ and L.T. Dăuceanu, *supra*, p. 136; L. Pop, *Tratat de drept civil. Obligaţiile. Volumul III ...* , *supra*, p. 222; L. Pop, *Tratat elementar ...* , *supra*, p. 418; L. Pop, *Curs de drept civil ...* ,

when the causation is direct (the damage being caused to the immediate victim) and indirect (when the damage is caused to another party as result of the damage suffered by the immediate victim) and is indirect only when no causal link exists between the damage and the illicit deed.[468] As such, from the Romanian's legal doctrine perspective, a direct damage is not equivalent with a damage caused directly to the victim.[469] Still, in this monograph, we will use the notion of "direct damage" to describe the situation in which a direct causal link exists between the damage and the tortious conduct and the notion of "indirect damage" to describe the situation in which the causal link between the two is indirect.

447. The Civil Code does not expressly regulate the problem of direct or indirect damages in the case or tortious liability (or, as a matter of fact, the problem of causation)[470] and our previously mentioned conclusions result from a systemic interpretation of the norms. The most relevant is Article 1.349, second paragraph, C.C.[471] which provides that the tortfeasor is obliged to repair "all the damages caused" by breaching a legal or social rule. The norm allows two interlinked conclusions. First, the tortfeasor is bound to repair all the damages, as long as, of course, the law does not otherwise provide. Or, no legal norm provides that in the case of tortious liability only direct damages entitle the victim to compensation as it does, as we shall see, in other domains. Second, in order for the damage to be repairable, it must be "caused" by the tortious conduct, which means that a causal link must exist between the deed and the damage. Though the causal link may be direct or indirect, the norm does not make any difference and *ubi lex non distinguit, nec nos distinguere debemus*. Thus, the norm may be interpreted as entitling both the direct and indirect victims to compensation.

448. Furthermore, by the very definition of tortious liability, it is undoubtable that direct victims may ask for compensation. Therefore, the only problem refers to indirect victim, who were defined by the legal doctrine as any individual that is connected with the direct victim by a family or interests relation and who, because of the damage inflicted to direct victims, also suffers a pecuniary or nonpecuniary damage.[472] Referring to the legal framework, apart from the already mentioned arguments, it is beyond any doubt that the indirect victims were not excluded, as there are specific hypotheses that directly refer to them. One such example, considered a classic example of indirect damage,[473] is Article 1.390 C.C. which provides the right to compensation for the ones who were maintained by the direct victim, who died

---

supra, p. 335; F.I. Mangu, *Răspunderea civilă. Constantele* … , *supra*, p. 168.

468. *See* L. Pop, *Tratat de drept civil. Obligaţiile. Volumul III* … , *supra*, p. 223; V. Stoica, *supra*, p. 35.
469. *See* L. Pop, *Tratat elementar* … , *supra*, p. 418; F.I. Mangu, *Răspunderea civilă. Constantele* … , *supra*, p. 168.
470. *See* F.I. Mangu, *Răspunderea civilă. Constantele* … , *supra*, p. 169.
471. We must emphasize once more that Art. 1.349 C.C. is the norm that prescribes the general legal regime of tortious liability.
472. *See* L. Pop, *Tratat elementar* … , *supra*, p. 419. For a similar definition, *see* P. Vasilescu, *supra*, p. 598.
473. *See* L. Pop, *Tratat elementar* … , *supra*, p. 419.

as a result of the tortious act.[474] In this case, the creditors are indirect victims but still the law provides their entitlement to compensation. Furthermore, Article 1.392 C.C. provides that the one who paid the victim's medical care or funeral expenses is entitled to ask for restitution from the one liable for the damage inflicted to the victim. Referring to this norm, it must be underlined that no special connection must exist between the victim and the one who paid for the mentioned expense. The payment itself is enough to justify the entitlement to restitution.

449. Even though there is a strong connection between the direct victim and the indirect victim, as the damage suffered by one determines the other one's damage,[475] the damage caused to the indirect victim gives rise to an autonomous right to compensation, which is independent in relation to the right belonging to the direct victim. For this reason, the compensation is determined considering the extent and gravity of the negative consequences suffered only by the indirect victim.[476]

450. In any case, the right of indirect victims to ask for compensation is one of the key distinctions between tortious liability and contractual liability, as, according to the law, the last entitles only direct victims to compensation. In this regard, Article 1.533 C.C. provides that even when the breach of a contractual obligation is committed with intention or gross negligence, the victim is still entitled only to those damages that are the direct and necessary result of the breach. As such, unlike tortious liability, when it comes to contractual liability, the law expressly provides that only direct damages entitle the victim to compensation.

§3. Pecuniary and Nonpecuniary

451. The existence of a damage that can be repaired lies at the very core of tortious liability. The damage is nothing else than the negative consequences endured by the victims resulting from the violation of a subjective right or legitimate interest.[477] The problem is that both the subjective rights and the legitimate interests are highly diverse, and this diversity also reflects the nature of damages that are caused when they are breached. When it comes to classifying the subjective rights and legitimate interest, one of the most common distinction is between pecuniary (or patrimonial) subjective rights/legitimate interest (the ones that have an economic value, such as property right) and nonpecuniary (or nonpatrimonial) subjective rights/legitimate interest (the ones that do not have an economic value, but are intimately linked to the individual, such as the right to personal integrity, reputation,

474. Article 1.390 C.C. provides that one can ask form compensation if he was entitled, according to the law, to maintenance from the deceased. Also, considering all the circumstances, the court may oblige the tortfeasor to pay a compensation to the one that was regularly maintained by the deceased without any legal obligation. The last hypothesis is considered to be a classical example in which the civil norms protect a legitimate interest as in the mentioned scenario where the indirect victim had no right to maintenance from the direct victim, but only a legal interest.

475. *See* L. Pop, *Curs de drept civil ...* , *supra*, p. 335.

476. *Ibid.*, p. 420.

477. *See* I.I. Neamţ, *Poate frica ...* , *supra*, p. 228.

private life).[478] Considering this classification, the negative consequences of a tortious act are as well pecuniary, when they can be economically assessed (e.g., when jewelry of the victim was stolen) or moral, when they cannot be economically evaluated (e.g., the pain endured by the victim due to a body injury caused by the tortfeasor). Still, there is no perfect correlation between the type of subjective right or legitimate interest breached and type of damage that is caused, as a violation of a patrimonial subjective right may lead to a moral damage or vice versa.[479] For example, if the tortfeasor kills the victim's pet, a patrimonial subjective right is violated, because, from the perspective of civil law, a pet is a patrimonial asset, but most often, besides the pecuniary damage, a moral damage will also be inflected, as the victim will endure a moral pain because of the loss. On the same line, the violation of a nonpatrimonial subjective right may lead to a pecuniary damage as for example when the reputation of a lawyer is affected, this leads to a loss of clients, or when a body harm leads to work incapacity.

452. Before communism it was unanimously accepted that the victim of a tortious act is entitled to both pecuniary and nonpecuniary damages.[480] Things have changed when a binding decision of the formal Supreme Court of Justice stated that in case of tortious liability no compensation may be afforded to the victim when a nonpecuniary damage was caused on the ground that there was an incompatibility between the fundamental principles of socialist legislation and the conversion into money of the moral sufferance. Furthermore, it has been stated that for the moral damages there are other mechanisms than pecuniary compensation, such as publishing the judicial decision that condemns the actions of the tortfeasor.[481] Because the decision was mandatory for the lower courts, the jurisprudence has changed, and the victims were no longer afforded nonpecuniary damages. Nevertheless, the solution was criticized by the legal doctrine, among others on the grounds that sometimes it is impossible to mark a clear boundary between pecuniary and nonpecuniary harm, such as in the case of body injury.[482] As a result of the legal doctrine reaction, things have gradually once again started to change, but this time into the right direction, as courts started to admit the entitlement of the victim to compensation when a moral damage was inflicted.[483] After the 1990s, the solution was expressly provided by some legislation[484] and it was almost unanimously accepted by legal doctrine and jurisprudence.[485]

---

478. *Ibid.*
479. *Ibid.*, p. 229. *See also* L. Pop, *Tratat de drept civil. Obligaţiile. Volumul III …* , *supra*, p. 204; L. Pop, *Tratat elementar …* , *supra*, pp. 413–414; C. Stătescu and C. Bîrsan, *supra*, p. 148.
480. *See* C. Stătescu and C. Bîrsan, *supra*, p. 149.
481. *See* Supreme Tribunal, Guidance Decision No. VII/29 December 1952, in *Culegerea de decizii ale Plenului şi Colegiilor Tribunalului Suprem, 1 August 1952–31 Decembrie 1954*, pp. 25–26.
482. For a synthesis of the arguments, *see* C. Stătescu and C. Bîrsan, *supra*, pp. 150–151.
483. *See* C. Stătescu and C. Bîrsan, *supra*, p. 152.
484. *See*, *e.g.*, Art. 11 of Law No. 29/1990 referring to administrative suits, published in Official Monitor (M. Of.) No. 122/8 November 1990.
485. *See*, *e.g.*, C.S.J., s. pen., Decision No. 2073/1992, in V. Terzea, *supra*, p. 404.

453. The new Civil Code allows no doubt in this direction. Aside the fact that Article 1.349(2) C.C. provides that the tortfeasor shall be bound to repair all the damages, there are a series of norms that refer exactly to the pecuniary compensation of moral damages or, in other words, to nonpecuniary damages.

454. Thus, according to the new legislation, the victim is entitled to monetary compensation for both pecuniary and nonpecuniary damage, with the underline, belonging to the doctrine and jurisprudence, that in the case of nonpecuniary damage the compensation is not meant to repair the damage, as such damages cannot be repaired by money, but to ease the victim's situation.[486]

455. The *pecuniary damage*, meaning the negative consequences of a tortious act that can be economically evaluated,[487] may have a very complex nature. In most of the cases they result from a violation of the victim's economic subjective rights and economic interest[488] which are extremely diverse, from the classical ones, such as the property right (in which case the tortious act may lead to an asset destruction or damaging, a stolen asset, a limitation of the property prerogatives or others similar) to the ones related to competition law (when in most of the cases the victim will end up buying a good or service to a higher price the normal) or environmental law (as, for example, when an illegal water pollution kill the fish population and diminish the income of a fisher). Nevertheless, some of the most complex situations arise when the violation of a nonpatrimonial right or legal interest leads to a patrimonial damage. The best example in this case is the bodily injury.[489]

456. Whenever the tortious deed damages the victim's physical, mental or health integrity, the negative consequences are extremely heterogeneous and diverse.[490] If the immediate result is the mental or physical pain, the negative consequences do not stop, in most of the cases, at this point, but are followed by a series of economical loses. Furthermore, when the damage is serious enough, expenses will be made by the victim in order to restore his bodily integrity. Moreover, in some extreme cases, the tortious act may lead to a temporary or permanent work incapacity, which means that the victim will be deprived of the main source of income. The huge number of particularities associated to bodily injuries made the legal doctrine to consider the resulting damage a distinct category.[491] Thus, bodily damage was defined

---

486. *See* I.I. Neamţ and L.T. Dăuceanu, *supra*, p. 135. *See also* the High Court of Cassation and Justice, Decision No. 1657/2011, available at www.scj.ro, last checked on Apr. 17, 2020.
487. *See* I.I. Neamţ and L.T. Dăuceanu, *supra*, p. 135; L. Pop, *Tratat de drept civil. Obligaţiile. Volumul III ...* , *supra*, p. 203; L. Pop, *Tratat elementar ...* , *supra*, p. 413; L. Pop, *Curs de drept civil ...* , *supra*, p. 331; P. Vasilescu, *supra*, p. 595; F.I. Mangu, *Răspunderea civilă. Constantele ...* , *supra*, p. 178.
488. *See* L. Pop, *Tratat de drept civil. Obligaţiile. Volumul III ...* , *supra*, p. 203; L. Pop, *Tratat elementar ...* , *supra*, p. 413; L. Pop, *Curs de drept civil ...* , *supra*, p. 331.
489. *See* F.I. Mangu, *Răspunderea civilă. Constantele ...* , *supra*, pp. 178–179.
490. *See* P. Vasilescu, *supra*, p. 596.
491. *See* I.I. Neamţ, *Poate frica ...* , *supra*, p. 229.

as the one resulting from the violation of those personal, nonpatrimonial, subjective rights that construct the physical personality of an individual, such as the right to life, health and bodily integrity.[492]

457. Considering their importance, the law has also paid a lot of attention to bodily damages, by providing which negative consequences are reparable and in which way. In this regard, no less than three articles of the Civil Code regulate the problem of bodily damage.

458. Referring strictly to the pecuniary damage, Article 1.387, first paragraph, C.C., provides that the compensation afforded to the victim shall incorporate the equivalent of the work income the victim was deprived of or can no longer obtain it because of the total or partial loss of work capacity. Therefore, in case of complete or partial loss of work capacity, the victim is entitled to the income that can no longer be obtained by working. The work incapacity must be proven by the victim through a medical expertise. Furthermore, according to the same legal norm, the victim is also entitled to the medical expenses, the expenses determined by the increased needs of the victim or any other material damages. Falling within this category are the expenses with medical devices such as wheelchair, the need to pay a personal attender and the cost of trainings needed to obtain a new work qualification adapted to the victims' work capacity.

459. Bodily harm may also lead to indirect pecuniary damages and the Civil Code provides two examples. First, according to Article 1.390 C.C., if the victim dies as a result of the tortious conduct, the one who was maintained by the victim is entitled to ask for the equivalence of maintenance from the tortfeasor. Then, Article 1.392 C.C. provides that the one who paid for the victim's medical care or funeral is entitled to restitution from the one held liable.

460. The *nonpecuniary damages* are defined as those negative consequences that emerge from a tortious conduct and which do not have an economical value or cannot be economically assessed.[493] Moral damages always take the shape of physical or mental pains[494] and, under this perspective, are more homogenous than pecuniary damages, which can take any form or shape that is economically assessable. In most of the cases, moral damages result from the violation of the nonpatrimonial subjective rights that define human personality in its triple dimensions: physical,

---

492. *See* I.I. Neamţ and L.T. Dăuceanu, *supra*, p. 135; L. Pop, *Tratat elementar … , supra*, p. 414; L. Pop, *Curs de drept civil … , supra*, p. 331. For a similar definition, *see* P. Vasilescu, *supra*, p. 596.
493. *See* I.I. Neamţ, *Poate frica … , supra*, pp. 228–229; I.I. Neamţ and L.T. Dăuceanu, *supra*, p. 135; L. Pop, *Tratat de drept civil. Obligaţiile. Volumul III … , supra*, p. 204; L. Pop, *Tratat elementar … , supra*, p. 413; L. Pop, *Curs de drept civil … , supra*, p. 331; P. Vasilescu, *supra*, p. 596; F.I. Mangu, *Răspunderea civilă. Constantele … , supra*, p. 179. *See also* C.A. Cluj, S. I. civ., dec. civ. 714/A/2015, in *supra*, p. 85; C.A. Constanta, s. civ., dec. No. 354/2008, in *supra*, p. 405.
494. *See* L. Pop, *Tratat elementar … , supra*, p. 413. The same scholar, in another landmark paper (*Tratat de drept civil. Obligatiile. Vol. II. Contractul* (*Civil Law Treaty. Obligations. 2nd Vol. The Contract*), Universul Juridic, Bucharest, 2009, 654–655) states that while in the field of contractual liability the most common damages are the economic one, in the case of tortious liability, the bodily damages take the lead.

moral and social. Nonetheless, the violation of a patrimonial subjective right, such as killing a pet, may also lead to a moral damage.[495]

461. Thus, the physical or mental pains may be the result of a bodily or health harm, the restrains of family and social life (social damage), of an aesthetic damage or of an emotional damage caused by the loss of a close person or loved object, the violation of one's dignity, honor, own image, private life.[496] In the section referring to tortious liability, the Civil Code expressly regulates only two types of moral damages: the social and family damage resulted from a bodily harm and the emotional damage resulted from the loss of a close person.

462. In which the social and family damage is concerned, Article 1.391, first paragraph, C.C. provides that when a bodily or health damage was inflicted, a compensation may be afforded to the victim for the life and social restrictions that result. The monetary compensation is not meant to repair the moral damage, but to compensate[497] for the pain suffered and for those social and family activities the victim was deprived off, such as attending a wedding, going to theatre or film, mountain hiking and others. Thus, the monetary compensation aims to offer the victim the pecuniary means by which to create a living environment which can ease the sufferance resulting from the new status quo.

463. Regarding the second, Article 1.391(2) C.C. provides that the court can also afford monetary compensation to decedents, ascendants, brothers, sisters and spouse for the pain caused by victim's death. Such compensation may also be afforded to any individual that is able to prove the fact the victim's death caused him an emotional sufferance. The legal doctrine has underlined that the fundament of this liability hypothesis is not the mere existence of a family connection between the direct victim, who died as a result of the tortious act, and the one that asks for compensation, but the emotional pain inflicted by the loss of someone dear. This is the reason why the list is open, and any individual who suffered an emotional pain is entitled to monetary compensation. Therefore, even if one is among the family members enumerated by the legal norm, this does not automatically mean that he is entitled to monetary compensation. In all circumstances, the moral damage consisting in emotional sufferance must also be proven,[498] meaning that the victim must prove the existence and the intensity of pain caused by the tortious act, even though the amount allowed as compensation is left at the discretion of the court. Finally, the right to monetary compensation is not inherited as a consequence of victim's death (*jure hereditatis*), but it is a personal subjective right belonging to the one that suffered an emotional pain (*nomine et jure proprio*).[499]

495. *See* L. Pop, *Tratat de drept civil. Obligaţiile. Volumul III* ... , *supra*, p. 204.
496. *See* I.I. Neamţ and L.T. Dăuceanu, *supra*, p. 135; L. Pop, *Tratat elementar* ... , *supra*, pp. 413–414; L. Pop, *Curs de drept civil* ... , *supra*, p. 331.
497. *See* I.I. Neamţ, *Poate frica* ... , *supra*, p. 231; P. Vasilescu, *supra*, p. 596.
498. *See* I.I. Neamţ and L.T. Dăuceanu, *supra*, p. 176.
499. *Ibid.*

464. Because of its purely personal nature, the right to be compensated for a moral damaged cannot, as a general rule, be transmitted to others by the victim neither through *inter vivos* acts nor *mortis causa* and is not inherited by the legal successor. Still, there are two exceptions. First, the right to compensation may be transmitted *inter vivos* if it was first settled or established by a court decision.[500] Then, the successor may continue a trial that was initiated by the victim, even though the claim refers to the compensation of moral damages.[501]

465. Though the Civil Code only mentions the two hypotheses in which a moral damage can be compensated, there are plenty of other situations in which the victim of a moral damage is entitled to monetary compensation. This result from the provision of the Article 1.391(3) C.C. which, regulating the possibility to sell the right to monetary compensation, refers to the violation of any subjective rights inherent to individual, without limiting them to the ones provided by the first two paragraphs. Furthermore, the fifth paragraph of the same Article provides that Articles 253–256 are further applicable, whereas Article 253(4) C.C., referring to any infringement of a nonpatrimonial subjective right, provides that the victim may ask for a monetary compensation even for the moral damage, as long as the tortious act is imputable to the tortfeasor. As such, any violation of the victim's subjective right to life, health, physical and mental integrity, dignity, private life, freedom of consciousness, etc. entitles the victim to ask for both a nonpatrimonial remedy and a monetary compensation.

§4. Pure Economic Loss

466. The Romanian law does not provide a set of general norms for tortious liability in the case of pure economic loss. Considering the principle of full compensation such loss can be compensated just as any other pecuniary damage, as long as the victim is able to prove the existence of a damage and a causation between the tortious act and the damage. Thus, no physical damage to the person or property of the victim is required in order for his to be entitled to monetary compensation. For example, if someone builds an apartment block with the violation of height limit and this reduces the value of the neighboring buildings, the neighbors are entitled to ask for monetary compensation, even though no material damage was inflicted to their property. Another example is offered by Article 1.392 C.C. which states that one is entitled to be refunded for the expenses made in order to restore the victim's heath, or, when the victim died, with his funerals.

500. *See* Art. 1.391(3) C.C.
501. *See* Art. 1.391(4) C.C.

§5. Actual and Future

467. The existence of a damage is, as shown, one of the most important conditions for engaging tortious liability, as no tortious liability may exist without a damage, the damage being both a condition and the limit of tortious liability.[502] In this regard, to be repairable, a damage must be certain, which meant that its existence is undoubtable and its amplitude determinable.[503]

468. An actual damage is always certain, as once it occurred its existence is beyond doubt and the amplitude may be proven by the victims using proof such as technical or accounting expertise, witness testimony, and documents.[504] Furthermore, as Article 1.381(2) C.C. provides, the victim's right for compensation is born the moment the damage has produced. It would thus appear that only the actual damage is repairable, as before the damage occurs, the victim has no right to ask for compensation.

469. Nevertheless, such a solution would lead to inadmissible results, especially in those hypotheses when the damage occurs gradually. One such example is the case when the victim lost the work capacity as a result of the tortious deed. In this case, the victim loses each month the equivalent of work income. If only the actual damage could be compensated, the victim should file a new claim each month, which, obviously, would mean a tremendous burden.

470. For this reason, Article 1.385(2) C.C. provides that monetary compensation can be afforded for future loss if it is certain that it will occur. Thus, as long as the victim may prove the fact that it is certain that a damage will occur in the future and the extent of that damage, a claim for compensation is admissible even though the damage has not yet occurred. Still, the fact that the damage is just potential and not actual leads to further consequences when it comes to the effect of court decision. Among others, the victim or the doer may, at any time, ask for a revision of the damage, if new elements led to the conclusion that the initial damage was not correctly assessed.[505]

471. Furthermore, the principle of full compensation entitles the victim not only to actual harm (*damnum emergens*) but also for the consequential loss which may have been caused by the tortious act (*lucrum cessans*). Such loss may include the loss of gains or profits which the victim has been deprived of, because of the damageable deed.[506] This future harm is a direct consequence of the *damnum emergens*. As with any other allegations, the victim is bound to prove the existence and amplitude of *lucrum cessans*. In some circumstances, the law provides a series of presumptions meant to ease the victim's task. For example, if *damnum emergens*

502. *See* I.I. Neamţ, *Poate frica* ... , *supra*, p. 228; I.M. Anghel, Fr. Deack, M.F. Popa, *supra*, p. 81; P. Vasilescu, *supra*, p. 592.
503. *See* L. Pop, *Tratat de drept civil. Obligaţiile. Volumul III* ... , , *supra*, p. 217.
504. *Ibid.*
505. *See* Art. 1.386(4) C.C.
506. *See* Art. 1.385(3) C.C.

consists of a monetary loss, the victim is presumed to have suffered a *lucrum cessans* equal to legal increase.[507] In any case, the victim does not have to prove that it is for sure that the alleged benefit would have occurred if not the tortious act, as a reasonable proof is enough. Furthermore, in the case of tortious liability, *lucrum cessans* does not have to be foreseeable in order for the victim to be entitled to compensation. As long as the victim reasonably proves that the tortious act led to a gain or profit deprivation, the doer is bound to compensate the damage, even if it was not foreseeable at the time of the deed.

§6. Other Costs

472. Based on the principle of full compensation, the victim is entitled to any costs that are the direct consequence of the tortious act. In this regard, Article 1.385(3) C.C. expressly provides that, aside *damnum emergens* and *lucrum cessans*, the victim is entitled to compensation for the expenses made in order to prevent or limit the damage. Therefore, the victim, who wanted to prevent the damage, after the illicit deed was committed, or to reduce the amplitude of the negative consequences, performed any expenses, is entitled for compensation of those damages. Though the law does not expressly provide so in the case of tortious liability, the expenses must be reasonable, as the victim cannot abuse of his right and produce grater expenses then the potential benefit.

473. On the grounds of tortious liability, the victim is entitled to compensation only for the *damnum emergens, lucrum cessans* and the expenses that are related to preventing or reducing the damages. For other expenses, such as the costs for assessing the damages and liability or obtaining judicial or extrajudicial payment, there are other mechanisms available. For example, if the parties do not get to a mutual deal, the victim has the possibility to file a court claim. In such case, when it comes to the judicial costs, including court fees, lawyer expenses and the costs with the administration of proof, such as expert fees, the Civil Procedure Code provides the rule looser pay, meaning if the claim of the victim is granted, the defendant shall pay all the court costs. If the claim is only partially granted, the court will decide the extent to which each party shall pay for the costs.[508]

474. After the victim obtained a favorable court decision and the defendant refuses to voluntarily pay the monetary compensation decided by the court, the victim may use the force execution proceedings and ask the intervention of a bailiff. In such case, all the costs with the force execution proceedings shall be borne by the debtor.[509]

507. For further detail, *see* the section dedicated to full compensation.
508. *See* Art. 453 Civil Procedure Code.
509. *See* Art. 669(2) C.C.

§7. Mitigation of Damages

475. The Civil Code does not expressly provide a duty of the victim to mitigate the damage. The only reference to this aspect is provided by Article 1.385(3) C.C which states that the victim is entitled for monetary compensation for the expenses made in order to avoid or limit the damage. Referring to this norm, the legal doctrine has opposite view. While some legal scholars see it as a source of a duty to mitigate,[510] others consider that the victim has no obligation to mitigate the damage and that the norm only provides a victim's right to compensation, based on the principle of equity, for the expenses if the victim decides to do so.[511] According to the last, regulating such an obligation for the victim should be carefully considered as the possibilities of the victim to retain the amplification of the damage or its very manifestation should be realistically assessed.[512]

476. Despite the opposite opinion, there are some arguments in favor of the first optic, that cannot be dismissed. Aside the fact that the law provides the right of the victim to ask for compensation for the expenses made in order to prevent or reduce the damage, it must be remembered that Article 1.371, first paragraph, C.C. provides that the tortfeasor shall not be held liable for the damage which the victim did not avoid though it could have been avoided. Thus, on one hand, the law provides that when the victim could have avoided, in whole or in part, the damage the tortfeasor is not liable for the avoidable damage and, on the other hand, the victim is entitled to the compensation of the expanses made for reducing or avoiding the damage.[513] By systematically and teleologically interpreting these provisions the resulting reasonable conclusion is that a victim's duty to mitigate the damage exists.

477. The limits of such obligation result from the same Article 1.371, first paragraph, C.C. The victim is bound to reduce or avoid the damage only when such an act is possible. The first question that arises is what is the standard on which the victim's possibility to avoid the damage is assessed? As the law does not provide any answer and considering the rationality behind tortious liability, the principle of full compensation, the principle of equity and the deterrent function of tort law, the only rational answer is that an *in concreto* analysis shall be performed. Therefore, the judge will have to consider all the circumstances in which the damage has produced and the effective capabilities of the victim, having in mind elements such as age, education, financial capabilities or physical strength. It is thus irrelevant that another individual, found in the same situation as the victim, could have avoided or reduced the damage, if for the victim itself such a task was impossible.

478. The second question is to what limits does the victim's obligation to mitigate the damage exist? In other words, as long as it is possible, should the victim

510. *See* L. Pop, *Tratat de drept civil. Obligațiile. Volumul III* … , *supra*, p. 495; L. Pop, *Tratat elementar* … , *supra*, pp. 563–564; L. Pop, *Curs de drept civil* … , *supra*, p. 415.
511. *See* C. Jugastru, *Prejudiciul* … , *supra*, pp. 17–18.
512. *Ibid.*, p. 19.
513. For the idea that Art. 1.371 C.C. provides a duty to mitigate the damage, *see also* F.I. Mangu, *Despre formele* … , *supra*, p. 172.

deploy any effort and expenses in order to avoid or reduce the damage, considering that all the expenses shall be refunded? In order to answer this question, the reason behind the victim's obligation must be considered. The victim's duty to mitigate the damage aims to reduce the amplitude, especially economic, of the negative consequences that arise from the tortious act. For this reason, the obligation's fundament exists only as long as what is reduced or avoided is more important than the resources put in to fulfill such a task. Thus, even if the damages can be reduced or avoided, when the resources required to do so overpass the damage itself, no obligation subsists for the victim.[514] Once again, such evaluation must be done considering the victim and his possibility to assess the potential amplitude of the damage without the intervention.

514. This is expressly provided in the case or contractual liability by Art. 1.531(2) C.C. which provides that the victim is entitled to compensation only for the reasonable expenses made to reduce or avoid the damage. Though the reasonable criterion is not expressly provided in the case of tortious liability, it is *mutatis mutandis* applicable, because *ubi eadem ratio ibi idem jus*. Still, a conclusion is difficult to draw in those cases when mitigating the damages implies undergoing a medical treatment or medical intervention, as such medical procedures also interfere with the right to bodily integrity and, sometimes, freedom of religion. *See* F.I. Mangu, *Despre formele ...* , *supra*, pp. 173–174.

Chapter 3. Assessment and Compensation of Damage

479. The finality of tortious liability is the damage reparation. As seen, there are two main principles that govern tortious liability: the principle of full compensation and the principle of in-kind reparation. The two act as landmarks during the entire process of assessing and individualizing the remedy. In any case, while the principle of full compensation is incident no matter the remedy requested by the victim, the principle of in-kind reparation is applicable only when the damage can be in-kind repaired and the victims did not ask instead for compensation, as it usually happens.

480. Furthermore, as a general matter, the law does not provide any special procedural norms for assessing or compensating the damage caused by a tortious act. Therefore, the general rules shall apply, the most important of which is the victim's obligation to prove all the conditions of tortious liability, including the existence and the extent of the damage, except the case when the law does otherwise provide.[515] Any proof are admissible, from expert reports or testimony to witness testimony or written documents. In most of the cases, the extent of economic damage is proven using expert reports or written documents while for the assessment of moral damage, witness testimony seems to be playing the major role. Moreover, expect some particular situations, the law does not provide with any criteria for assessing the damage, the only landmark being the principle of full compensation.

§1. Objective Versus Subjective

481. The Romanian law and jurisprudence does not make any distinction between the objective and subjective approach when it comes to damage assessment and compensation. Nevertheless, as we shall further see, there are undoubtable situations in which the assessment is objective, in the sense that the court decision is based on actual loss. This is the case in most of actual pecuniary damages. As long as the damage is pecuniary and actual, in most of the cases it can be objectively assessed by determining the value of it using criteria such as market value, replacement costs, and reparation costs. For example, when a victim's asset was destroyed, the compensation will be objectively determined by considering the value of that asset.

482. In other cases, the assessment is subjective either because the determined value of the loss is prospective or because, by default, no objective criteria may be used. Regarding the first situation, the assessment is not based on actual loss, but more on a prospective evaluation in most of the cases when *lucrum cessans* is determined, in the cases of the damage for lost chance and when the damage has not yet occurred. In the last situation the compensation may be revised after the damage has

515. Expressing the principle *actor incubit probatio*, Art. 249 Civil Procedure Code provides that the one that makes any claim before the court is bound to prove it.

occurred if the compensation is not equivalent to the damage, while in all the others, once a court decision was passed, the compensation can no longer be questioned. Then, the assessment is even more subjective when a monetary compensation is allowed for moral damage. In such cases, the law does not offer any criteria,[516] leaving the judge the complete freedom to decide which criteria should be considered, in what manner and, in the end, the value of the compensation. Nonetheless, the jurisprudence has constantly underlined that the decision must still be based on objective criteria and that the compensation allowed should be neither symbolic nor a source of enrichment for the victim.[517]

§2. Concrete Versus Abstract

483. Based on the principle of full compensation and considering the scope of tortious liability—*restitutio in integrum*, as a general matter—the damage shall be *in concreto* determined. This is especially the case when the victim seeks for an in-kind remedy, as such remedies require, by default, a concrete analysis of the negative consequences arising from the tortious act. The same applies to monetary compensation, in all those situations in which a concrete assessment of damage is possible, because despite the fact that the damage is not repaired in kind, the value of monetary compensation must be equivalent to the value of the loss. Thus, the court must consider all the negative consequences and the value of the infringed right or legitimate interest for the victim. For example, if the victim's car was destroyed in a car accident, the court shall not consider only the abstract value of a similar car but also eventual upgrades of the victim's car. The same applies to monetary compensation for moral damages, even though in this case the situation is somewhere in between. It is impossible to economically assess the value of a moral damage, considering that they do not have an economic value. As such, no concrete assessment is possible. Still, before establishing the value of monetary compensation, the court must take into consideration all the concrete negative consequences endured by the victims and then decide a reasonable monetary compensation for those effects.[518] For example, if the plaintiff's dad was killed in a car accident by the defendant, the court shall first consider the impact of the deed over the plaintiff based on elements such as the relation with the deceased, the way in which the plaintiff reacted to the drama, if he required any medical or psychological help, and then, value all these elements when establishing the monetary compensation.

516. *See* C.A. Constanta, s. civ., dec. No. 354/2008, in *supra*, p. 405.
517. *See, e.g.*, Bucharest Court of Appeal, third section, Civil Decision No. 647/2019, available at rolii.com, last checked on Jan. 18, 2020, and Constanta Court of Appeal, Decision No. 354/2008 in V. Terzea, *supra*, p. 405. The main elements of reference in such cases are the concrete sufferance endured by the victim, the principal of equity and the need to find a proper balance between the values that were breached by the tortious act and the compensation afforded to the victim. *See, e.g.*, High Court of Cassation and Justice, Decision No. 5567/2011, available at www.scj.ro, last checked on Apr. 17, 2020.
518. *See* High Court of Cassation and Justice, Decision No. 10211/2009, in V. Terzea, *supra*, p. 416.

484. A particular situation exists in the case of personal injury that resulted in work incapacity. In this case, the law expressly provides for both concrete and abstract evaluation, depending on the circumstances. If at the time of the deed the victim was employed or obtained income from any other job or profession, then the compensation shall be equivalent to that income.[519] On the contrary, if the victim was not employed and had no income, the monetary compensation shall be determined *in abstracto*, considering the income that the victim could have obtained based on the professional qualification. If the victim had no professional qualification nor was on the way of obtaining one at the time of the deed, the compensation shall be equivalent to the minimum wage.[520] Therefore, in the latter cases, the court will refer to an abstract, potential damage when determining the monetary compensation, and not the concrete damage. The same abstract evaluation will be used when the compensation is for a lost chance or for future loss.

§3. Methods of Assessing the Damage

485. Considering the principle of full compensation, the court invested with a tortious liability claim must determine, based on all the relevant circumstances of the case, the exact loss and the correspondent remedy. Regardless of the remedy sought, in-kind reparation or monetary compensation, the first step is to assess all the negative consequences of the deed in relation to the victim: the asset was destroyed or only damaged, the type of injury inflicted to the victim, the gravity of the injury, the impact of the deed over the victim's physical or mental status, etc. Then, starting from this, the court shall analyze whether the remedy sought by the victim is or not just.

486. It must be underlined that Romanian courts have, with minor exceptions,[521] the full competence to assess both the facts (the loss) and the value of the monetary compensation granted or the extent of the in-kind remedy. Nonetheless, the court cannot award more than the plaintiff asked for (*ultra petita*) or something else (*extra petita*), but it can only assess the justness of the claim with which it was invested.[522]

487. The plaintiff is the one who must first evaluate the damage through the claim addressed to the court and to propose the evidence that sustains the claim.[523] The value of the claim can be later modified if the evidence administrated before

519. *See* Art. 1.388, first and second paragraphs, C.C. for adults and Art. 1.289(2) C.C. for minors.
520. *See* Art. 1.388, first and third paragraphs, C.C. for adults and Art. 1.289, first paragraph, C.C. for minors.
521. Such as when the parties settled when the court analysis is limited to only to the legality of the settlement.
522. *See* Art. 397, first paragraph, Civil Procedure Code.
523. *See* Art. 194, let. (a) and (e), Civil Procedure Code.

the court reveal a different value[524] and, in exceptional circumstances, new evidence can be proposed during trial.[525] The defendant may accept the plaintiff's claims, in which case the court can grant it without further analysis, or it can defend arguing, among others, that the loss or the value of the loss does not reflect the reality. In this case, the defendant shall propose its own set of evidence. Furthermore, when finding the truth regarding the claims, the court itself may decide to bring new evidence, which was not requested by the parties, or ask the parties to provide further evidence.[526]

488. In the case of pecuniary damages, if the value of the monetary compensation requested by the victim is contested by the defendant, most often the value of the compensation will be determined based on expert evaluations[527] or on elements such as market value (where there are no particularities),[528] accounting documents, and written documents.[529] For the lost profit, when the damage is pecuniary, the victim may either accept a lost profit equivalent with legal interest or, if a higher amount is requested, the extent of the damage must be proven. As previously shown, an exception is provided by the law when as a result of the tortious act the victim partially or totally lost the work capacity. In such case, the compensation, for this loss, shall be equal to the victim's income before the deed, or, depending on the circumstances, the income that could have been obtained, considering the qualification, or the minimum wage. Thus, the victim will only have to prove the loss of work capacity and the previous income or the qualification and, in some circumstances (when the income for that qualification is not regulated), the income obtained by others with a similar qualification. When a moral damage was caused, the victim must only prove the negative moral effects of the deed[530] and the court is sovereign in determining the value of the monetary compensation. Despite the fact that when it comes to monetary compensation for moral harm the law does not even provide any criteria that should be considered by the court, let alone potential values; the jurisprudence seems to be quite uniform. Nonetheless, the lack of such criteria and landmarks has sometimes led to out-of-the-ordinary decisions.[531] Finally, when the liability of a tortfeasor who lacked discernment is engaged, the

524. *See* Art. 204(2) Civil Procedure Code.
525. *See* Art. 254(2) Civil Procedure Code.
526. *See* Art. 254(5) Civil Procedure Code.
527. *See* P. Vasilescu, *supra*, p. 595.
528. For example, if one abusively refuses to evacuate an apartment, the owner is entitled to a damage equivalent to the rent usually paid on the market for such an apartment. *See* Contanta Tribunal, Decision No. 59/2010 in V. Terzea, *supra*, p. 394 and Court of Appeal Timisoara, Decision No. 268/2007 in *ibid*.
529. Written documents are, for example, the main proof used by natural persons when it comes to prove the pecuniary damage that has already occurred and its dimension. *See* Supreme Tribunal, Decision No. 924/1973 in V. Terzea, *supra*, p. 407.
530. *See* High Court of Cassation and Justice, Decision No. 1130/2012, available at www.scj.ro, last checked on Apr. 17, 2020.
531. *See*, *e.g.*, the Decision No. 1827/2014, delivered by the High Court of Cassation and Justice, second section, available at www.scj.ro, last checked on Nov. 26, 2019, in which the court granted the victim who lost the right forearm in a car accident a monetary compensation of EUR 1 million. About the incoherence of jurisprudence when it comes to moral damages, because of the lack of legal criteria, *see* O. Ghiţă, *Consideraţii Teoretice şi practice cu privire la daunele morale în cazul*

court must afford an equitable compensation, considering the patrimonial situation of the parties. Thus, in this case, if such solution would seem inequitable, the victim will not be afforded a full compensation. The criteria provided by law to determine the equitable compensation is the patrimonial status quo of the parties, which means that the victim will have to prove both the personal economic situation and the one of the defendant and why the requested compensation is equitable given the two. In any case, the court will have to decide in the end, after considering all the evidences and the arguments, what monetary compensation is equitable.

§4. Equitable Limitation of Damage

489. As a general matter, the Romanian law does not allow an equitable limitation of damage. The principle of full compensation entitles the victim to a compensation for all the damages, no matter how inequitable this may seem, caused by the fault of the doer or the form of tortious liability. The only exception is provided by Article 1.368 C.C. which, as mentioned, derogate from the principle of full compensation and entitles the victim only to an equitable indemnification, when the liability of a doer who lacks discernment is engaged. In any other case, full compensation shall be granted.

§5. Methods of Payment

490. Regarding the way in which the damage may be paid, from the provision of Article 1.386 and 1.387 C.C. it results that a distinction must be drawn between the *uno ictu* damages (the damages that have only one manifestation) and continuous or gradual damages.

491. When the negative consequences of the tortious act produce *uno ictu* or when all the negative consequences have already happened at the time the court was invested with the claim, the global sum is the only way in which the payment may be established. In this regard, Article 1.386, first paragraph, C.C. provides that if the in-kind reparation of the damage is not possible or if the victim does not want an in-kind reparation, the damage shall be repaired by paying "a compensation" determined by the court or decided by the parties. The use of singular, together with the fact that the law expressly provides some exception, allows the above-mentioned conclusion.

492. On the other hand, the third paragraph of the same Article states that when the damage is continuous, the payment shall be in the form of periodic sums. *Mutatis mutandis*, the same applies when the damage is gradual. The classical example is the one in which the plaintiff asks for a monetary compensation equivalent of the

---

dreptului la despăgubiri prevăzut de art. 388 din Codul civil (Theoretical and Practical Considerations Relating to Non-material Damages in the Case of Right to Damages Provided for by Art. 388 of the Civil Code), in Revista Română de Drept Privat No. 3/2020, p. 100.

maintenance he was lacked because the one who used to perform the maintenance was killed. In such case, the defendant will be obliged to a monthly payment the extent of which shall be determined considering the damage that was actually caused to the victim and not the criteria set by the law for legal maintenance.[532] Furthermore, Article 1.387(2) C.C. provided that the compensation for lost income when the victim lost the work capacity shall be in the form of periodical payments. The final thesis of the same norm also provides an exception, allowing, for solid grounds, the compensation to be determined in the form of a unique sum. The victim is the only one entitled to ask for a global sum and the solid grounds put forward may be extremely diverse, from the fact that the victim plans to leave the country and in such case the periodic payment may lead to difficulties,[533] to a substantial possibility that the defendant may become insolvent in the future or hide assets in order to avoid force execution proceedings.

493. In most of the cases, when the payment is established in the form of periodic sums, the sums are determined in Euro, as this allows a more constant value of compensation over time and the victim does not have to upgrade the sums periodically.[534] Also, the victim may ask for the sum to be periodically indexed with the inflation index, in order to keep the value of compensation constant.

494. In any case, no matter the type of payment, whenever a compensation was established for a damage that did not yet occurred, both the victim and the tortfeasor may later ask for its revision if new elements allow the conclusion that the initial compensation is no longer in correlation with the value of the damage infringed to the victim or when the damage did not occurred or ceased to happen.[535] Thus, in such case, res judicata is incident only as long as the circumstances din not changed.[536]

532. *See*, *e.g.*, the Supreme Court of Justice, Decision No. 1720/1991, in V. Terzea, *supra*, p. 423.
533. *See* Supreme Tribunal, Decision No. 1589/1974 in V. Terzea, *supra*, p. 411.
534. If the compensation is established in national currency and the amount due no longer reflects the damage, the victim is entitled to file a new claim and ask for the difference. *See* Salaj Tribunal, Decision No. 137/1991 in V. Terzea, *supra*, p. 412.
535. *See* Art. 1.386(4) C.C.
536. *See* F.I. Mangu, *Răspunderea civilă. Constantele* ... , *supra*, p. 151.

Chapter 4. Personal Injury and Death

495. Specific rules concerning compensation for personal injury and death have been adopted in the Civil Code, namely Articles 1.387–1.395. The full compensation principle creates an obligation for the responsible to compensate all pecuniary losses deriving directly from the wrongful act as well as nonpecuniary losses.

496. Given the fact that harming a person or causing his a wrongful death also represents a crime, in order to accommodate the different prescription terms between the civil and criminal proceedings, the legislator opted for the possibility to prorogate the civil prescription term to be as long as the one provided for the prescription of the criminal responsibility which is usually longer. In the same time, given the interference with social security rights, the civil prescription is suspended until the social security pension or support is established.

§1. Pecuniary Losses

497. In the particular case of body or health damage the pecuniary losses translate in the compensation of the victim's loss of work earnings (past and future), its medical care expenses and the expenses caused by the increasing life needs resulting directly from the damage as well as any other material damage.

498. Thus, the compensation must include the equivalent to the work earnings that the victim was deprived or that is impeded to earn by the effect of the loss or reduction of work capacity.

499. The Civil Code establishes precise rules to determine the value of this compensation. Thus, this value will be established according to the monthly net income of the victim from the year before the loss or the reduction of the work capacity. If this circumstance does not apply to the victim, the value of the compensation will be calculated on the basis of the average monthly net income that he could have earned according to his professional qualification. The same criteria also apply if the victim was in the process of acquiring a professional qualification. Even if the training of the victim was not complete, the value will be established according to the average monthly net income of a professional who would have had finalized the training in order to obtain the qualification. However, if the victim can prove that he had the possibility to obtain a higher work income on the basis of a contract signed in the year previous to work capacity loss or reduction but which had not entered into force, this amount has to be taken into consideration.

500. If the victim had no professional qualification and he neither was in the progress of obtaining one, the compensation will be established on the basis of minimum net income.

501. When the victim is a minor, the above considerations are applicable but the compensation is due from the day in which he would have normally acquired the professional qualification that he was following. Before that date, if the minor had an income at the moment of the wrongful act, he is entitled to receive the equivalent of this income until the compensation mentioned before would apply. If the minor had no income and he was not in the progress of obtaining one, the compensation will be established on the basis of minimum net income. In these last two cases, this compensation is due only from the day the minor comes to the legal age to be part of an employment contract.

502. As a rule, the compensation for the loss of work earnings will be awarded in periodical installments by taking into account the increasing life needs of the victim. However, on the victim's demand, for ground reasons, a lump sum may also be awarded. Before the final judgment, for urgent needs, the judge will be able to grant a provisory compensation.

503. Concerning the medical care expenses, the expenses caused by the increasing life needs or other pecuniary losses suffered by the victim, there are not any special rules provided by the Civil Code. Therefore, the general rules regarding the proof of damage will apply.

504. Besides the victim, a third party might have made expenses for the medical care of the victim. In this case, the Civil Code recognizes the third party's right to demand compensation for damage against the responsible. It is most commonly the case of public hospitals that provided medical care for the victim.

505. In case the victim died, there are two different categories of pecuniary losses that the Civil Code regulates.

506. First, it is the loss of third parties—indirect victims, that were financially supported by the deceased. The right to compensation is granted in all the cases in which the indirect victim was according to law benefiting from the financial support from the deceased. Therefore, it is the situation in which the law recognizes the victim's subjective right to financial support.

507. However, in the case of wrongful death, the legislator also admits the reparation of damage for the person who can only display a legal interest, namely the person that received constant financial support from the deceased although the law did not prescribe any such obligation. Thus, according to circumstances, the judge can grant compensation to such victim.

508. In order to establish the amount of the compensation, the judge will assess the needs of the victim and the income the deceased would have normally earned during the time for which the compensation is granted. To this end, the work earnings will be estimated according to the rules abovementioned concerning the health and body harm.

509. Second, in the category of expressly mentioned damages, the medical treatment costs that a third party made for the victim incurred as a result of the injury prior to death and the funeral and burial costs incurred are included. In this case as well, the legislator grants the subjective right to compensation to an indirect victim who suffers from a direct damage of the wrongful death.

510. Lastly, in the case of both body or health harm and wrongful death, it has to be mentioned that if the victim is entitled to social security benefits, the compensation will be awarded accordingly. Namely, if the social security benefits cover the damage suffered by the victim, he is no longer entitled to compensation. If this is not the case, the responsible will have to pay the difference between the amount received as social security benefit and the amount of the compensations the victim is entitled to. Therefore, as long as the pension (invalidity or survivors') or social aid (including death grant) has not been granted or declined to the victim, the judge can only grant a provisory compensation.

511. This is the legal regime established by the Civil Code and it sets rules concerning the most common types of pecuniary damages that occur in case of personal injury and death. However, if there are victims that can prove other pecuniary losses, the rule of full compensation gives right to demand the reparation of such losses according to the common rules.

§2. NONPECUNIARY LOSSES

512. For body or health damage, the Civil Code expressly admits the possibility to grant compensation for the restrictions of the victim's possibilities to develop a normal family and social life. So, it basically concerns the loss of amenities of life. This does not imply however that the victim is not entitled to an award for pain and suffering which will be awarded and evaluated separately.

513. The right to demand such compensation is granted only to the victim and it cannot be inherited as long as the deceased did not claim it before his death. However, if the right to compensate nonpecuniary losses was claimed before the death of the victim, the heirs are entitled to continue the civil action.

514. In case of the victim's death, compensation could be granted for the pain and suffering of relatives (ascendants, descendants, brothers, sisters, spouse) or any other person who can prove the existence of such prejudice.

515. Awarding compensation in order to attenuate the nonpecuniary losses suffered by the direct or indirect victims does not impede upon the victim's possibility to demand the protection of the nonpecuniary subjective rights of the person by nonpecuniary means such as injunction or other means.

516. The right to compensate nonpecuniary losses cannot be transmitted to third parties until it has been established by a transaction between the parties or by final judgment.

517. Determining the amount of compensation is usually the attribute of the judge as long as the parties involved do not reach an agreement. As a rule, there are no legal or jurisprudential guidelines concerning the amount of compensation that can be awarded and this usually leads to very different solutions rendered by judges.

518. By the adoption of Law No. 132/2017 concerning the compulsory third-party liability insurance referring by damages caused by vehicles and trams accidents,[537] the legislator made a frail attempt to change this reality. For the situation in which the parties agree to set the compensation for body and health damage amicably, the legislator establishes five general criteria: a general amount set by common order between the Ministry of Health and the Financial Supervisory Authority under the score communicated by the National Institute of Legal Medicine; the compensation takes into consideration the medium level presumed of a harmed person; the value of a traumatic point is equal to the double of the minimum base gross salary at the date of the accident; the compensation may be adjusted to each case according to the circumstances, on the base of supporting documents; the scoring concerns only the physical pain caused by body and health damage, for the psychological trauma, the victim may bring documents to prove it. However, the secondary legislation that should establish the traumatic point has not been adopted yet; circumstance delays the application of these legal provisions.

537. Published in the O.J. No. 431 of Jun. 12, 2017.

Chapter 5. Various Damages *(Property)*

519. In the Romanian legal system property is one of the main guiding principles enshrined in the Constitution, the Civil Code as well as in different international treatises and conventions to whom Romania adhered.

520. Private and public property are both granted constitutional protection that is further developed in the legal regime established by the Civil Code.

521. Property is defended by civil, administrative and criminal actions aimed to discourage and prohibit any damage brought to it. Civil actions imply both real and personal actions issued out of the main legal report of property right or out of the legal report of obligation that arose from the infringement brought to the property right.

522. Real actions include a claim for restitution if the good is no longer in the possession of the owner or otherwise, a negative action against any person who claims to be the holder of any real right, other than property, over his property. Principally, these actions have no limit in time. If the good can no longer be

523. If the claim is admitted, the defendant will be obliged to return the good or to pay a compensation if the good has perished due to his fault or it has been alienated. The defendant will also be obliged to return the products or their value. In all cases, the compensation will be assessed according to the moment of restitution. Also, the holder in bad faith or the precarious holder will be obliged, upon request, to return the fruit produced by the good until it is returned to the owner. However, the owner may be obliged, on request, to reimburse the defendant for the necessary expenses he has incurred for the preservation of the good. The useful expenses shall be reimbursed, upon request, within the limit of the value increase, unless otherwise provided by law. The owner may also be obliged, on request, to reimburse the expenses necessary for the production and collection of the fruit or products.

524. The holder in good faith of the good has no obligation to return the fruit produced by the good as he become owner of the fruits according to the law. In order to become owner, the holder must be in good faith at the time of harvesting the fruit. Good faith of the holder exists when he is convinced that he is the owner of the good under a translational deed of property whose causes of ineffectiveness he does not know and should not, under the circumstances, know. In the case of fruit produced by immovable property entered in the land register, good faith is assessed in relation to the conditions required of the acquiring third parties to reject the rectification action. His good faith ceases the moment the causes of ineffectiveness of his title are known to him.

525. The owner is also entitled to personal actions that arise from civil liability grounds in case of damage brought to the property. The damage will be evaluated according to the general rules of tortious liability and the compensation will comprise: the value of the deterioration of the good, the value of the lack of use and the value of other damages that are linked directly to the wrongful act.

526. Damage to property caused by other person's property may exist even in situations where there is no fault and as a consequence no liability for one's own act. Set as a judiciary limit to property, the Civil Code admits a strict form of liability in charge of the owner that causes, by exercising his right, greater inconveniences than normal in the neighborly relations. In this case, the court may, for equity reasons, oblige him to compensate the injured party, as well as to restore the previous situation when this is possible.[538] If the damage caused would be minor in relation to the necessity or usefulness of the harmful activity by the owner, the court will be able to approve the performance of that activity. However, the injured party will have the right to compensation. If the damage is imminent or very probable, the court may approve, by way of a presidential order, the necessary measures to prevent the damage, here included an injunction relief.

527. This form of strict liability incurs only when the exercise of the property right is in the limits of the law. If the right exercised by the owner constitutes an abuse or exceeds the material limits of the good, the ground for the claim will be tortious liability for one's own deed. The compensation however, in both of the cases, will be established according to the general rules of tortious liability.

528. An additional measure to protect the property is established by the legislator that it is aimed mainly at the protection of the good. Under the denomination of "Taking measures for the preservation of the owned property," Article 952 of the Civil Code states that "If there are reasonable grounds to believe that the property possessed may be destroyed or damaged by property in the possession of another person or as a result of some works, such as the erection of a building, the cutting of trees or the excavation of a neighboring plot, the owner may request that the necessary measures be taken to avoid the danger or, if necessary, the cessation of the works. Pending the settlement of the application, the holder or, as the case may be, the other person may be obliged to pay a bail, left to the discretion of the court, only in the following situations: a) if the court provisionally orders the removal of the work or the cessation of the works, the bail shall be established in the charge of the possessor, so that the damage that would be caused to the defendant by this measure can be repaired; b) if the court approves the maintenance of the work in its current state or the continuation of the works, the bail is established in the charge of the defendant so as to ensure to the possessor the necessary amounts for restoring the previous situation."

529. Enshrined in the chapter dedicated to possession and its protection, this measure actually represents a limit to the property as it does not allow the owner to exercise his right in accordance to the limits of the law regardless of the fact that his use is not abusive.

---

538. Article 630 of the C.C.

Chapter 6. Interference with Collateral Benefits

§1. Insurance

530. There are two cases that need to be taken into consideration: the situation in which the author of the wrongful act is insured and the situation in which the victim is insured.

531. In the first case, the victim has an autonomous right to be paid directly by the insurance company. The amount of the compensation will be set amicably between the victim, the author of the damage and the insurance company. If the parties cannot reach an agreement, it will be set by the judge. If the value of the prejudice is larger than the maximum insurance allowance, the victim can demand the responsible according to the law to pay the difference.

532. As a rule, the assurance company has no right of recourse against the author of the wrongful act. Exceptions can be met in the case of the compulsory third-party liability insurance.

533. In the second case, a distinction has to be made regarding the type of insurance. If the victim insured the good that has been damaged, the insurance replaces the value of the good at the moment of the wrongful act. Thus, the victim can no longer demand compensation from the author or other person who can be held liable. However, if the insurance does not cover the prejudice, the victim can demand the compensation for the difference. In all cases, the assurance company has, by subrogation in the rights of the victim, a right of recourse against the author of the wrongdoing and the person who can be held liable for the amount paid.

534. If the victim was insured against body or health damage, the solution is different because the insurance allowance is being regarded as the victim's savings and not as a compensation for the harm suffered. Thus, the victim is entitled both to the insurance allowance and the compensation from the responsible and consequently, the insurance company has no right of recourse against the responsible. Given its nature, this type of insurance can also be cumulated with the social security benefits that the victim is entitled to.

§2. Social Security

535. Social security benefits can interfere with the tortious liability compensation mainly in two situations.

536. An invalidity pension is being granted in the case of health or body damage that made the victim partially or completely unable to work. Persons can receive an invalidity pension if: (i) they are or have been insured under the public pension system; (ii) they have lost at least half of their capacity to work; (iii) the state of their health has been classified in a category of disability according to a decision issued by the social insurance medical expert and (iv) their age is lower than the standard retirement age.

537. Another situation concerns the wrongful death and the social security rights of which the family members of the deceased benefit such as the survivors' pensions and the death grants.[539] Survivors' pensions are paid to the children and surviving spouse if the deceased person who supported them was a pensioner or met the requirements to receive any type of pension paid from the public pension system. Death grants are paid in the events of the death of both an insured person or pensioner under the public pension system and family members who were supported by them and have no entitlement of their own to social insurance if the person proves that he has paid expenses related to the death.

538. These social security rights are meant to compensate for the damage of the victim (direct or indirect). Thus, if the victim is entitled to social security benefits, first, these rights have to be established in favor of the victim and only if this amount does not cover the victim's prejudice, he has the right to demand from the responsible the difference between the amount of the prejudice and the social security benefit. Another consequence is that as long as the social security rights of the victim have not been established, the civil judge can only grant a provisory compensation.

§3. Others

539. Another situation that might occur is that of a third party, not responsible for the damage, that decides to pay the compensation for the victim.

540. In this case, if the third party pays the compensation with the intent to make a donation or payment for the responsible, the victim will no longer have a right to compensation toward the responsible as his prejudice would have been repaired. The right of recourse will follow the general rules of the theory of obligation. For instance, if there was a donation, there would be no right of recourse but if a subrogation has taken place at the moment of the payment, the third party will have a right of recourse against the responsible.

541. If the victim received a donation from a third party motivated by the harm he had suffered, this sum could not be considered reparation of the prejudice and thus the victim will have the right to demand the compensation from the responsible. However, if the victim agrees to renounce his right of compensation toward the responsible in consideration of the donation he received, his rights toward the responsible will be extinguished.

---

539. *Ibid.*

Chapter 7. Other Remedies

§1. Restitution *(For Injust Enrichment)*

542. Whenever the conditions for tortious liability are not met, the victim of the injury cannot claim compensation in order to repair its damage from the responsible. However, in some of the cases in which exemption causes intervene, the principle of equity motivated the legislator to find another remedy that gives right to the victim to obtain a certain indemnity.

543. It is the case of self-defense, necessity, and whenever the damage was caused by a person lacking discernment and the person responsible to supervise cannot be held liable.

544. Regarding self-defense, the Civil Code states that "The one who, being in self-defense, caused a damage to the aggressor shall not owe compensation. However, the offender that caused a crime by exceeding the limits of self-defense may be obliged to pay an adequate and fair compensation."[540] It is considered to act by exceeding the limits of self-defense when the person who was initially in self-defense exceeds the limit of a defense proportional to the gravity of the attack and the circumstances in which it occurred, without being able to establish that the perpetrator was in a state of disturbance or fear induced by the attack and justifying the perpetration. In this case, there are no limits established by the law concerning the amount of the indemnity that can be awarded, the principle of equity being the only criteria applicable. Thus, the judge will take into consideration, the value of damage, the victim's and the offender's economic state and the circumstances in which the offense occurred.

545. A different approach is established by the legislator concerning the damage produced in a state of necessity. Thus, "a person who, in a state of necessity, has destroyed or damaged another's property in order to defend himself or his own property from imminent damage or danger is obliged to repair the damage caused, according to the rules applicable to enrichment without just cause." The same approach characterizes the situation in which the harmful act was committed in the interest of a third person: in the case in which the damage was caused by exceeding the limits of self-defense or in a state of necessity, the victim is entitled to claim an indemnity on the basis of enrichment without just cause from the third person.

546. In this case, the indemnity will be circumscribed to the limits inferred by the unjust enrichment regime of obligation. Thus, the indemnity will amount to the extent of the patrimonial loss suffered by the other person, but it is not possible to go beyond the limit of the debtor's own enrichment. Applying the rules of unjust enrichment in this case has been critiqued as it makes very difficult its application in the situations in which the value protected was nonpecuniary. Thus, whenever the

540. Article 1.360 of the C.C.

act of self-defense or state of necessity was aimed to protect the life, body or health of another person, applying the rules of unjust enrichment supposes appreciating the enrichment of the person, namely putting a price on these invaluable items.

547. The last situation in which an alternative remedy has been recognized concerns the situation in which the damage was caused by a person lacking discernment and the person responsible to supervise him cannot be held liable. In this case, the victim can claim an indemnity against the author of the damage. The indemnity will be established in a fair amount, taking into account the patrimonial status of the parties. Thus, there are no legal limits that apply.

§2. Injunctive Relief

548. Injunctive relief is not a remedy that is associated with tortious liability, as it lacks the reparation component that is considered essential for tortious liability in the Romanian legal system.

549. Even in these circumstances, this mechanism is not absent in our legal system and it has been consecrated both in the Civil Code and in the Civil Procedural Code.

550. As we have mentioned before, the victim or the potential victim is entitled to demand injunctive relief whenever there is an injury or potential injury to a non-pecuniary subjective right.[541] In this case, it is considered to be one of the main and specific means of protection granted by the legislator to this category of rights.

551. Also, an injunctive relief can be demanded in front of the court in order to protect imminent damage to property rights, like in the case of overcoming the abnormal inconveniences of neighborhood or taking measures for the preservation of the owned property.[542]

552. However, the general framework for injunctive relief can be found in the article of the Civil Procedure Code. Article 33 that regulates the legal interest for the claim or any civil action states that, "The interest must be determined, legitimate, personal, born and current. However, even if the interest is not innate and current, a claim may be made in order to prevent the infringement of a threatened subjective right or to prevent the occurrence of an imminent and irreparable damage."

553. On this ground, an injunctive relief may be claimed not only in the specific cases regulated by the Civil Code but also in order to protect and prevent an imminent and irreparable damage to any subjective right.

541. For more details, *see* Part I, Chapter 2, §4.
542. For more details, *see* Part VI, Chapter 5.

§3. Punitive Damages

554. Romanian law does not provide a legal framework for the punitive damages. Originating in common law[543] and having as a role to punish and deter the tortfeasor and not to compensate the victim,[544] usually in case of intentional or profit torts,[545] punitive damages were long seen as incompatible with the general principles of civil liability and thus reputed as inadmissible.[546] In this regard, it was underlined that the punitive damages contravene the full compensation principle, allowing the victim to be afforded more than the actual damages,[547] and elude the reparatory function of civil liability, emplacing it with a sanctionatory one, although in our civil legal system the sanctionatory function belongs to the state, and not the individuals.[548]

555. Nevertheless, an increasing number of scholars are starting to question this allegation and to underline that in one form or another, punitive damages have already found their place in our legal system. Even where a legal norm is missing, the punitive damages may find a fertile ground in those cases where the two above-mentioned obstacles can be avoided. One such domain is the moral damages. The principle of full compensation is highly diluted when it comes to moral damages, and so is its impact on punitive damages. Because no direct and objective correspondence may be established between the sum granted to the victim and the moral suffering, the doctrine has noticed that in many cases this amount includes a punitive component.[549] Moreover, it has been stated that if the role of moral damages is to alleviate the victim's suffering, then it must be considered that this may sometimes involve a punishment to the doer for the wrong committed.[550]

556. Furthermore, in particular circumstances, the courts started to explicitly refer to a punitive component of the moral damages granted to the victim. For example, a labor case, after noting that the employee had to address the course several times in order to protect from the illicit deeds of the employer and even so, the

---

543. *See* A. Tamba, *Danunele punitive în Common Law. În România acest tip de daune ... (Punitive Damages in the Common Law. In Romania This Type of Damages ...)*, in Revista Română de Drept Privat No. 2/2020, pp. 289–291; M.I. Floare, *Observaţii privind daunele punitive şi oportunitatea introducerii lor în sistemele de drept civil de tip continetal (Remarks Regarding Punitive Damages and the Feasibility of Their Introduction in Contract in Continental Civil Law Systems)*, in Studia Universitatis Babeş-Bolyai Iurisprudentia No. 2/2014, pp. 27–32; D. Gîrbovan, *Criterii de stabilire a daunelor morale: caracterul punitiv al daunelor ca satisfacţie pentru victimă. Repere europene şi naţionale (Criteria of Establishing Non-material Damages: The Punitive Nature of Damages as a Satisfaction for the Victim. European and National Milestones)*, in Revista Română de Drept Privat No. 2/2020, pp. 53–60.

544. *See* A. Tamba, *supra*, pp. 287; M.I. Floare, *supra*, p. 27; D. Gîrbovan, *supra*, p. 54.

545. *See* A. Tamba, *supra*, pp. 288; M.I. Floare, *supra*, p. 28.

546. *See* I.I. Neamţ and L.T. Dăuceanu, *supra*, p. 134. *See also* High Court of Cassation and Justice, Decision No. 3717/2014, unpublished.

547. *See* M.I. Floare, *supra*, p. 34.

548. *Ibid.*, p. 36.

549. *See* M.I. Floare, *supra*, p. 36; D. Gîrbovan, *supra*, p. 69.

550. *See* D. Gîrbovan, *supra*, p. 72.

latter did not seem to stop mobbing the employee, the court decided that such a conduct must be sanctioned and this sanction should reflect the moral damages afforded.[551] Even though not as explicit, a similar rationing may be found in other courts' decisions as well.[552]

557. Beyond the domain of moral damages, there are some legal provisions that entitle the creditor to more than the actual damage suffered. So is the case, for example, of Article 139(2) of Law No. 8/1996 (which, in some circumstances, entitles the owner of an intellectual property right to a compassion equivalent the triple amount that would have been legally due by the one who breached the right), or Article 10 of Law No. 72/2013 (which entitles the creditor to an extra compensation damages of minimum EUR 40).[553] Finally, Article 906 of the Civil Procedure Code provides with a legal mechanism specially designed to enforce intuitu personae or negative obligations. As such obligations cannot be directly enforced, the norm provides that the debtor may be sentenced to pay the creditor per diem penalties which go between 100 lei and 1,000 lei[554] when the obligation is nonpecuniary and 0.1% to 1% in case of pecuniary obligations. As the High Court of Cassation and Justice has stated, the penalties are not meant to cover any damages caused to the creditor by the nonexecution of the obligation, but to force the debtor to act accordingly with the obligation.[555] Therefore, the penalties cumulate with eventual damages caused to the creditor by the delay in executing a positive intuitu personae obligation or by breaching a negative obligation. Even though, there are some differences between the above-mentioned examples and the classical punitive damages,[556] especially the fact that they do not regularly depend on the form of guilt and are not usually meant to deter, but more to force an execution of the obligation, high similarities exist. For example, in the case of Article 906 of Civil Procedure Code, the penalties will always lead to an over compensation of the victim; they are meant to sanction the wrongdoer and though in direct correlation with the compensation, the penalties are different and autonomous.

558. All in all, despite the fact that the Romanian legal system does not provide a general set of norms when it comes to punitive damages and the high majority of jurisprudence and doctrine pleads for their inadmissibility, they still found in particular circumstance a way through, either as component of moral damages, or in special cases prescribed by law.

551. *See* Cluj Court of Appeal, Civil Decision No. 2658/A/2016, available at www.juridice.ro, last checked on Apr. 3, 2021.
552. *See*, *e.g.*, Bucharest Court of Appeal, Civil Decision No. 393/2016, available at www.rolii.ro, last checked on Apr. 3, 2021.
553. For further details about these norms, *see* M.I. Floare, *supra*, p. 39.
554. The actual currency of Romania.
555. *See* High Court of Cassation and Justice, Decision No. 16/2017, available at www.scj.ro, last checked on Apr. 3, 2021.
556. For the opinion that Art. 906 of Civil Procedure Code does not provide with an example of punitive damages, *see* A. Tamba, *supra*, p. 303.

Selected Bibliography

General Works and Treatises

Baias, F.A., E. Chelaru, R. Constantinovici, & I. Macovei (coord), *Noul Cod Civil. Comenariu pe Articole. Ediţia 2. Revizuită şi adăugită (New Civil Code. Comment on Articles. 2nd ed., revised and consolidated)*, C.H. Beck, Bucharest, 2014.

Cantacuzino, M.B., *Elementele dreptului civil (The Elements of Civil Law)*, Cartea Românească, Bucharest, 1921.

Neamţ, I.I. & L.T. Dăuceanu, *Drept Civil. Obligaţiile. Caiet de seminar. Ediţia a II a. revăzută şi adăugită (Civil Law. Obligations. Seminar Book. 2nd ed., revised and consolidated)*, Universul Juridic, Bucharest, 2019.

Nicolae, M., *Drept civil. Teoria Generală. Vol. I. Teoria dreptului civil (Civil Law. General Theory. First Volume. The Theory of Civil Law)*.

Pop, L., *Tratat. Drept civil. Teoria generală a obligaţiilor (Treaty. Civil Law. General Theory of Obligations)*, Chemarea, Iaşi, 1998.

Pop, L., *Tratat de drept civil. Obligaţiile. Volumul III. Raporturile obligaţionale extracontractuale (Civil Law Treaty. Obligations. IIIrd Volume. Extracontractual Legal Relations)*, Universul Juridic, Bucharest, 2020.

Pop, L., *Drept civil român. Teoria generală a obligţiilor (Romanian Civil Law. General Theory of Obligations)*, Lumina Lex, Bucharest, 2000.

Pop, L., Obligaţiile născute din faptele juridice cauzatoare de prejudicii sau răspunderea civilă extracontractulă (delictuală), in L. Pop, I.Fl. Popa, & S.I. Vidu, *Tratat elementar de drept civil. Obligaţiile conform noului Cod civil (Basic Treaty on Civil Law. Obligations According to the New Civil Code)*, Universul Juridic, Bucharest, 2012.

Pop, L., I.Fl. Popa, & S.I. Vidu, *Curs de drept civil. Obligaţiile (Civil Law Course. Obligations)*, Universul Juridic, Bucharest, 2015.

Stătescu, C. & C. Bîrsan, *Drept civil. Teoria generală a obligaţiilor. Ediţia a IX-a, revăzuta şi adăugită (Civil Law. General Theory of Obligations. 9th ed., revised and added)*, Hamangiu, Bucharest, 2008.

Vasilescu, P., *Drept civil. Obligaţiile. Ediţia a 2-a revizuită (Civil Law. Obligations. 2nd Edition, revised)*, Hamangiu, Bucharest, 2017.

Selected Bibliography

Monographies

Deleanu, I., *Instituţii şi proceduri constituţionale în dreptul român şi în dreptul comparat (Constitutional Institutions and Proceedings in Romanian Comparative Law)*, C.H. Beck, Bucureşti, 2006.

Jugastru, C., *Prejudiciul. Repere româneşti în context european (The Damage. Romanian Landmarks in European Context)*, Hamangiu, Bucharest, 2013.

Mangu, F.I., *Răspunderea civilă. Constantele răspunderii civile (Civil Liability. The Constants of Civil Liability)*, Universul Juridic, Bucharest, 2014.

Mangu, F.I., *Răspunderea civilă delictuală obiectivă (Objective Civil Liability)*, Universul Juridic, Bucharest, 2015.

Neamţ, I., *Acţiunea colectivă ca mijloc de reparare a prejudiciilor în masă. O analiză din perspectiva dreptului comparat (The Class Action as an Instrument for Repairing Mass Torts. A Comparative Law Analysis)*, Universul Juridic, Bucharest, 2017.

Pop, L., *Răspunderea civilă (Civil Liability)*, Alma Maters Timisienis Mirton, 2001.

Articles

Boilă, L.R., *Consideraţii referitoare la răspunderea delictuală a persoanei lipsite de discernământ reglementată prin art. 1368 din actualul Cod civil (Reflections on the Tortious Liability of the Person Who Lacks Discernment Regulated by Article 1368 from the Current Civil Code)*, in Dreptul, No. 5/2014.

Dincă, R., *Comparaison de la réforme du droit francais de la responsabilité civile avec le nouveau Code civil roumain. Volume 1 sous la direction Patrice Jourdain, Mireille Bacache*, IRJS, 2018.

Floare, M.I., *Observaţii privind daunele punitive şi oportunitatea introducerii lor în sistemele de drept civil de tip continetal (Remarks Regarding Punitive Damages and the Feasibility of Their Introduction in Contract in Continental Civil Law Systems)* in Studia Universitatis Babeş-Bolyai Iurisprudentia No. 2/2014.

Gîrbovan, D., *Criterii de stabilire a daunelor morale: caracterul punitiv al daunelor ca satisfacţie pentru victimă. Repere europene şi naţionale (Criteria for Determining Moral Damages: The Punitive Characteristic of the Damages Allowed as a Satisfaction for the Victim)* in Revista Română de Drept Privat, No. 2/2020, pp. 50–73.

Gherdan, S.V., *Răspunderea delictuală subsidară (Subsidiary Civil Liability)*, in Pandectele Române No. 6/2012.

Ghiţă, O., *Consideraţii Teoretice şi practice cu privire la daunele morale în cazul dreptului la despăgubiri prevăzut de art. 388 din Codul civil (Theoretical and Practical Considerations Relating to Non-material Damages in the Case of Right to Damages Provided for by Art. 388 of the Civil Code)*, in Revista Română de Drept Privat No. 3/2020.

Mangu, F.I., *Funcţiile răspunderii civile în filosofia actualului Cod civil (Functions of Civil Liability in the Philosophy of the Current Civil Code)*, in Analele Ştiinţifice ale Universităţii "AL. I. Cuza" Iaşi, Tomul LIX, Ştiinţe Juridie, No. 1, 2013.

Neamţ, I.I., *Instrumente vechi pentru probleme noi. Prejudiciile în masă faţă-n faţă cu răspunderea civilă (Old Instruments for New Problems. Collective Damages Face to Face with Civil Liability)*, in Revista Română de Drept Privat No. 2/2020.

Neamţ, I.I., *Poate frica faţă de un prejudiu viitor constitui un temei sufficient pentru o răspundere civilă delictuală actuală. O privire în cutia Pandorei (Is the Fear of a Future Damage Likely to Be a Sufficient Basis for a Current Tort Liability? An Insight into Pandora's Box)*, in Revista Română de Drept Privat, No. 3/2020.

Neamţ, I.I., *Class action la porţile cetăţii! (?) (Class Action at City Gates),* in Liber Amicorum Liviu Pop, Universul Juridic, Bucharest, 2015.

Neamţ, I.I., *Executarea silită a dreptului de a avea legături personale cu minorul. Iluzie sau realitate? (Enforcement of the Right to Have Personal Connection with the Minor Child. Illusion or Reality?)*, in Revista de Dreptul Familiei, No. 1–2/2019.

Podaru, O. & A. Buciuman, *Despre pierderea sansei în contenciosul administrativ (About Loss of Opportunity in Administrative Litigation)*, in Revista Română de Drept Privat No. 3/2020, pp. 303–308.

Pop, L., *Încercare de sinteză a evoluţiei principalelor teorii cu privire la fundamentul răspunderii civile delictuale (Attempt to Summarize the Evolution of the Main Theories Regarding the Fundaments of Tortious Liability)*, în L. Pop, *"Contribuţii la studiul obligaţiilor civile" (Contributions to the Study of Civil Obligations)*, Universul Juridic, Bucharest, 2010.

Stoica, V., *Pot fi drepturile potestative exercitate abuziv? (May Potestative Rights Be Exerted Abusively?)*, available at https://www.juridice.ro/essentials/517/pot-fi-drepturile-potestative-exercitate-abuziv, last checked on April 17, 2021.

Tamba, A., *Fundamentul obligatiei de reparare a prejudiciului de către persoana lipsită de discernământ (The Fundament of the Obligation to Repair the Damage by the Person Who Lacked Discernment)* in Dreptul, No. 11/2011.

Tamba, A., *Danunele punitive în Common Law. În România acest tip de daune... (Punitive Damages in the Common Law. In Romania, This Type of Damages ...)*, in Revista Română de Drept Privat No. 2/2020, pp. 289–291.

Selected Bibliography

Index

The numbers here refer to paragraph numbers.

Index

www.ingramcontent.com/pod-product-compliance
Ingram Content Group UK Ltd.
Pitfield, Milton Keynes, MK11 3LW, UK
UKHW020144290926
15471UKWH00004B/695